SECOND EDITION

A GUIDE TO
BENEFIT-COST
ANALYSIS

EDWARD M. GRAMLICH

The University of Michigan

Prentice Hall, Englewood Cliffs, New Jersey, 07632

Library of Congrss Cataloging-in-Publication Data

GRAMLICH, EDWARD M.
  A guide to benefit-cost analysis/EDWARD M. GRAMLICH. — 2nd ed.
  p.   cm.
  Updated ed. of: Benefit-cost analysis of government programs. c1981.
  Bibliography:
  Includes index.
  ISBN 0-13-074543-X
  1. Expenditures, Public—Cost effectiveness. I. Gramlich, Edward
M. Benefit-cost analysis of government programs. II. Title.
HJ7451.G72   1990
351.007'8—dc20   89-35575

Editorial/production supervision
  and interior design: Edith Riker/Bea Marcks
Cover Design: Lundgren Graphics
Manufacturing buyer: Ed O'Dougherty

Previously published under the title: *Benefit-Cost Analysis of Government Programs*

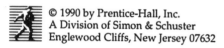
ISBN   0-13-074543-X

Prentice-Hall International (UK) Limited, *London*
Prentice-Hall of Australia Pty. Limited, *Sydney*
Prentice-Hall Canada Inc., *Toronto*
Prentice-Hall Hispanoamericana, S.A., *Mexico*
Prentice-Hall of India Private Limited, *New Delhi*
Prentice-Hall of Japan, Inc., *Tokyo*
Simon & Schuster Asia Pte Ltd., *Singapore*
Editora Prentice-Hall do Brasil, Ltda., *Rio de Janeiro*

To
Ruth

CONTENTS

PREFACE

For more than a decade now I have been teaching a course in benefit-cost analysis. This course is a required part of the two-year sequence for students of the Institute of Public Policy Studies at the University of Michigan. It is a valuable part of the sequence because it teaches public policy students how to think about the benefits and costs of policy measures. It also provides many applications of principles learned in other courses—microeconomics, public finance, macroeconomics, and statistics, to name a few.

In 1986–87 I took a leave from my academic duties to serve first as Deputy Director and then as Acting Director of the Congressional Budget Office. As for any academic, this Washington tour was valuable in teaching, or beginning to teach, some of the ins and outs of dealing with politicians. But I also was surprised to see just how often benefit-cost analysis is actually used in Washington. The Congressional Budget Office prepares analytical reports on different policy issues—acid rain, minimum wages, public employment, matching grants, cost efficiency in the provision of health care, national defense. I found my old benefit-cost experience being called on more or less continuously as I reviewed reports in these areas, and I have used many of these topics in this book.

In 1981, after teaching the benefit-cost course for four years, I screwed up my courage and wrote a textbook, *Benefit-Cost Analysis of Government Programs*. At the time there were not many good reading materials that could be assigned public policy students in such a course. The book has certainly proven very useful in teaching here over the years, and the number of adoptions at other colleges and universities has seemed quite good for a specialty book. By this time there is a much broader range of public finance and public policy texts available, but still not many books that make benefit-cost analysis their sole focus.

This edition updates the previous version, bringing in new material, improving the treatment of some old material, and using new real-world examples, many of them drawn from my Congressional Budget Office experience. But while much of the material is new, this book has the same basic goals as did the earlier version:

- to show how the logic of benefit-cost analysis can be applied to a wide range of policy measures

- to translate the technical debates of economists to those with a good bit less training.

As before, the book can either be used as part of a public policy curriculum, as at Michigan, or for an undergraduate specialty course or section.

Many people have helped shape my thinking on benefit-cost analysis in general, and on this book in particular. Harvey Brazer, Roy Bahl, Paul Courant, Ronald Ehrenberg, Robert Haveman, George Johnson, Richard Porter, Hal Varian, and Michael Wolkoff read and made comments on all or large parts of the earlier version. For this version both Courant and Porter have reread large segments and made many new helpful comments. I have also benefited greatly from the comments of outside reader Tom Teitenberg. My latest two classes of students have gone through the draft manuscript in detail, pointing out passages that were wrong or opaque, and in some cases even finding errors in my answers to the problems at the end of the chapters. My teaching assistant, Thomas Lenaghan, has been particularly helpful in this regard. In addition I wish to thank the reviewers of this edition, Professor Abdul Qayum of Portland State University, Professor Herbert Mohring of the University of Minnesota, and Professor Barry Weingast of Washington University.

I owe much to the Institute of Public Policy Studies at the University of Michigan for giving me the opportunity to teach this course, and supplying both demanding and interested students as well as cooperative and helpful faculty. I could not ask for a better place to work. I also could not ask for a more supportive and helpful family. My wife Ruth has shown great tolerance and humor over the years in putting up with my idiosyncratic work habits. Last time around the most I could ask of my children, Sarah and Robert, was to understand their father's need to get some work done. This time they have grown in size and understanding, and have also read and made comments on parts of the book.

ONE
INTRODUCTION

In the affair of so much importance to you, wherein you ask my advice, I cannot, for want of sufficient premises, advise you what to determine, but if you please I will tell you how. When those difficult cases occur, they are difficult, chiefly because while we have them under consideration, all the reasons pro and con are not present to the mind at the same time; but sometimes one set present themselves, and at other times another, the first being out of sight. Hence the various purposes or inclinations that alternately prevail, and the uncertainty that perplexes us. To get over this, my way is to divide half a sheet of paper by a line into two columns; writing over the one Pro, and over the other Con. Then, during three or four days consideration, I put down under the different heads short hints of the different motives, that at different times occur to me, for or against the measure. When I have thus got them all together in one view, I endeavor to estimate their respective weights; and where I find two, one on each side, that seem equal, I strike them both out. If I find a reason pro equal to some two reasons cons, I strike out three. If I judge some two reasons con, equal to some three reasons pro, I strike out five; and thus proceeding I find at length where the balance lies; and if, after a day or two of further consideration, nothing new that is of importance occurs on either side, I come to a determination accordingly. And, though the weight of reasons cannot be taken with the precision of algebraic quantities, yet when each is thus considered, separately and comparatively, and the whole lies before me, I think I can judge better, and am less liable to take a rash step, and in fact I have found great advantage from this kind of equation, in what may be called moral or prudential algebra.

Benjamin Franklin, London, September 19, 1772

The true rule, in determining to embrace or reject any thing is not whether it have any evil in it; but whether it have more of evil, than of good. There are few things wholly evil, or wholly good. Almost every thing, especially of government policy, is an inseparable compound of the two; so that our best judgment of the preponderance between them is continually demanded. On this principle the president, his friends, and the world generally, act on most subjects. Why not apply it, then, upon this question? Why, as to improvements, magnify the evil, and stoutly refuse to see any good in them?...

The surplus—that which is produced in one place, to be consumed in another; the capacity of each locality for producing a greater surplus; the natural means of transportation, and their susceptibility of improvement; the hindrances, delays, and losses of life and property during transportation, and the causes of each, would be among the most valuable statistics in this connection. From these, it would readily appear where a given amount of expenditure would do the most good. These statistics might be equally accessible, as they would be equally useful, to both the nation and the states.

Representative Abraham Lincoln, Washington, June 20, 1848

It turns out that two of the greatest early American heroes were proponents of benefit-cost analysis. But they certainly are not the only ones. Modern U.S. presidents as well have been captivated by the notion. Under President Franklin Roosevelt the U.S. Flood Control Act first enunciated the now familiar standard that "the benefits to whomsoever they may accrue (be) in excess of the estimated costs." Under President Harry Truman the Budget Bureau adopted a formal set of rules to be used in making project decisions. Under President Lyndon Johnson the government tried to adopt a Planning Programming Budgeting System to aid in making spending decisions. Under President Jimmy Carter the Office of Management and Budget tried to adopt a Zero-Based Budgeting System to achieve the same end. And under President Ronald Reagan the government tried to apply formal cost-benefit analysis to health, safety, and environmental regulations.

With all this attention, there must be something here. Benefit-cost analysis is beguiling in its simplicity and seems to have very wide ramifications. In evaluating any choice, just add up the benefits, subtract the costs, and choose the alternative that maximizes the net benefits. It is not surprising that all these presidents would make benefit-cost analysis a key initiative of their administration.

But they may have gone too far. Although the benefit-cost framework is simple and useful as an organizing device, it is also easy to see more in benefit-cost analysis than there really is. It could naively be felt that benefit-cost analysis provides more answers than it really does, or makes questions easier than they really are.

This book tries to clarify these issues. It first discusses what benefit-cost analysis is and is not, showing how it can help frame questions but also where it has limitations. It then tries to teach benefit-cost analysis, to show how one actually does a benefit-cost analysis. The techniques of benefit-cost analysis are shown not only for dams and water projects, the traditional subjects, but also for other types of spending projects, human investment projects, grants to other governments, tax subsidies, and regulations. Increasingly, public needs are being dealt with through these other activities, and if an aspiring benefit-cost analyst wants to be useful, he or she must have the ability to operate in these newer areas.

In principle one can do a benefit-cost analysis of any choice—to go to this restaurant or that, to remain in school or work, to buy a used car now or a new car later. Sometimes some of the principles discussed here, such as knowing how to compare benefits received now and later, will help in making such personal choices. But most of the attention here is to public policy choices—should the government institute this spending program or that, use a tax subsidy or a regulation? Part of the reason for this attention to public policy is institutional—benefit-cost courses or modules are usually taught in connection with a public finance course, or as part of a public policy curriculum. Part is historical—there has simply been much more discussion of benefit-cost analysis of government activities than of any other activities. And part is substantive. Government has more complex and varied responsibilities than private decision makers. Private households can take market prices as given, but governments have an obligation to see if these prices accurately reflect social costs. Private households can analyze problems from their own perspective, but governments should analyze them from the perspective of all groups in a community. Hence government benefit-cost studies of a particular are more interesting than most corresponding private studies.

Just as this book tries to teach about the limitations of benefit-cost analysis, its own limitations should be noted. One main limitation is that it is kept fairly short. Benefit-cost analysis is not really a self-contained field of economics, but rather sits uneasily between microeconomics and public finance, with occasional doses of macroeconomics thrown in. When concepts are used from these other fields, they obviously cannot be explained in as much detail as in books about the other fields. Moreover, not all topics in these other fields are considered, only those that involve benefit-cost analysis in an important way.

A related warning involves program activities. There are lots of government activities these days, and one reasonably sized book cannot discuss all of them. Two important program areas that get fairly light treatment are health and defense—not because the issues are unimportant, but because it is impossible for one book written by one author to deal with everything.

Third, while benefit-cost analysis, and its larger field of program evaluation, are interdisciplinary fields, this book concentrates on the economic side of benefit-cost analysis. Again, this is not because political or sociological issues are unimportant, but simply because one has to draw the line somewhere. There is certainly enough to talk about from a primarily economic standpoint: that there is more to talk about from other standpoints should be viewed as a challenge to the student to take more courses in these other areas.

In terms of difficulty, the book is written mainly for students with a reasonable knowledge of the principles of microeconomics. Graphs are used extensively, as in most other economics books, and fairly simple equations are used occasionally. But while the book is beamed at this general audience, it should also benefit students with a little less and a little more background in economics. Sometimes those with a little less economics may have to take some things on faith, but most of the relevant arguments should be comprehensible.

BENEFIT-COST ANALYSIS AND THE GOVERNMENT

Is there any reason that it becomes particularly difficult to do benefit-cost analysis for government programs? There are three considerations.

A first is that the government is not an entity separate from its citizens, but really the collective expression of the will of citizens. The benefits and costs of some government project are then not the increases or decreases in government revenues but the gains or losses to all members of the community. Moreover, the government has a responsibility to look beyond the simple monetary gains and losses of some activities and consider whether projects lead to nonmonetary changes in atmospheric pollution, health and safety risks, or even wastes of people's time. Changes in any of these should be considered as much a benefit or a cost of a project as a monetary gain or loss.

A second reason why a government evaluation activity raises more complicated issues is in the pricing of resources used or the benefits created by a project. To maximize profits, private producers make decisions on the basis of market prices. But a public decision maker has the added responsibility of asking whether these prices give a correct measure of social benefits or costs. If the answer is no, public decision makers may have to adjust market prices to account for certain nonmarket effects. As will be seen, the question of exactly how to do that can become very complicated.

A third complication is that the government's policy purview can be very broad. There is a basic quandary that returns over and over on what to assume about other policies. Say that agreed-upon objectives of government policy are to reduce unemployment, to devote more resources to investment, and to equalize the distribution of incomes. If a government project has an impact on one or more of these objectives, for good or ill, should that be taken into account in the benefit-cost analysis? On one side, it could be argued that since society has already dealt with these other issues in its wisdom, what is can be considered optimal, and analysts should just ignore these other ramifications in doing a benefit-cost analysis. The counterargument, of course, is that since it is not easy to achieve any of these other objectives, any gain that the project makes in raising the income of the poor should be given added weight. Presumably what both sides could agree to is that the benefit-cost analyst should at least try to determine the impact on these other objectives of policy, and at least make this known to ultimate decision makers.

MISCONCEPTIONS

There are three common misconceptions about benefit-cost analysis. One is that benefit-cost analysis is a mechanical substitute for common sense. Nothing could be further from the truth. Benefit-cost analysis is a framework for organizing thoughts, or considerations: nothing more and nothing less. For any real world choice, there will always be some considerations that cannot easily be enumerated or valued, and where the analysis becomes quite conjectural. Benefit-cost analysis does not, and should not, try to hide this uncertainty. The sensible way to deal with uncertainty about some aspects of a benefit or a cost is to quantify what can be quantified, to array and rank nonquantifiable factors, and to proceed as far as possible. To use an example, suppose it can be shown that a mandatory container return law (bottle bill) costs state taxpayers about $X apiece, but reduces roadside litter substantially. The benefit-cost analyst will be hard pressed to know whether the bottle bill should be adopted, but in working out these numbers, it is much easier for legislators to see what is really going on with the bottle bill. Viewed in this light, even if benefit-cost analysis alone does not make any decisions, it can serve a valuable purpose in focusing decisions on the critical elements.

A second misconception is that it is unethical to use benefit-cost analysis in public policy decisions. The reason for the misconception is that often public policy decisions involve weighty matters. If the government builds a bridge, some construction workers may lose their lives. The government has to decide how much to spend on cancer research, which may save lives. The saving or losing of lives then becomes an important component of the gains or losses from a project. What to do?

Some commentators have an understandable reluctance to turn such weighty matters over to the benefit-cost analysts, and indeed these matters should not be completely turned over to the benefit-cost analysts. But even here the benefit-cost analysts might be helpful. Suppose that a careful study of construction wages indicates that workers are fully aware of the risks that they are taking in building a bridge, that they have plenty of other job opportunities, and that they get paid handsomely by the bridge authority for undergoing risk. Then it is possible to conclude that the risks are already incorporated into the market costs of the project. Or, the careful study may indicate that the risks are not accounted for and that the market cost of the project understates the true social cost. In such a way, it is possible to estimate the true social cost of the project, to compare this true cost with the expected benefits, and to provide in addition real data on expected loss of life in the construction phase. If compiled properly and used properly, this information can better inform the decision of whether or not to build the bridge. If compiled and used improperly, that is too bad, but it does not mean that it was unethical to compile the information. And it should always be remembered that society does have to make these decisions somehow, and that society can never shun *all* risk of life—then it would never have any bridges, and it would spend its entire budget on cancer research. There has to be a balancing of considerations, even when matters are weighty, and it seems best to get the most information that can be gotten carefully through benefit-cost analysis.

A final misconception regards the difference between a net improvement and a panacea. Too often government programs are over-advertised—program X can cure poverty, program Y can stop illiteracy. And too often they are evaluated in popular discussion on this basis—we did X, poverty still exists, so X must have failed. In this age of cynicism about public policy, it will not surprise anybody to say that government panaceas, which by themselves can cure some deep social problem, are hard to come by. But whether or not a panacea exists, surely this is the wrong standard to apply in making decisions about X. As both Franklin and Lincoln said, a policy measure is worth adopting if its benefits exceed its costs, and thereby makes a net improvement, even if it does not cure some deep problem all by itself. Its net benefits may be small relative to the scope of the problem, but if they are larger than for alternative choices, the program is worthy of consideration. Society can ill afford to reject worthwhile programs because they do not meet a standard that is far too demanding.

POSITIVE AND NORMATIVE—THE ROLE OF POLICY ADVICE

Another ground rule that must be clarified at the outset is just what role is to be played by benefit-cost analyses. Benefit-cost analysts are typically social science graduates working either in an administrative bureaucracy, for a consultant firm, for a lobbyist group, or on a legislative staff. Only rarely do they rise to the rarefied air of being actual politicians or decision makers. Their work, benefit-cost analyses and supporting studies, will usually be an input to a policy decision, and the world might actually be better off if it is an important input. But benefit-cost analyses are not policy decisions. The role of benefit-cost analysis is to aid in decisions, but not actually to make them. It also follows that whatever information is of value in this decision, such as the gains and losses that different groups are likely to receive as a result of a program, should also be provided.

These considerations lean on the side of preventing benefit-cost analysts from getting too cocky. But analysts should not get too humble either. Sometimes it is felt that because special interests pull a lot of weight in the legislature, or because some policies are like sacred cows that will never be carefully examined, it is useless to do benefit-cost analyses. And sometimes it probably is useless to do them. But not always and everywhere. Special interests pull a lot of weight, but sometimes the underlying analytics of a project can be so negative that even the strongest lobby in the world cannot get a program continued. The only hope is to keep doing the benefit-cost analyses, anticipating that at some point the burden of the negative results will become persuasive. And sacred cows do not have infinite lives either. Today's sacred cows can easily become tomorrow's sacrificial lambs if budgets get too tight or if other conditions change.

A key distinction here, and throughout the book, is that between the positive and the normative. Positive social science refers to attempts to describe the way the world is; normative social science refers to attempts to describe the way the world should be. Most benefit-cost analysis is done from a normative standpoint, where the true gains and losses from a policy are listed, quantified, and compared. Positive considerations play their role by helping to do this analysis, if for example it is necessary to know the answer to the positive, or descriptive, question of how many units of a good consumers will buy at what price. And some students of actual governmental decision making will be much more interested in the positive question of how certain policy decisions are made than the normative question of what choices should be made.

TYPES OF EVALUATIONS

Program analysts make much of the distinction between summative evaluations and formative evaluations. Summative evaluations ask whether a program is beneficial or not, given the structure of the program. Formative evaluations ask how a program could be made to work better.

Although there is a clear distinction between these questions, in general the economist's view of benefit-cost analysis downplays the distinction. As will be seen, the so-called fundamental principle of benefit-cost analysis, discussed at length in Chapter 3, requires that in any choice situation, the analyst or decision maker should choose the alternative that maximizes net benefits. If the policy question is the summative one of whether to do a program or not, the fundamental principle says to do it if net benefits are positive. If it is the formative question of whether some other version of the program is preferred, the fundamental principle says yes if the net benefits of the new conception of the program are positive. Either way, a good operational principle is to determine all variants of a program, measure gains and losses from each, and recommend the alternative that maximizes net benefits.

SUMMARY

It is very easy to define benefit-cost analysis: simply add up all the gains from a policy alternative, subtract all the losses, and choose the alternative that maximizes net benefits. Everybody does something like this all the time, and the extension to the world of public policy is natural and obvious.

There are, at the same time, several respects in which benefit-cost analysis of government programs is both trickier and more interesting than a corresponding analysis at the private level. On the one hand, the government represents all groups in a community, so the gains and losses of all of these groups should be considered. Government has an obligation to look at true social costs and benefits, as opposed to market prices. And governmental decision makers might want to weigh the benefits and costs differently if projects alter the distribution of income, the level of unemployment, or affect some other goal of policy.

Benefit-cost analysis is sometimes accused of being a mechanical substitute for common sense, and sometimes even of being unethical. Neither criticism is appropriate. Benefit-cost analysis is really a framework for comparing the pros (benefits) and cons (costs) of project choices. Benefits and costs should be quantified when they can be and not when they cannot be, but whether quantified or not, they should never be ignored. Even when they cannot be quantified, perhaps because they involve weighty matters of life and death, there are ways of setting up the analysis to focus public decisions properly.

TWO

WHY SHOULD THE GOVERNMENT INTERVENE IN A MARKET ECONOMY?

By 1987 total government spending at all levels in the United States had reached $1.4 trillion, 35 percent of the gross national product. At the federal level, this spending included everything from national defense to public assistance to postal subsidies. At the local level it included items ranging from education to trash collection to public hospitals. Obviously, any attempt to catalogue such a wide array of activities will not be perfect and may lead to awkwardly mixed cases. Yet we must do some simplifying to give some order to our attempt to analyze the workings of various programs.

This chapter has two objectives. First it identifies the normative rationales for government intervention in a market economy—the range of things the government might be trying to accomplish and why it is necessary for the public sector rather than the private sector to accomplish them. Second, it gives a quick review of the actual spending programs at the federal, state, and local level, classified by these objectives.

GOVERNMENT AND THE MARKET

Some years ago Richard Musgrave developed a useful way to classify the vast array of government programs. He divided government activities into those that effect the allocation of resources, the distribution of incomes, and stabilization objectives.[1] Allocation programs include measures to affect relative prices and/or the allocation of resources in the economy, motivated by considerations of economic efficiency. Distribution programs consist of efforts to alter the distribution of incomes, motivated by considerations of distributive equity. Stabilization measures are designed to achieve various macroeconomic objectives—stable prices, high employment, reasonable growth of overall output levels. Since this third set of objectives can be accomplished by manipulating overall tax and spending levels, they do not arise in a very central way in a study of benefit-cost analysis, though macroeconomic considerations do enter into topics such as the valuation of the labor incomes of otherwise unemployed workers or the valuation of benefits and costs realized at different times. But the first two objectives do involve specific programs and will be discussed extensively.

It should be noted at the outset that this classification scheme is not perfect. Many programs are undertaken for a mixture of allocation, distribution, and stabilization reasons, and programs undertaken for allocation reasons involve taxation that automatically affects the distribution of income. Yet as a broad way of sorting out what the government does, Musgrave's trichotomy is still useful.

To see how the allocation and distribution objectives come into play, it is first necessary to review the role of prices in a market economy. (Readers who are familiar with intermediate microeconomics can read this material lightly.) Suppose first that we are examining the market for good X. On one side of the market we have the consumers who demand this good. They operate under a demand function, more commonly referred to as a demand curve. This demand function is shown in Figure 2.1 as downward sloping (and uncurved!). It tells how many units of good X consumers will buy at various price levels. The price (P) is the independent variable and the quantity purchased (Q) is the dependent variable. The downward slope then means that as the price falls, the quantity demanded rises.

An alternative way to interpret the demand function is to analyze the willingness of consumers to pay for various units of the good. At quantity Q, consumers are willing to pay just P, but no more than that, for the last unit. We have switched the variables so that the quantity is now the independent variable and the price is the dependent variable: for this reason a demand function expressed this way is called an inverse demand function. Under this interpretation, we can also see that the price that consumers are willing to pay exactly equals the marginal utility (MU) of consumers for the good

(1) $MU_x = P_x$

The downward slope can then also be rationalized by the principle of diminishing marginal utility: the more of the good is possessed by consum-

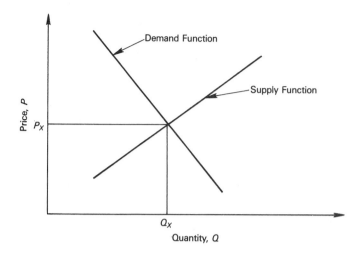

Consumers equate MU_X to P_X
Producers equate MC_X to P_X
P_X is the price that clears the market and makes marginal utility of consumers
   (MU_X) equal to marginal cost of producers (MC_X).

FIGURE 2.1   Economically Efficient Allocation of Resources, One Good

ers, the less is their marginal valuation of the last unit, and the less they are
willing to pay for one more unit.

The supply function is also drawn in the figure. In a competitive market,
suppliers will only supply the good if the price equals the marginal cost (MC)
of the good, so that

(2) $MC_x = P_x$

The upward slope of the supply function reflects the fact that for most goods
it becomes increasingly costly to raise supply: higher prices for the good are
necessary to elicit increased supplies as the amount already supplied rises.

The market-clearing price of the good is then determined by the inter-
play of demand and supply. At all prices below P_x quantity demanded
exceeds quantity supplied, and the excess demand tends to bid up the price.
At all prices above P_x the excess supply tends to bid down the price. At the
equilibrium price (P_x) there is no excess demand or supply. P_x is then referred
to as an equilibrium price because there is no tendency for it to change.

Putting these two functions together illustrates the genius of Adam
Smith's famous invisible hand. If the market price is free to vary, it clears the
market so that there are neither excess demands nor supplies. Consumers
look at this price charged and choose the quantity that equates their marginal
utility to price. Producers look at this price to be earned and equate their
marginal cost to price. Hence in market equilibrium production will equal

consumer demand, and consumers' marginal utility will equal producers' marginal cost

(3) $MU_x = MC_x$

Production will be at the socially optimal level because it takes place as long as its marginal valuation exceeds its marginal cost, but no further.

And the genius of this market solution extends even further. Not only is the level of production optimal, but it is allocated properly on both sides of the market. On the demand side, all those consumers with a willingness to pay greater than P_x will buy the good; and all those with a willingness to pay less than P_x will not. Hence the production is consumed by those who most value this production. On the supply side, all those producers who can supply the good for less than P_x will; all those who cannot will not. Hence the production is done by those who can supply the good most cheaply. Production is at the right level, it is consumed by those with the greatest demand, and it is done by those for whom it is cheapest.

All of this applies to one good, but the formal analysis can also be made in terms of many goods. The reason other goods are relevant is that markets are interdependent. If, for example, consumers desire to spend a little more on good X, they spend a little less on good Y. Or if producers use more resources to produce X, they have less available for Y. To deal with these complications, economists move from what is known as the partial equilibrium analysis of one market, an example of which was given in Figure 2.1, to a general equilibrium analysis of the whole economy.

A very simple form of this general equilibrium analysis is shown in Figure 2.2. On the axes are supplies of two goods, X and Y. To keep things simple, Y can be thought of as all goods other than X. The curve analogous to the supply function is known as the production possibilities (PP) curve. As its name indicates, this curve shows how much the economy *can* produce of the two goods with its present level of resources. The economy can devote all of its resources to the production of X at point A, or all to the production of Y at point B, or some intermediate combination.

The slope of this curve is known as the marginal rate of transformation (MRT). As the economy moves from point C to point D, it gives up CE of good Y and gains ED of good X. The saving in resources equals $(\Delta Y)(MC_Y)$, the change in Y (ΔY) times the marginal resource cost of producing Y (MC_Y). Since the PP curve measures maximum feasible production, we assume that all of these saved resources are devoted to the production of X. This means that

(4) $(\Delta Y)(MC_Y) = (\Delta X)(MC_X)$

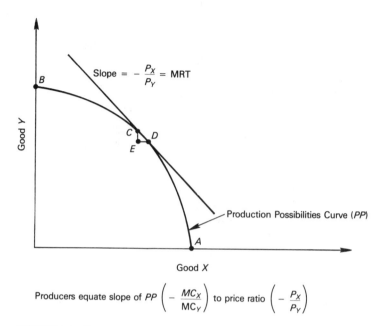

Producers equate slope of PP $\left(-\dfrac{MC_X}{MC_Y}\right)$ to price ratio $\left(-\dfrac{P_X}{P_Y}\right)$

FIGURE 2.2   Economically Efficient Production, Two Goods

Remembering from high school algebra that the slope of this PP curve over the interval is $-\Delta Y/\Delta X$, we get the following set of equalities

(5) Slope of $PP = \text{MRT} = -\Delta Y/\Delta X = -MC_X/MC_Y$

In this sense the marginal rate of transformation can be shown to equal the ratios of the marginal costs.

We note further that as the economy tries to produce more and more of good X, it would need to draw on more and more resources that are better suited for producing good Y. Hence the marginal cost of X rises, just as shown in the partial equilibrium analysis of Figure 2.1, and the marginal cost of Y falls. By equation (5), this means that the MRT gets more negative as we move rightward, or that the PP curve is concave to the origin.

When producers of all goods produce at the point where price equals marginal cost, as they do when there is perfect competition, the economy automatically moves to a point where the MRT (marginal cost ratio) equals the price ratio. Since the MRT is the slope of the PP curve, this MRT is also equal to the slope of a line tangent to the PP curve, as is also drawn on Figure 2.2

(6) Slope of $PP = \text{MRT} = -MC_X/MC_Y = $ Slope of tangent $= -P_X/P_Y$

A similar analysis can be done on the consumer side of the market, analogous to the demand function of Figure 2.1. Consumer tastes are measured along what is known as an indifference curve, shown in Figure 2.3. The *PP* curve takes resources as given and measures how much production of X and Y can be undertaken; the indifference curve takes consumer satisfaction as given and measures combinations of X and Y that yield exactly this overall level of satisfaction. If we compare two indifference curves, one going through point C and one through point E, the one through C represents a higher level of satisfaction because a household consumes the same amount of X but more Y.

The slope of this indifference curve can be similarly derived as just shown. If the household were to move from point C to point F, it would sacrifice $(\Delta Y)(MU_Y)$ units of utility—the change in Y times its marginal utility of consuming Y. To get back on the same indifference curve, it must gain back this utility, so that $(\Delta Y)(MU_Y) = (\Delta X)(MU_X)$. Hence just as before, the slope of the indifference curve, known as the marginal rate of substitution (MRS), over this interval is

$$(7) \text{ Slope} = MRS = -\Delta Y/\Delta X = -MU_X/MU_Y$$

FIGURE 2.3   Economically Efficient Allocation of Resources, Two Goods

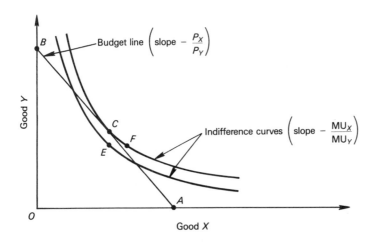

Good Y

B

Budget line $\left(\text{slope} - \dfrac{P_X}{P_Y}\right)$

C

F

E

Indifference curves $\left(\text{slope} - \dfrac{MU_X}{MU_Y}\right)$

A

O

Good X

Consumers maximize satisfaction by equating slope of indifference curve $\left(-\dfrac{MU_X}{MU_Y}\right)$ to slope of budget line $\left(-\dfrac{P_X}{P_Y}\right)$. When they do

$$\dfrac{MC_X}{MC_Y} = \dfrac{P_X}{P_Y} = \dfrac{MU_X}{MU_Y}$$

This time as we move rightward and consume more X and less Y, the MU_X will decline because of diminishing marginal utility, and the MU_Y will rise for the same reason. Hence the slope gets less negative, or the indifference curve is convex to the origin.

We can now use these indifference curves to show how households will maximize their satisfaction levels given their income (or spendable resources). This is done by drawing in the household's budget line. The budget line shows the combination of goods that the household can consume with its fixed income. If the household spends all income on Y, it can go to point B. Income must then equal $(OB)(P_Y)$, the amount of consumption of Y (OB) times the given price of Y (P_Y). If the household spends all on good X, it can go to point A with income defined as $(OA)(P_X)$. Since $(OB)(P_Y) = (OA)(P_X)$ by definition, we have

(8) Slope of budget line = $-OB/OA = -P_X/P_Y$

Note that this budget line cannot be changed by the household, because it depends on the fixed outside level of income and the ratio of prices determined by the economy.

The optimizing household will try to get to the highest indifference level given its income and prevailing price levels. It moves along its fixed budget line until it attains this highest indifference level. This will occur at point C where the slope of its indifference curve, the MRS, equals the slope of the budget line, the price ratio. But this is just the same price ratio that equaled the marginal cost ratio (MRT) on the production side. Hence in competitive equilibrium we have

(9) $MU_X/MU_Y = P_X/P_Y = MC_X/MC_Y$

This is the two good, general equilibrium, analogue of the marginal utility equals marginal cost condition in the partial equilibrium analysis. The only thing different between the two good equation (9) and the one good equation (3) is that consumers now equate their *ratio* of marginal utilities (MRS) to the price *ratio*, and producers equate their *ratio* of marginal costs (MRT) to the same price *ratio*. As before, production of each good takes place at the optimal level, consumers with the highest valuation get the output, and producers with the cheapest costs produce the good.

This all sounds so wonderful that one might be puzzled that a case for government intervention can be made at all. Just let the market work, and the right amount of production will be done by the right people for the right people. But remember that we made some assumptions along the way. If these assumptions are not fulfilled, we have a case for government intervention. A few of the prominent ways in which the assumptions may not be fulfilled are as follows:

> Monopolies. Suppose there were monopolistic sellers of goods. Monopolies hold back production to create excess profits: in these terms their price exceeds their marginal cost. Hence when consumers equate marginal utility to price, marginal utility exceeds marginal cost, and too little production would take place in a free but monopolized market.
>
> Environmental costs. Suppose the production of a good entails environmental costs to citizens outside the firm. In this case, the marginal social cost would exceed the marginal cost to producers and the marginal utility to consumers. Here too much production would take place in a free market.
>
> The distribution of income. Any set of market demand curves is based on an income distribution that gives rich people with many dollars to spend more weight than poor people without many dollars to spend. If this distribution of income does not satisfy equity goals of society, there is again a case for government intervention to promote equity objectives.

These are examples of market failure, where the free private market allocation of resources for one reason or another falls short of the social optimum, giving a rationale for government intervention.

ALLOCATIVE EFFICIENCY

In this section we consider some deviations from economic efficiency that might be taken care of through government allocation measures. We do not explicitly consider problems of establishing workable competition, for it is assumed that those deviations from a competitive equilibrium can best be dealt with through some form of antitrust or pro-competition policy. We focus only on inefficiencies that would exist even if all markets were perfectly competitive.

Public Goods

One type of allocative inefficiency involves what is known as the public goods problem. Consider Figure 2.4(a), dealing with a private good. There we assume that the good is supplied along the competitive supply function MC and that there are three consumers, with demand functions drawn as the three parallel downward sloping lines D_A, D_B, and D_C. The market demand function can be derived by summing the demands of the three individuals at each price, or the horizontal sum. That yields the heavy line and the market equilibrium Q^*, where A buys the amount read from his demand function, B the amount read from hers, and C the amount read from hers. Note that for each consumer $MU = P$, and since $P = MC$ from the supply function, the

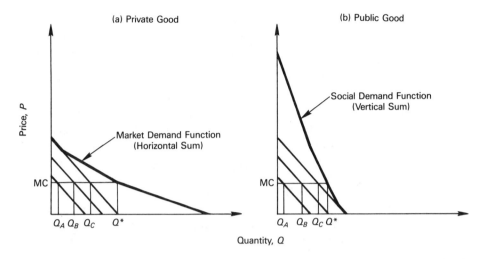

(a) For private goods, each consumer faces the same price (= MC), and market demand $Q^* = Q_A + Q_B + Q_C$, the horizontal sum. At Q^*, MC equals each consumer's MU.

(b) For public goods, all consumers automatically consume the same amount. Social demand is the sum of the MUs of each consumer at each Q, the vertical sum. At Q^*, the sum of the MUs equals the MC.

FIGURE 2.4   Private and Public Goods

solution is economically efficient. Each consumer values the last unit of output exactly at its marginal cost.

Now consider a class of goods known as public goods, shown in Figure 2.4(b). The supply function and the demand function for each individual are exactly the same as before, but now the physical properties of the good are different. Imagine that the good is something like a public park, a lighthouse, or even a national defense system. For these goods if one consumer consumes it, all others automatically consume exactly the same amount. The consumption by these other consumers does not change the consumption of the first. To put it another way, for these goods it is either technically infeasible or very costly to exclude others from consuming the good when one person does: the "exclusion" principle does not apply. For a private good exclusion is possible and all consumers consume different amounts at the same price; now things are turned around so that all consumers automatically consume the same amount.

To find the economically efficient equilibrium it is necessary to derive a market demand function from the individual demands. Previously we saw that demand functions could be interpreted either as showing how much a consumer will consume at each price, or the consumer's marginal utility, or willingness to pay, at each quantity. In the public goods case we take the second interpretation. Combining this with the physical constraint that each consumer must consume the same amount yields a strange result: to get the community demand curve for a public good we must sum the individual demand functions vertically, not horizontally. At Q_A, for example, we know that A's willingness to pay is just the value MC. But B also consumes Q_A automatically, and her willingness to pay is read from her demand function. And C automatically consumes Q_A, and her willingness to pay can also be read from her demand function. The marginal satisfaction yielded to all three consumers, each of whom consumes Q_A, is then the vertical sum of the marginal utility values of each consumer. This community, or social, demand function is plotted as the heavy line.

Why does the physical constraint that consumption must be the same require government intervention? Technically it does not. But we can see that if A was left to his own devices, he would consume Q_A. He would equate his own marginal utility to marginal cost, and the good would be under-consumed because the added utility of B and C would be ignored. Similarly, if left to her own devices, B would consume Q_B. This is greater, but still less than the social optimum because the utility of A and C is ignored. The proper solution is at Q^*, where the combined marginal benefits of all consumers are set equal to the marginal cost. Ronald Coase has shown that under certain conditions, A, B, and C could work toward this social optimum by having a system of side payments to get one consumer to consume more, since the other two consumers would benefit.[2] But in complex societies with many consumers, a complete system of side payments is very difficult to work out, and it often becomes much more feasible for the government to intervene in the market directly and provide spending closer to the social optimum.

Externalities

A second phenomenon that could justify government intervention in even a freely competitive market economy is known as an externality. As the name suggests, an externality designates a benefit or a cost of a market transaction that is neither paid for nor received by those making the transaction, and is therefore not incorporated into the market demand or supply. The example just alluded to was where a manufacturing plant might emit smoke and cause acid rain or other damage to groups that are neither producers nor consumers of the good. On the other side, if a firm were to sell a product that made outsiders better off, such as a drug that cures a communicable disease, the firm would not capture all of the benefits of its production in its selling price.

Figure 2.5 displays examples of externalities on both the benefit and the cost side. The left panel gives the case of external benefits, such as for drugs for communicable diseases. Here the social benefits from the good are not

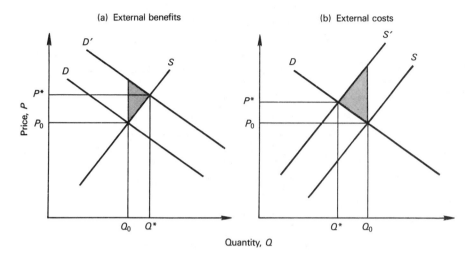

For external benefits, the true social demand (D') exceeds the private demand, and either a demand or supply subsidy can be given to expand output toward the social optimum, Q^*. The cost of not doing so, or the dead weight loss, is given by the shaded triangle.

For external costs, the true social cost (S') exceeds the private cost, and either demand or supply taxes can be assessed to contract output toward the social optimum, Q^*. The cost of not doing so is again given by the shaded triangle.

FIGURE 2.5 Externalities

entirely included in the consumers' demand function and the firm's selling price. The free market equilibrium is at the intersection of the market demand function, D, and the supply function, S, at Q_0 and P_0. But the point of optimal economic efficiency is where the demand function including the externalities, D', intersects the supply curve at Q^* and P^*. One policy measure that would move society toward Q^* would be a rebate to demanders of the distance between the two demand curves. In this case at each quantity willingness to pay is increased because of the subsidy. Or, at each price quantity demanded is increased because of the subsidy. The demand function is shifted up by just the amount of the subsidy to the social demand function, and equilibrium quantity would be at the social optimum level Q^*. The same subsidy could also be given to suppliers, with the same outcome (just shift down the supply curve the requisite amount). In either case, the government could provide these subsidies and correct this externality.

What is the cost of not correcting the externality? This cost is the same as the value of the government intervention, and it is obviously a key notion in the benefit-cost analysis of this and other programs. Given its importance, we introduce it here even though a more systematic discussion of benefit-cost analysis comes later. The cost of not correcting the externality is known as the dead weight loss or excess burden, and is shown in the left panel of Figure 2.5 as the shaded triangle. It can be derived very simply. Without intervention the market goes to Q_0. At this quantity, the marginal social benefit of production is read from the social demand function and the marginal cost is read from the supply function. The difference is the base of the triangle. These differences are then summed for all output from Q_0 to Q^* to give the dead weight loss triangle. Not intervening in the market causes this social loss.

The logic is precisely the same in the case of external costs, shown in the right panel of Figure 2.5. If these costs were not "internal to" the firm, or charged to the firm by the market, the free market solution of Q_0 and P_0 would lead to more than the socially optimal amount of output, Q^*. The government could correct the inefficiency by incorporating the externality into the firm's supply, say by taxing it in the amount of the difference between the supply function including the externalities, S', and the old supply function. At each quantity the price required to supply the good is higher because the supplier has to pay the tax; or at each price, quantity supplied is less because of the tax. The tax moves the market to the social optimal level, Q^*, and avoids the dead weight loss. This dead weight loss or excess burden is again given by the difference between true marginal social costs and firm marginal costs, summed over the excess output in the free market (Q_0–Q^*).

Natural Monopolies

A third type of deviation involves what are known as natural monopolies, instances where the fixed costs of providing a good are very large, relative to the marginal costs, so that average costs are declining over the relevant consumption range. Illustrations would be a bridge, highway, or a public utility. The large fixed cost implies that the industry typically cannot support enough suppliers to make it competitive—hence the term natural monopoly.

An example is shown in Figure 2.6. Assume that the marginal cost of supplying the service, say crossings of a bridge, is given by the MC curve. This MC curve could be rising or falling over this range: in the figure it is drawn as horizontal. The important thing is that the MC must be low relative to the average total cost (ATC). As long as it is, it will pull down this average and lead to the phenomenon of falling average costs. This ATC is by definition equal to the sum of the fixed cost of building the bridge, averaged over the number of users, plus the marginal cost. Hence at any point the average fixed cost is given by the difference between the ATC curve and the MC curve. It can be seen from the figure that this distance declines as the number of users (Q) over which the fixed costs are averaged increases.

How should such a service be provided? There are several options. One is to leave things up to the free market. In this case our natural monopoly becomes a real monopoly. The way any firm maximizes profits

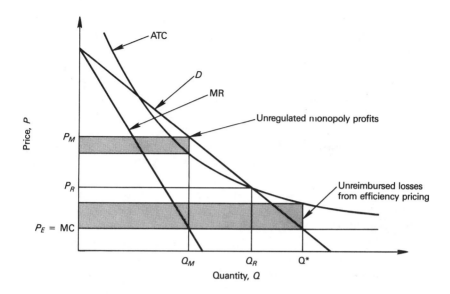

The physical properties of the good are such that MC is low relative to ATC, pulling down the ATC. There are three pricing options:

1. Unregulated monopoly prices at P_M, with Q_M users, makes excess profits given by the top shaded rectangle, and has dead weight loss given by the triangle with base $Q^* - Q_M$ and height $P_M - P_E$.
2. Regulated monopoly prices at P_R (= ATC), has Q_R users and makes no excess profits, but still has dead weight loss given by the triangle with base $Q^* - Q_R$ and height $P_R - P_E$.
3. Efficient price is at P_E = MC with Q^* users and no dead weight loss. But the firm must now be subsidized by the bottom shaded rectangle.

FIGURE 2.6 Natural Monopoly

is to produce at the quantity where the marginal revenue from an expansion of output equals the marginal cost. A competitive firm has a horizontal demand function with an infinite elasticity of demand. Such a firm can produce all the output it wants with no reduction in price, so the MR equals the price which in turn equals both the MC (through profit maximization) and MU (through consumer optimization). This is another way of seeing that the market outcome is economically efficient. A monopolist, by contrast, has enough market power that the demand function slopes downward. This means that the monopolist can only expand output by cutting prices on all units of output, so that the MR is below the demand function (as drawn in Figure 2.6) by just the loss of revenue from the price cuts on previous levels of output.

Hence when our natural monopoly becomes a real monopoly, it sets MR equal to MC to find the profit-maximizing quantity Q_M. It reads the price from the demand curve at P_M. This solution is not politically attractive because at Q_M the price charged exceeds the ATC, which means that the firm owning the bridge makes excess profits given by the top shaded rectangle. In economic terms, it is not attractive either, but this time it is because consumers are equating MU to P, which is greater than MC. The solution is economically inefficient in that it would be possible for the bridge to supply more crossings where MU exceeds MC. The dead weight loss of the real monopoly is defined in the legend, again the difference between MU and MC summed over the output gap.

A second option, and one commonly followed in practice, is to regulate away the profits of this monopoly. The way this is usually done is to force the regulated monopoly to price where excess profits are zero, or just at P_R = ATC, with Q_R bridge crossers. Although this outcome may solve the political problem of excess profits, notice that MU still exceeds MC. At the margin, the benefits of crossing the bridge still exceed the low marginal costs, and society could gain by permitting added crossings. The new dead weight loss is smaller, but still not zero.

The third option is the one that is economically efficient. The toll should be P_E = MC, with Q^* crossers. Since MU now equals MC, there is no dead weight loss. The problem here is that at this toll, the bridge authority recovers only the marginal cost of crossing the bridge, but is not reimbursed for its average fixed cost. At this economically efficient quantity level, the bridge authority loses the bottom shaded rectangle. Hence there is no reason why a monopoly regulated this way will build the bridge in the first place. One solution is for the government to build and own the bridge and just permit the bridge operator to charge marginal costs. Another is to subsidize the bridge owners in some way for their fixed costs. Either way, some form of government intervention is necessary, first to prevent the natural monopoly from becoming a real monopoly and second to insure economically efficient pricing of the facility.

DISTRIBUTIVE EQUITY

To this point we have concerned ourselves exclusively with problems of allocative efficiency, but now we can broaden the focus to deal with income distribution issues as well. As was said before, distribution is an objective of government intervention because even a freely competitive market only insures that workers get paid their marginal product in production, not necessarily enough to live on. Moreover, distributional standards are in part relative: as living standards rise in general, social norms of what is a living wage may also rise. We now discuss some rationales for government distributional programs.

Direct Tax and Transfer Programs

The obvious way of narrowing the distribution of income is to tax the rich to support the poor. To see how this works, the solid line in Figure 2.7 gives the distribution of income with no government distributional policy. As an empirical matter, this distribution is generally skewed: some people do not even earn a poverty level living standard (about $9000 per year for a family of three in 1987), and some people earn an income many times that of the poverty level.

If there were such a redistributive tax-transfer system, those on the lower side of the median would be the beneficiaries and those on the upper side would pay for the redistribution. The distribution would be shifted to the small dashed line, with very few people left below the poverty line, and higher incomes also reduced. To use a statistical term, the variance of the income distribution would be reduced by the tax and transfer measures.

The advantage of this form of transfer is that it is the most direct. Low-income families would be eligible for payments and high-income families would make them. Payments could also be directed to the neediest relatively easily. But there are also some disadvantages. One is that recipients are getting a form of "welfare" payment, with all the social stigma that goes with it. A second is that there could be some economic inefficiency in this form of payment. To get the payments, low-income families would have an incentive to keep their income low—not work as hard. To avoid making the payments, high-income families would have precisely the same incentive. Arthur Okun has referred to both of these inefficiencies as the "leaky bucket" problem: families would like to transfer water, but some of the water will leak in the process.[3] The upshot is that direct transfers involve delicate balances between the equity goal of helping poor people and the efficiency goal of not diluting incentives to work.

Human Investment

A second type of redistribution focuses on the long run, much like preventive medicine. Rather than giving the poor transfer payments, this type of redistribution involves education and training of people to make them more productive, called human investment programs. In the parlance of politicians, rather than giving handouts, society is extending a helping hand. Whereas transfer programs try to reduce the variance of the income distribution, human investment programs could, in principle, shift up the entire distribution as is shown by the large dashed line in Figure 2.7.

The advantage of this approach is obvious. Now equity and efficiency goals are not necessarily in conflict; indeed many helping hand programs make sense in their own right in terms of productivity increases, regardless

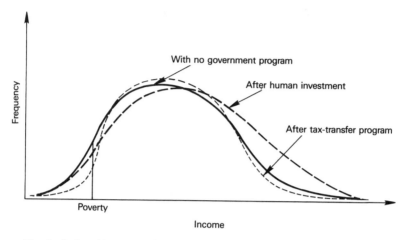

The distribution of income can be compacted by tax and transfer programs or shifted up by human investment programs.

FIGURE 2.7   Distribution of Income

of their impact on the distribution of income. The disadvantages are that such programs are harder to make work—they may not raise incomes at all—and they may well not work for all of the poor. Hence there are likely to be larger numbers left in poverty status, even with a successful education program that did raise the average income in society. And even if successful with the poor, the rewards for these educational types of activities are very long in coming, perhaps taking a generation or more to realize sizable gains.

Social Insurance

A third type of income redistribution cannot easily be shown in diagrams such as Figure 2.7, and in a long-run sense it might not even be called redistribution. It involves social insurance. Because there are some social risks that people cannot easily insure against, the government sets up programs to insure against risks. The classic example of this type of program is social security, where the government protects people against destitution in their old age by setting up a trust fund into which workers pay while working and from which they receive benefits once they retire. There are similar trust fund arrangements for unemployment insurance and to cover the medical costs of the aged (medicare).

One might ask why there would not be private insurance against these social risks. There are two answers:

In some cases the risks are sufficiently general, say the risk of unemployment in a recession, that it would simply be too expensive for private companies to provide it.

In other cases we run up against what economists call the adverse selection problem. Suppose that a private company tried to provide health insurance. Since it generally cannot tell who needs lots of health insurance and who needs very little, it might charge an average amount, only to find that the only people who buy the insurance are those who are very sickly and use the insurance extensively. The insurance companies lose, they either raise rates or go out of business, healthy people use insurance even less, and we again get a situation where insufficient amounts of private insurance are provided. In both cases the solution to the missing insurance problem would be to have the government set up a general scheme to insure the entire population against the risk.

These social insurance programs are clearly not redistributive in the same sense as previously shown, because the benefits received by the typical retiree or unemployed worker are related to payroll taxes that the same worker has already paid. But these social insurance programs still have some of the same incentive problems as redistributive transfers. On the one side, there is a tax on workers that could discourage work (though less so than in the human investment example if workers feel they will get some back some day). On the other side, there is an incentive for unemployed workers to extend their benefits by staying unemployed a bit longer, or for retirees to spend more than the minimum necessary on health care because medicare is paying.

ACTUAL SPENDING LEVELS

The preceding normative discussion can be given a realistic flavor by showing how much various governments actually do of the previously described activities. For regulatory interventions and taxes, there are intrinsic difficulties in measuring the size of the impact, and it is difficult to come up with numbers indicating the size of governmental activity. But for direct spending it is easy to come up with such numbers, since the size of the impact is approximately related to the size of the spending. Hence the following discussion tries to categorize spending into various allocation and distribution classes for the federal, state, and local governments in the United States.

The Federal Government

Table 2.1 shows the categorization of federal spending. Spending is shown for two years—1960 and 1985—to give some idea not only how extensive the spending is but how it has grown over time. For each year the number shown is not spending itself, which naturally grows through time with population, prices, and productivity, but spending as a percentage of gross national product (GNP), to correct for changes in the scale of the

TABLE 2.1   Spending of the Federal Government, 1960 and 1985
Percentage Share of Gross National Product

	1960	1985
Total expenditures	18.4	24.6
Allocation	11.2	8.4
National defense and international affairs	9.4	6.9
Domestic	1.8	1.6
Distribution	4.2	11.7
Transfers	3.4	11.2
Social Security and Medicare	2.2	8.3
Agriculture	0.6	0.8
Other	0.6	2.1
Human Investment	0.8	0.5
Housekeeping	3.0	4.4
Veterans	1.1	0.7
Interest	1.3	3.2
Other	0.6	0.5

Components may not sum to total because of rounding error.
Source: *Survey of Current Business*, various issues.

economy. And the activities are classified into allocation, distribution, and a last catchall category called housekeeping—paying interest on the debt, administering the tax system, and providing pensions to veterans or other past employees of the federal government.

One technical note is that since these spending totals include grants from one government to another, spending at different governmental levels cannot simply be added to measure the aggregate size of government. A typical grant program involves having the federal government pay money to state governments for spending on some public service. The same money is thus simultaneously included in the spending of the federal government and the states, and a simple addition of these spending totals would "double-count" the grant. To avoid double-counting, it is necessary to sum all spending and then deduct all intergovernmental grants. In 1985, for example, the sum of the spending shares of the federal, state, and local governments from Tables 2.1, 2.2, and 2.3 is 40 percent, but the true share of government spending at all levels after deducting grants is 35 percent.[4]

As can be seen from the table, federal spending has grown from 18.4 percent of GNP in 1960 to 24.6 percent by 1985. Allocation spending has actually declined over the interval, mainly because of the drop in spending for national defense and international affairs. Spending for housekeeping has risen over the period, mainly because of the rise in spending for interest on the federal outstanding debt, in turn related to the large federal deficits of recent years.

**TABLE 2.2   Spending of State Governments 1960 and 1985
Percentage Share of Gross National Product**

	1960	1985
Total expenditures	5.2	8.2
Allocation	1.6	2.5
Distribution	3.0	4.9
Transfers	1.2	2.0
Public assistance	0.7	1.4
Health	0.4	0.6
Human investment	1.8	2.9
Housekeeping	0.5	0.7
Interest	-0.1	—
Other	0.6	0.7

Components may not sum to total because of rounding error.

Source: *Survey of Current Business*, various issues.

But even with the growth in interest payments, the big change in the table involves spending for social insurance programs, social security, and medicare. These social insurance expenditures are the largest component of spending now, and their change alone accounts for the entire growth in federal spending as a share of GNP over the 25-year interval. Payments for farmers, essentially distributional in that their main object is supporting farm prices and incomes, have stayed roughly stable at slightly less than one percent of GNP, and other distributional payments largely for low-income persons have grown as a share of GNP, but are still only slightly more than two percent.

**TABLE 2.3   Spending of Local Governments 1960 and 1985
Percentage Share of Gross National Product**

	1960	1985
Total expenditures	6.5	7.7
Allocation	1.9	1.8
Distribution	3.8	4.9
Transfers	0.8	1.1
Human investment	3.0	3.8
Housekeeping	0.8	1.0
Interest	0.1	0.1
Other	0.7	0.9

Components may not sum to total because of rounding error.

Source: *Survey of Current Business*, various issues.

State Governments

The next level in the U.S. governmental hierarchy is the states. States have some supervisory role over their local governments, and they also maintain statewide functions such as state road systems and state universities. They are intermediate with respect to the grant system as well—they receive most of the grants from the federal government (included in federal spending) and they give other grants to local governments (included as state spending).

State spending has risen from 5.2 percent of GNP in 1960 to 8.2 percent in 1985. Interest payments and other housekeeping expenses have been low and have not changed significantly, but both allocation and distributional spending have risen moderately over the years. Within the distributional category, both public assistance transfers and human investment spending for education and training have also risen moderately. By 1985 allocation, transfers, and human investment spending were all between two to three percent of GNP.

Local Governments

Spending by the approximately 82,000 local governments in the United States has also risen moderately in the past 25 years, from 6.5 to 7.7 percent of GNP. Sometime in this period state spending passed local spending in size.

Roughly half of local spending, and most of the growth in local spending, can be attributed to just one function, operating public school systems. Otherwise, the shares look much like those for states—about two percent to allocation (police, fire, trash collection, roads), one percent to income transfers, and slightly less than that to housekeeping.

SUMMARY

This chapter has reviewed the main objectives of government intervention in a market economy. There is a rationale for so-called allocation activities to correct what would otherwise be distortions in the allocation of resources by a free market. These distortions involve problems with public goods, externalities, and natural monopolies: in each case even a competitive market would not inevitably gravitate to the right solution from the standpoint of overall economic efficiency.

There is also a rationale for distribution activities in the event that the free market distribution of income does not conform to basic notions of distributive equity. These activities could either feature tax and transfer programs, which raise all low incomes but may have efficiency costs, longer run education and training programs to raise incomes across the board for those who take advantage, or social insurance programs to compensate for people's inability to get private insurance against certain risks.

In terms of actual spending levels, federal spending is now almost one-fourth of GNP, with state and local spending adding another 8 percent apiece. Aggregate government spending of 35 percent of GNP (after correcting for intergovernmental grants) is low, relative to the levels in European countries, as is the growth in this share over time. The largest component of spending at any level, and the main growth in the past 25 years has come in federal spending for social insurance. Federal national defense spending is now a close second, but unlike social security and medicare, it has fallen as a share of GNP over the past 25 years.

NOTES

[1]Musgrave's book, *The Theory of Public Finance* (New York: McGraw-Hill) came out in 1959. Its latest incarnation is Richard A. Musgrave and Peggy B. Musgrave, *Public Finance in Theory and Practice*, 5th edition, (New York: McGraw-Hill, 1989).

[2]Ronald Coase, "The Problem of Social Cost," *Journal of Law and Economics*, October 1960.

[3]Arthur M. Okun, *Equality and Efficiency: The Big Tradeoff* (Washington D.C.: The Brookings Institution, 1975), Chapter 4.

[4]Perceptive readers may wonder what happens if states respond to federal grants by cutting their own taxes. That does happen fairly extensively, as later chapters will show. But it does not change the addition rule proposed, because in that case the federal grant simply replaces a state tax, and should not be included in total spending.

THREE
THE FUNDAMENTAL PRINCIPLE OF BENEFIT-COST ANALYSIS

Until now we have examined certain respects in which a free market may fail to yield an allocation of resources that is judged to be economically efficient or a distribution of income that is judged to be equitable. Certain types of governmental activities—direct spending, tax subsidies, or regulations—can conceivably improve the situation. But how do we know whether they will? The answer is straightforward—do a benefit-cost analysis of the intervention. In this chapter we introduce that topic.

The rationale for benefit-cost analysis can be drawn from three different intellectual traditions. One tradition uses the logic of a field known as welfare economics, one uses microeconomics, and one uses a field known as public choice. We will review each tradition to see how it answers the benefit-cost question, and then try to show how ultimately all three traditions converge to the same operational rule of thumb for the aspiring benefit-cost analyst, called the fundamental principle of benefit-cost analysis. The chapter concludes by giving some examples of how to use the fundamental principle.

THE WELFARE ECONOMICS TRADITION

The first thing to recognize about any intervention in a market economy, however much it improves the welfare of society as a whole, is that it will probably make at least some people worse off. In the examples used in the previous chapter, there may be an excellent public goods rationale for building a new public park that could benefit the entire citizenry, but the owners of a private amusement park may be made worse off. Taxes to correct air pollution will improve everybody's health, but will surely hurt the business of the firms that had been polluting the air. Transfers to aid poor people will aid them but hurt those who have to foot the bill.

How should society deal with these cases where policies will help some and hurt others? The issue has troubled social scientists for more than a century, and moral philosophers even longer than that. Remarkably little progress has been made. The basic sticking point is economists' reluctance to make interpersonal utility comparisons. How can we know whether the social value of the gain to one person exceeds the social cost of the loss to others? Most people may gain from the public park, but do they count for more than those who own the amusement park?

The logical criterion for proving that a policy change, or any other change, is beneficial was first stated by a nineteenth century Italian social scientist, Vilfredo Pareto. Pareto's rule is very simple:

> Program X improves the welfare of society if it makes at least one person better off and no one worse off.

It is hard to argue with that, but also hard to apply it, because almost every public program will make at least someone worse off.

Pareto's rule has more practical applicability than might at first be apparent because it could allow for a system of side payments from those who gain from a policy to those who lose. If the winners from a policy change compensate the losers for their pain and suffering, these winners can still be better off without anybody being worse off. Explicit side payments are known as bribes and are generally illegal, but there are many more subtle ways in which side payments can be and have been made. In U.S. legislative history, the 1974 Trade Readjustment Assistance Act tried to make most U.S. consumers better off by lowering tariff barriers; but it also contained a provision for side payments, in the form of assistance payments, for industries that were hurt by the tariff reductions. The Tax Reform Act of 1986 tried to eliminate tax-induced distortions in the allocation of resources by lowering tax rates generally, but there were many temporary provisions to cushion the blow for those industries that had been previously benefiting from distortionary treatment. Although good government proponents often rail at these apparent handouts, they have a very strong philosophical justification that goes right back to Pareto's rule.

But not every complex public policy issue can be resolved by making side payments. It may often be impossible to devise a system of side payments, and even when side payments are made, they are generally not complete compensation for the losses felt by some groups. Moreover, if side payments were made for every issue with policy losers, the system of public laws would get impossibly cluttered. The U.S. tax code would be much more complicated than it is now, and most people figure it is already far too complicated. Trade bills would be much more complicated, defense bases would be much more difficult to close, and so forth. At some point in the policy process, decisions will have to be made that entail losses. What to do then?

From an economic efficiency standpoint alone, net national welfare can be maximized by following a rule that comes from the work of two British economists, Nicholas Kaldor and John Hicks.[1] What is now known as the Kaldor-Hicks rule can be stated as:

> Program X has positive net benefits if the gainers *could* compensate the losers and still be better off.

Notice that under this Kaldor-Hicks rule the side payments do not have to be made. If they are made, the winners would make the payments and have some gains left over—these are the positive net benefits, and in this case the policy change satisfies the Pareto rule too. If side payments are not made, the winners gain more than the losers lose, and there are positive net benefits for society as a whole. But not for every person in society, and if we are unwilling to make interpersonal utility comparisons, we can no longer actually be sure that program X makes society better off. When the side payments are not made, the change no longer satisfies the Pareto rule.

Why has the Kaldor-Hicks rule become so popular? Simply because the Pareto rule is so demanding that it can hardly ever be adhered to. The difference between the two rules can be illustrated with a concept that has also proven useful in statistics. Suppose decision makers are reviewing policy proposals as they come along, trying to minimize the social cost of errors they make. They can make two types of errors:

> Type I errors, where the policy change is really beneficial but decision makers reject it.
> Type II errors, where the policy change is really not beneficial, but decision makers fail to reject it.

When decision makers follow the Pareto rule, they will reject almost all policies, because they can almost never be sure that nobody is worse off. They almost never make a type II error, but in rejecting almost all ideas they make many type I errors. The Kaldor-Hicks rule can be viewed as an answer to the innate conservatism of the Pareto rule because it permits decision makers to use a less demanding screen, accepting those ideas where there is potential, if not actual, Pareto improvement. Under this Kaldor-Hicks rule, decision makers will make more type II errors but many fewer type I errors.

In any policy situation there will often be more than one policy under consideration. The government could build a park with only swings or with swings, tennis courts, and a swimming pool. To deal with the case of multiple options, the Kaldor-Hicks rule can be restated as what Edith Stokey and Richard Zeckhauser call the "fundamental principle" of benefit-cost analysis:[2]

> In any choice situation, select the (policy) alternative that produces the greatest net benefit.

Again, the implication is that the side payments need not be made, that we are simply asking whether the winners could compensate the losers and still have some net benefits left over. But this time we are applying the principle to find the best solution to a problem, that solution that leaves the most left over for the winners.

THE MICROECONOMIC TRADITION

The microeconomic tradition for making benefit-cost decisions goes back to the public goods example of the previous chapter. There we showed how individuals would underconsume public goods because they would ignore the benefits others received from that consumption. But we did not work the example all the way.

That is done with the aid of Figure 3.1. It is drawn with a larger scale to focus primarily on the situation for consumer A, but it describes the same overall situation as in the previous chapter. Again we have three demanders of the good, A the political conservative with the lowest demand at every price, C the political liberal with the highest, and B the middle-of-the-road demander. As before, the vertical sum is the social willingness-to-pay at each quantity, shown by the heavy line, and the optimal level of output is where this vertical sum equals the marginal cost of buying the good at Q^*. As before, we know if left to their own devices, consumers will underconsume, and that government intervention may be necessary to correct the distortion and move output levels toward Q^*. Point Q^* is sometimes called the Samuelsonian point, after Paul Samuelson, who first worked this analysis out completely.[3]

We know that Q^* is the optimal quantity by comparing the marginal social benefit and the marginal cost at each quantity. If this marginal social benefit exceeds marginal cost, we expand quantity a bit more and do the test again, safe in the knowledge that since marginal social benefits are declining, eventually they will equal marginal costs. And, as long as output is expanding with marginal benefits exceeding marginal costs, society is getting better off all the time.

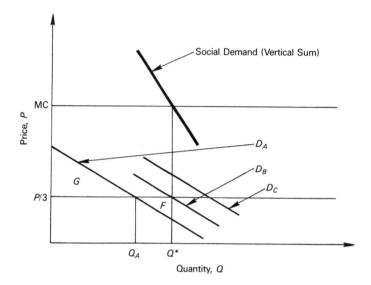

If A is charged a price of P/3, he would desire to consume Q_A and gain area G.

If A is forced to consume the social optimum Q^*, his net gain is area G-area F.

FIGURE 3.1   Does A Benefit from a Public Good?

There is another way to discover the optimal point, this time using an economist's concept called consumer surplus. In Figure 3.1, suppose each consumer is asked to pay for one-third of the public good, being faced with a price of P/3. Consumer A operates under the demand function labelled D_A in the diagram, and would be inclined to consume Q_A units at this price. Will A benefit from the provision of the public good? It depends on the level of consumption. If he could get to Q_A, he would benefit greatly. The first unit of output yields a marginal satisfaction much greater than the price of P/3. The second yields a bit less satisfaction. Only at A's preferred quantity Q_A is there no more marginal satisfaction. But the total satisfaction for A in consuming Q_A, his optimal quantity of the public good, is given by summing of the satisfaction achieved on each unit up to Q_A, triangle G. This triangle is A's net gain from consuming at Q_A, or A's consumer surplus.

Public goods are public goods, however, and A may not be able to achieve this amount of consumption. Remember that all consumers consume the same amount. Suppose now that society goes to the Samuelsonian point where the aggregate marginal social benefit equals the marginal cost at Q^*. Here A still gets all the surplus he had earlier on consumption up to Q_A, but beyond that he loses triangle F, the amount by which his cost (P/3) exceeds his willingness-to-pay from the demand function. Hence the net gain for A at Q^* equals triangle G less triangle F.

This type of reasoning can be used to express the Samuelsonian public goods optimum point in terms of the Kaldor-Hicks rule. Suppose the community were consuming the public good at Q_A and charging each of the three consumers $P/3$. Would it make sense to expand output to Q^*? According to the Samuelsonian logic previously described, clearly yes, because over the interval from Q_A to Q^* the marginal social benefits (given by the vertical sum) exceed the marginal cost. The Samuelsonian gain from expending output is shown by the heavily-shaded triangle in Figure 3.2.

Since this heavily-shaded Samuelsonian gain is derived by summing the individual demand curves, it can also be derived from the individual demands. We have already seen that A's loss in expanding output is the difference between A's price and A's marginal utility, triangle F. B gains in expanding output, because at Q_A she is consuming less than desired. If output is expanded, she values the marginal output from her demand func-

FIGURE 3.2   The Optimal Quantity of Public Goods

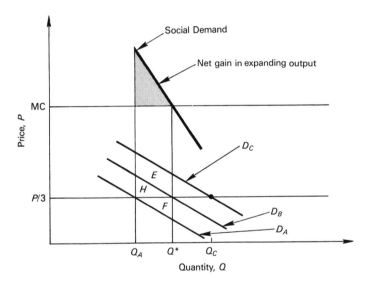

As output expands from Q_A to Q^*, A loses triangle F, B gains triangle H, and C gains trapezoid $H + E$.

The net $(H + E + H - F)$ equals the heavily-shaded Kaldor-Hicks gain.

tion and gains triangle H. Reasoning in the same way, C gains the trapezoid $E + H$ (the sum of the triangle and the extra parallelogram). The net of gains of B and C less the loss to A is just the heavily-shaded area under the social demand curve. That this claim is correct can be seen by working out the first problem at the end of this chapter.

Putting things in terms of these individual consumers shows how the Kaldor-Hicks rule can be applied. In the expansion of output from Q_A to Q^*, consumer A loses triangle F, while B and C gain. They could make side payments of triangle F to A and retain for themselves the heavily-shaded area. In this case the move would pass the Pareto test because A is compensated for his pain and is indifferent to the move, while B and C are made better off. If, on the other hand, B and C do not make the side payments, the move would not satisfy the Pareto standard because A is worse off, but it would pass the Kaldor-Hicks test because B and C could potentially make the payments and still be better off. It also satisfies the fundamental principle because it represents the policy alternative with the greatest net benefit. Ultimately, then, the Samuelsonian microeconomic efficiency point Q^* is also the point that satisfies both the Kaldor-Hicks rule and the fundamental principle.

THE PUBLIC CHOICE TRADITION

The public choice tradition moves from these normative ideas to a positive discussion of how decisions might actually be made in a democracy. Rather than having optimal levels of spending magically occur, this tradition tries to ascertain how democracies work in practice, and what might be the outcomes of different kinds of political processes.

Suppose A, B, and C are still each paying one-third of the marginal cost of a public good. As shown in Figure 3.2, A would favor Q_A, B would favor Q^*, and C would favor Q_C. What spending level would be adopted? For the demand functions shown in the figure, Q^* is the most likely outcome. This positive prediction has desirable normative implications, because it says that majority voting will lead to the social optimum outcome. But we should restrain our optimism because the necessary conditions turn out to be rather specialized.

With the public goods demand functions shown, A prefers Q_A to Q^* to Q_C. The reason his preferences are lined up this way is his consumer surplus: he loses nothing with his preferred choice Q_A, triangle F with his second choice Q^*, and an even bigger triangle with his third choice Q_C. C's preferences are just the reverse: she loses nothing with Q_C, a small triangle with Q^*, and a big triangle with Q_A. B is happy with Q^* and loses a moderate amount with either Q_A or Q_B.

Suppose the three voters had a referendum on whether to spend Q_A or Q^*—A would vote for Q_A but the other two would vote for Q^* and Q^* would win. Suppose the referendum were between Q_C and Q^*. Q^* would get two votes and Q_C would get one: again Q^* wins. If the election were between Q_A and Q_C, the winner is the one that gets B's vote (not clear from the diagram), but that winner then loses to Q^*. However we run the election, society gravitates to Q^*, that spending level favored by B, the voter in the middle or the "median" voter. This is our fortunate result that the median voter-predicted outcome of majority rule voting is also the Samuelsonian and Kaldor-Hicks social optimum outcome for this particular example.

But the example is particular, and there is no assurance that things would work out so nicely in practice. A first problem, of course, is that referenda are rarely confined to clear choices on how much to spend on a particular public good. Normally voters vote for political candidates who have positions on a host of issues, some of which a voter may agree with and some of which not, so voters are balancing a host of considerations when they make a vote. Indeed, rarely do voters have any idea what level of spending on a public good a particular candidate would favor. Given these information deficiencies, the clear prediction of this simple median voter model is unlikely to be realized in practice.

A more subtle problem involves the preferences themselves. Here they could be described as single-peaked. A, the political conservative, favors very little spending over moderate spending over high spending; C, the liberal, has tastes that are reversed. What if a voter favored Q_A over Q_C over Q^*. Or, what if voters have preferences that differ for different types of spending? The voting scheme breaks down in these cases, as can be seen from the second problem at the end of this chapter.

But even if voters have good information on what they are voting for, or what candidates will do once in office, and single-peaked preferences, the median voter predicted outcome does not necessarily lead to the Samuelsonian and Kaldor-Hicks social optimum outcome. Suppose tastes are asymmetric, as shown in Figure 3.3. Everything is the same as in Figure 3.2 except that we now add to C's demand for the public good. Since we have added to C's demand, we raise the social demand, which now intersects the marginal cost curve at Q^*, above the median voter outcome at Q_B. This median voter outcome is unchanged because the median voter outcome is determined entirely by B—the tastes of A and C have nothing to do with it as long as B remains the median voter. In this example, we left A's tastes unchanged but raised C's, hence the social optimum outcome at Q^* is greater than the median voter outcome at Q_B.

In this case the wishes of those believing in democratic theory and the wishes of those believing in economic efficiency come into conflict. The one-man-one-vote democratic outcome is at Q_B, but we also know that society as a whole gains if we raise spending above Q_B to Q^*. What to do?

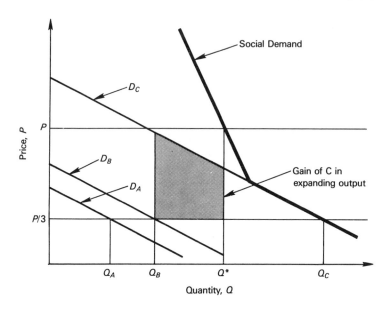

The median voter outcome is at Q_B. C is willing to bribe A and B the shaded area to get them to expand output to Q^*. This shaded area exceeds the losses of A and B because Q^* is the Samuelsonian and Kaldor-Hicks point.

FIGURE 3.3   Median Voter and Samuelsonian Outcome, Asymmetric Tastes

One way to resolve the conflict involves our old friend, side payments. Suppose that C could make side payments to A and B to get them to raise the Q they favor. C is prepared to pay her net gain of the shaded trapezoid to A and B to move them from Q_B to Q^*, and by the principle that the Samuelsonian point yields the maximum net benefit, C has enough gain to compensate A and B and still be better off. As before, these side payments may sound like an anti-democratic distortion of the one-man-one-vote principle, but in fact they are consistent with an even more democratic principle, the Pareto rule, because with this compensation, nobody loses and society gains in the move from Q_B to Q^*.

When previously discussing the Pareto principle, we had raised some practical difficulties with the payment of side payments—how could they be paid every time there were losers? Here we raise an additional theoretical objection. What if A and B knew that C had a large demand for public goods and was prepared to pay A and B's loss of surplus to get them to expand output? It would not take too much subtlety to realize that A and B would have an incentive to understate their demands to get more payments, and C as well, so that she has to make less payments. But if everybody is misstating demands, how will we know where Q^* is?

Economists, quite expert in the theory of bribes, have devised a whole set of answers to the paradox, known as demand revealing mechanisms. One of the most well-known is the institution of Clarke taxes.[4] Suppose that we made everybody pay their $P/3$ for the public good, and then had an additional tax as well. If there were just two choices, Q_B and Q^*, the pivotal voter, the one whose tastes changed output from the median voter point at Q_B to Q^*, would pay an additional Clarke tax. The amount of the tax would be just the loss felt by A and B in expanding output. In effect, this pivotal voter has to pay the cost of her intense preferences. That logic is just the same as with externalities discussed in the previous chapter. But unlike other types of side payments, the Clarke tax would not actually go to anybody, because if A and B knew they would receive bribes, they would misstate preferences.

In cases such as this one where any level of public output can be chosen, it gets very complicated to work out the Clarke taxes. For each voter one has to compute the Q chosen by the others, and then the Clarke tax for that voter. To illustrate, the Clarke taxes for C are computed by finding the choice A and B would make, were C absent; and computing how much C must bribe A and B to move from their choice to the social optimum. The government planner then collects all these bribes, or Clarke taxes, for the three voters and moves society to the social optimum. A set of Clarke taxes can be worked out in the first problem at the end of this chapter.

The key principles of Clarke taxes are:

They are assessed when a pivotal voter wants to change the outcome from the majority rule outcome voted on by everybody else.

This pivotal voter must pay the compensation that equals the loss imposed on everybody else in changing output.

Her decision to change reflects the Kaldor-Hicks principle: if she gains over and above payment of her Clarke tax, she will do it.

But Clarke taxes cannot go to anybody, because then recipients will misstate preferences.

If Clarke taxes were assessed for all cases of asymmetric preferences, there would at least in principle be excess revenues, the disposal of which might generate further economic efficiency problems.

Although Clarke taxes represent an ingenious solution to the problem of conflict between the majority rule outcome and the social optimum outcome, they are not yet ready for adoption in the rough and tumble world of practical politics. Very sophisticated social scientists have had great difficulties in explaining and implementing much simpler concepts. But it is ironic that this rough and ready political world has evolved several mechanisms for dealing with the underlying problem of asymmetric tastes. These mechanisms fall under the general heading of preference-weighted voting, a name given by James Buchanan and Gordon Tullock.[5] Some of them have rather nefarious connotations, which adds to the irony.

One of these nefarious practices is logrolling, the process by which legislators agree to support projects in other districts in exchange for the support of those other legislators on their own projects. The logrolling solution to the preceding preference-weighted voting problem is for C to compensate A and B with support on another issue in exchange for the votes of A and B for Q^*. Logrolling examples can approximate the Pareto rule, because C actually pays the compensation. But unlike Clarke taxes, logrolling compensation is actually paid to somebody, and since A and B now have an incentive to misstate their preferences, it can and often does get out of hand.

Another nefarious practice is the filibuster, the process by which C would hold out so strongly for Q^* that she would be willing to filibuster the Senate until A and B cave in. Filibusters are similar to Clarke taxes in that C pays—she has to stay awake all night talking—while A and B do not get anything back. There is not as serious a problem with preference revelation, but in this case A and B are definite losers (of sleep as well as surplus) so successful filibusters do not pass the Pareto test.

A third widely condemned phenomenon is low turnout in local spending elections. Low turnout rates are often described as an example of democracy not working, but in fact they may show that democracy is working very well. The desired spending levels of voters like A and B may be close enough to Q^* that many of these citizens do not care enough about the difference to vote, while voters like C, with intense preferences, do care enough to vote. If an election is held and many of the type A and B voters do not vote, that may seem anti-democratic but is again a device to move society toward the social optimum level of Q^* with majority-rule voting.

There are also devices for eliminating the losses of surplus that come from divergent tastes. Erik Lindahl devised a scheme, shown in Figure 3.4, to make all voters happy with the optimum quantity of public goods. Instead of charging $P/3$ to each voter, charge them their willingness-to-pay at Q^*. Society goes to the optimum quantity, and each voter votes for exactly this quantity. Then all of the voting problems just described can be dispensed with.[6]

As with the preference-weighted voting schemes previously described, it might seem impossible to institute a full system of Lindahl tax shares, but again there are ways. One is user fees, according to which those who are heavy users of some public facilities such as roads, golf courses, and swimming pools pay more. These high demanders are forced to reveal their tastes for swimming pools if they want to benefit from them in the first place. Another device, which does not solve the preference-revelation problem but does work toward a Lindahl solution to the provision issue, is the common practice of paying for public goods with either an income tax or a property tax. If tastes for public goods are correlated with income and/or property wealth, income and property taxes charge more to the high demanders (rich) than the low demanders (poor).

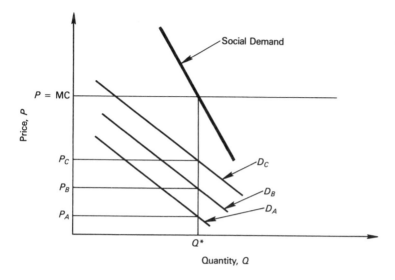

If instead of charging all voters $P/3$ for their public goods, society lets those with high demands pay more and those with low demands pay less, all voters would agree on Q^*.

FIGURE 3.4 Lindahl Tax Shares

Migration among communities also may have the effect of resolving the problem of how to get majority voting schemes to yield the social optimum output. Charles Tiebout first pointed out that if citizens were free to migrate from community to community, all those with tastes similar to those of A could form their own community and consume Q_A, all those with tastes similar to B could live with her and consume Q_B, and all those with tastes similar to C could live with her and consume Q_C.[7] In this way each community could achieve the optimum for that community without the difficult voting problems.

THE FUNDAMENTAL PRINCIPLE OF BENEFIT-COST ANALYSIS

Wherever we start, with the welfare economics tradition, with the microeconomic tradition, or with public choice, we get to the same bottom line. When choosing among programs, the best all-purpose rule is to choose the one that maximizes net social benefits. Compensation may be paid to those who lose in the policy change, in which event the change satisfies the Pareto rule as well, but compensation is not necessary and there are both operational and theoretical problems in devising compensation schemes.

TABLE 3.1   Benefits and Costs of Different Projects

PROJECT	GAIN TO CONSUMERS	LOSS TO SUPPLIERS	COST TO TAXPAYERS	NET BENEFITS	BENEFIT-COST RATIO*
A	200	50	100	50	1.50
B	200	50	200	-50	0.75
C	450	50	300	100	1.33
D	100	10	100	-10	0.90
E	650	0	500	150	1.30

*Using taxpayer costs as the denominator.

To see how this net benefits principle can be applied, let us say policy makers are confronted by the projects listed in Table 3.1. Each is assumed to make something cheaper for consumers and thereby cause consumer surplus gains. But each will hurt somebody, say alternative suppliers, and each will cost taxpayers. For every project we have listed these gains and losses, along with two overall statistics. The net benefits to society (under the Kaldor-Hicks rule) are derived by adding all gains and subtracting all losses and costs. The commonly calculated benefit-cost ratio is derived by dividing gains to consumers less losses to suppliers by taxpayer costs.

It is clear first off that projects that pass the Kaldor-Hicks test will have positive net benefits and a benefit-cost ratio greater than one. In most real world cases either indicator will prove adequate, but we will discover some instances where the rules give different signals. In such cases the net benefits rule should be used. This means ultimately, of course, that there is never any point in calculating a benefit-cost ratio. Either it says the same thing as the net benefits rule, in which case the ratio is redundant, or it says a different thing, in which case the ratio gives the wrong answer.

Suppose first the question is which of the projects on the list should be picked. All numbers in the table are known, and decision makers are free to select any projects they want. Projects A, C, and E—those with positive net benefits—or passing the Kaldor-Hicks test, are the ones selected.

But usually it is not so simple. Sometimes decision makers will not have all of this information, or they will have constraints on their freedom of action. In such cases the fundamental principle is still useful, but it has different applications.

Missing Information

One common example is where some information is missing. As we will see throughout the book, there are cases where it is simply impossible to fill in all values in Table 3.1. Suppose, for example, that we could not estimate the consumer gains from project A. We knew that it cost taxpayers 100 and suppliers 50, but we did not know how much it benefited consumers.

A moment's reflection indicates that this is almost exactly the buyer's choice most people have most of the time. They are offered a good for a price, here 150, without being told their marginal utility. They must make up their mind somehow. Is it helpful to do benefit-cost analysis in this case? Yes, because it is better to know that the price is 150 than to know nothing at all about the price. Does benefit-cost analysis eliminate judgment, discretion, political balancing, and so forth? Obviously not, because politicians still have to decide whether to initiate the project. It would obviously be preferable if the benefit-cost analysts could fill in all the blanks, but they are doing useful work if they can only fill in some.

Cost Effectiveness

Suppose next we have a different problem. We still cannot measure the consumer gains from projects A and B, but we know that these two projects are substitutes that accomplish the same end, such as transporting handicapped persons. Since the two projects do the same thing, only one should be chosen. How should the two be compared?

The answer is to do what is known as a "cost effectiveness" test. Rather than computing the net benefits for each alternative, which is impossible in this case, a cost effectiveness evaluation looks at two or more ways of accomplishing some objective, and takes the cheapest. In the case at hand, A is clearly the better way to provide a particular service—it costs 150 while B costs 250. We cannot fully apply the fundamental principle to all program alternatives because of missing information, but we can apply this principle to two or more alternatives by the simple expedient of taking the alternative that maximizes net benefits, or minimizes costs.

Constraints

The fundamental principle can also be applied subject to constraints. Let us go back to the complete information case, but say that the President only allows the budget office to propose projects with budget or taxpayer costs of 400. In this case the maximizing package consists of A and C. The alternative choice, E, does not fit in the budget even though it is the project with the largest net benefits. If the budget were to rise to 800, the maximizing package now becomes C and E. The project with the highest benefit-cost ratio of all, A, will not even be chosen. This is an example of the previously mentioned proposition that the benefit-cost ratio can be a misleading guide to decisions and really should not even be calculated.

And constraints can be applied in dealing with legislative bargainers. Suppose we had a logrolling situation under which you could not get your preferred package A, C, and E unless you were prepared to give some Senator project D. Would you do it? Under the fundamental principle, yes. Including D the whole package yields net benefits of 290, still much greater than zero, which is what would have happened if you had not rolled logs with the good Senator.

A final problem is an old favorite of economists, the difference between something on average and something at the margin. Let us assume now that projects C and D are really components of the same program. Say that both involve the job training of unemployed teenagers. These jobs benefit the teenagers but they entail costs to other workers, who have a harder time getting good jobs once the teenagers become more productive. Project C involves running full-day training programs, and D extends these programs to provide after-school instruction. If we had complete information and no decision-making constraints, we could see that C passes the net benefits test and D does not. If for some reason C and D were tied together and proposed as a package, the package would pass the test with net benefits of 90; but social efficiency would be enhanced by a more fine-grained evaluation that could distinguish the good program (C) from the uneconomic marginal extension (D).

SUMMARY

The chapter has discussed different traditions, or lines of thought, which have led to modern day benefit-cost analysis. The welfare economics tradition features the demanding Pareto rule for accepting projects, which is that a project can only be shown to be beneficial if at least some people gain from it and nobody loses. The way in which this can be assured is that the gainers in a project compensate the losers, and in fact such compensation is sometimes paid in public decisions. But there are both theoretical and practical problems in devising schemes for paying such compensation, and economists have come up with the less demanding Kaldor-Hicks standard under which a project is considered beneficial if the gainers *could* pay the losers and still have something left over, even if this compensation is not actually paid.

From the Kaldor-Hicks standard, one can derive the fundamental rule of benefit-cost analysis, under which that choice alternative should be selected that maximizes the net benefits to society. This fundamental rule turns out to give the same answer to public decisions as does the Samuelsonian rule for determining spending on public goods, which is to go to the point where marginal social benefits, the sum of the marginal willingness-to-pay of all consumers, equals the marginal social cost.

These normative standards are then compared with a positive standard for determining how output of public goods will be chosen in a majority rule democracy. The median voter rule, according to which voters' demands are arrayed and the winning outcome is that chosen by the median voter, is the likely outcome of a democratic voting process under some simplifying assumptions. If tastes are symmetric around this median, the median voter outcome will equal the Samuelsonian outcome, which is also the outcome dictated by the fundamental principle of benefit-cost analysis. If not, the two outcomes will differ, and there is a potential clash between the majority rule median voter outcome and the social optimum outcome from an economic efficiency standpoint. There are also various techniques (Clarke taxes, log-rolling, filibustering, incomplete turnout) that can yield outcomes closer to the social optimum within a majority rule voting context.

There are also some guides to use in applying the fundamental rule of benefit-cost analysis. One is not to compute benefit-cost ratios—the right measure of the gains or losses to society is program net benefits, and the benefit-cost ratio can be a misleading guide. A second is that a cost-effectiveness test can be used to get around missing information when the investigator is comparing two or more ways of accomplishing the same end. A third is that when projects are packaged together for some outside reason, either physical or political, the net benefits test should be applied to the whole package.

NOTES

[1]The Kaldor criterion is that gainers be able to compensate losers and still be better off. See Nicholas Kaldor, "Welfare Propositions of Economics and Interpersonal Comparisons of Utility," *Economic Journal*, September 1939. The Hicks criterion is that the losers should not be able profitably to bribe the gainers not to change. See John R. Hicks, "The Valuation of the Social Income," *Economica*, May 1940. Tibor Scitovsky suggested that both criteria be used, in "A Note on Welfare Propositions in Economics," *Review of Economic Studies*, November 1941.

[2]Edith Stokey and Richard Zeckhauser, *A Primer for Policy Analysis* (New York: Norton, 1978), p. 137.

[3]Paul A. Samuelson, "Pure Theory of Public Expenditures," *Review of Economics and Statistics*, November 1954, and "Diagrammatic Exposition of a Theory of Public Expenditures," *Review of Economics and Statistics*, November 1955.

[4]The designer of Clarke taxes is Edward H. Clarke, "Multi-part Pricing of Public Goods," *Public Choice*, Fall 1971. There are many other demand revealing mechanisms: a good discussion can be found in Robin W. Boadway and David E. Wildasin, *Public Sector Economics*, 2nd edition, (Toronto: Little, Brown and Company, 1984), p. 161.

[5]James M. Buchanan and Gordon Tullock, *The Calculus of Consent* (Ann Arbor: The University of Michigan Press, 1962).

[6]Erik Lindahl, "Just Taxation: A Positive Solution," in Richard A. Musgrave and Alan T. Peacock (eds.), *Classics in the Theory of Public Finance* (London: Macmillan, 1958).

[7]Charles M. Tiebout, "A Pure Theory of Local Expenditures," *Journal of Political Economy*, October 1956.

PROBLEMS

1. Say we have a jurisdiction made up of three consumers (or equally-sized groups). These consumers have the following inverse demand functions for a pure public service:

$$P_A = 26 - Q_A$$
$$P_B = 28 - Q_B$$
$$P_C = 33 - Q_C$$

where P refers to the marginal utility of the three consumers and Q to the quantity consumed. The physical properties of this public service are such that all consumers automatically consume the same amount.

a. What is the community demand function for this public service and how many units should the community consume when the cost per unit is 60?
b. What set of Lindahl taxes will induce all consumers to vote for the optimal quantity of public services?
c. If each consumer paid one-third of the cost of the public service, find the desired consumption of each, and their dead-weight burden if the community consumed the optimal amount.
d. If consumption amounts were voted on democratically with each consumer paying one-third and with no side payments, find community consumption and the dead-weight burden felt by each consumer.
e. Suppose now we allowed side payments. Find how much C would bribe A and B to change community output. Compute the Pareto gains of each consumer. Compute the Clarke taxes for each consumer.
f. As the community goes from the median voter outcome to the social optimum outcome, show that the Kaldor-Hicks gain derived from the compensation rule exactly equals the top-shaded triangle in Figure 3.2.

2. Using the inverse demand functions and equal tax shares of the previous problem, suppose a referendum were held between $Q = 6$ and $Q = 8$. Who would vote for which output, and which would win? Between $Q = 8$ and $Q = 13$ who would vote for which outcome and which would win? Between $Q = 6$ and $Q = 13$, with the winner going up against the other, who would vote for which outcome, and which spending level would ultimately prevail?

Those preferences could be described as single-peaked—each voter has one preferred outcome, and losses rise as Q moves away from that outcome on either side. Now we switch the example so that voter C prefers $Q = 6$ to $Q = 8$. Suppose a referendum were held between $Q = 6$ and $Q = 8$. Who would vote for which outcome and which would win? Between $Q = 8$ and $Q = 13$ who would vote for which and which would win? Between $Q = 6$ and $Q = 13$, with the winner to play the other which spending level would ultimately prevail?

3. The Army Corps of Engineers has proposals for building six dams, with the benefits (B) and costs (C) listed as follows:

Dam	B	C
1	40	20
2	30	10
3	30	20
4	10	20
5	15	10
6	15	20

Compute the net benefits and the benefit-cost ratio for each dam. Find the optimal-sized budget and the dams that should be built within it. Find the dams that should be built if the budget were limited to 20. If dams 3 through 6 were substitutes (in the same river basin), which should be built? How much have you used net benefits and the benefit-cost ratios in making these decisions?

FOUR
VALUATION OF BENEFITS AND COSTS

The examples in Chapter 3 assumed that we knew the gains and losses of different groups and showed how the fundamental principle of benefit-cost analysis should be applied. In this chapter we dig deeper to see how the underlying gains and losses can be estimated. We will focus on the true social gains and losses, which may or may not be reflected in market valuations. We will also try to distinguish true gains and losses felt by society from internal transfers, where one group gains what the other group loses with no net gain or loss to society. But in this chapter we only worry about partial equilibrium analysis—the gains and losses realized in one market—and we do not deal with questions of the timing of benefits and costs.

CONSUMER AND PRODUCER SURPLUS AND DEAD WEIGHT LOSS

Before we can measure gains and losses, we need to develop further the basic concepts of consumer and producer surplus. These fundamental concepts are shown with the aid of Figure 4.1.

Begin with consumers, who are operating along the demand function shown in the left panel in Figure 4.1(a). Suppose that the price of a good were

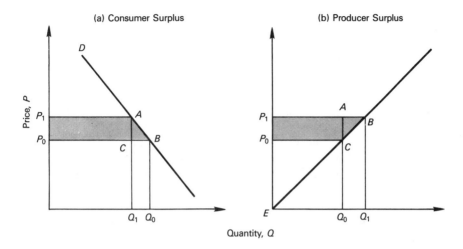

(a) Consumer Surplus

(b) Producer Surplus

(a) When the price falls from P_1 to P_0, consumers gain the shaded trapezoid—called the gain in consumer surplus.
(b) When the price falls from P_1 to P_0, producers lose the shaded trapezoid—called the loss in producer surplus.

FIGURE 4.1   Consumer and Producer Surplus

to fall from P_1 to P_0. Common sense suggests that consumers would be better off. They could buy what they had bought before, but not pay as much. In fact, they can do even better than that. If they bought the same amount as before, Q_1 in the figure, they would gain the distance P_1P_0 for each of Q_1 units, or the rectangle P_1ACP_0. But when the price falls they buy more, too, moving along their demand function to quantity Q_0. The difference between their marginal valuation, read from their demand function, and the new price P_0 at each quantity above Q_1, or the triangle ABC, is an added gain. The total gain is thus the shaded trapezoid P_1ABP_0, the sum of the pure price change effect with no quantity change (rectangle) and the added gain on their expanded buying (triangle). This trapezoid represents the gain in what is called consumer surplus, one of the most basic concepts in benefit-cost analysis.

The same price change would also affect producers. Just as we expected that consumers would gain when the price fell, we might expect that producers would lose. True, they do lose. Just as consumers gain a bit more than would be predicted from the price change alone by readjusting purchases, we might expect that producers would lose a bit less than from the price change alone because they can readjust. Right again.

This can be seen from the right panel in Figure 4.1(b). Making the standard assumption that the supply function is the competitive supply function, it shows the marginal cost of producing each level of output. At any quantity, say Q_1, producers will be indifferent between producing and not producing one more unit of output. The price received, P_1, just equals the marginal cost of production for this last unit of output. But since marginal cost is rising and price is the same for all units of output, producers make profits on their inframarginal units of output up to Q_1. These profits are given by the difference between the price line and the supply function on all units up to Q_1, or the triangle P_1BE.

Now we do the same experiment as before and imagine that the price were to fall from P_1 to P_0. Producers would seem to lose the difference, P_1P_0, on all units up to Q_1, their desired production at the initial price. But if the price were to fall, they would no longer produce Q_1. They would restrict production to Q_0, the highest they could go before their marginal cost equalled this new lower price. Hence their new profits would be given by the smaller triangle P_0CE. Profits would thus fall by the difference in the triangles, or the shaded trapezoid P_1BCP_0. This trapezoid represents the loss in what is called producer surplus, another basic concept.

The two concepts are combined in Figure 4.2. Suppose the government is considering the imposition of a commodity tax in some market. The original demand is given by the function labelled D and the original supply by the function labelled S. Imposition of the tax will shift up the supply

FIGURE 4.2   Dead Weight Loss

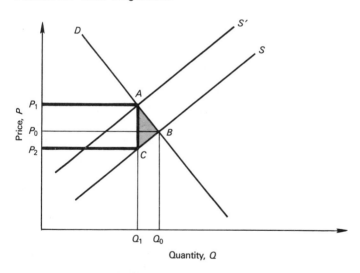

A tax is imposed that shifts the supply curve to S'.
(a) The market price increases from P_0 to P_1 and quantity falls from Q_0 to Q_1.
(b) Consumers suffer a loss of consumer surplus of P_1ABP_0.
(c) Producers suffer a loss of producer surplus of P_0BCP_2.
(d) The gain in tax revenue is P_1ACP_2.
(e) The net Kaldor-Hicks loss is shaded triangle ABC, called the dead weight loss from the tax.

function by just the amount of the tax, to the function labelled S'. The market price rises from P_0 to P_1 and the market quantity falls from Q_0 to Q_1.

Before there was a tax, producers required a compensation of P_2 to produce this final output, Q_1. Since they have shifted up the supply function to reflect the tax, that compensation of P_2 is their return after they have sold goods and paid their tax. Their before-tax return is obviously P_1. Total tax payments are then P_1-P_2 times output of Q_1, the rectangle P_1ACP_2.

Using the previous analysis, the loss of consumer surplus from the rise in price is given by the trapezoid P_1ABP_0. The loss of producer surplus from the fall in prices received by producers is P_0BCP_2. The Kaldor-Hicks tally for this tax is the gain of tax revenue less the loss of these two surpluses, which is a loss of the triangle ABC. This triangle is called the dead weight loss, or excess burden of the tax. In effect, consumers and producers lose more than taxpayers gain, the difference being a dead weight loss that goes to nobody.

The implication of all of this for tax policy is that other things being equal, society is better off when taxes minimize distortions, or dead weight losses. Since the dead weight loss triangle here has as its base the amount of the tax and as its height the change in market output, the economic cost of distortions will be less the less market output changes. That in turn happens when demand and/or supply functions become more vertical. This shows why economists try to design nondistortionary taxes, and in doing that, often end up proposing taxes on markets where at least one of the functions is inelastic.

The same considerations arise in benefit-cost analysis. One could do a benefit-cost analysis of this tax versus some other tax—the fundamental principle will say to pick the tax that implies the least dead weight loss. Or, one could do a benefit-cost analysis of an expenditure increase financed by a tax such as that shown in Figure 4.2—in this case the losses in this tax market should be subtracted from the full Kaldor-Hicks tally, complicating the analysis done in Chapter 3. In general, the net benefits for any public project will often be affected by surplus changes and dead weight losses of the sort shown here.

A SAMPLE BENEFIT-COST ANALYSIS

We now use these concepts of consumer and producer surplus in a simple example of a prototype benefit-cost analysis. The analysis could be of either a pure public good or a natural monopoly—the latter is chosen because it brings in one additional element. This natural monopoly is assumed to make some service cheaper for consumers, hence yielding consumer surplus gains. It also reduces the producer surplus of alternative suppliers of the service, and it costs taxpayers money.

Using the natural monopoly framework, suppose that a city is considering building a subway that will lower the cost of a subway ride to $.25. Presently buses cover the same routes and charge a fare of $.50, of which $.40 is the marginal cost of a bus ride and $.10 is profit. Transportation planners feel they know two points on the demand function. Presently at the $.50 fare there are 100,000 riders a year, and it is estimated that if the fare were $.40, there would be 140,000 riders. Perhaps this last point could have come from an earlier experience when the bus company may have been forced to charge a fare of $.40. The planners also know that the annual fixed cost of the subway will be $20,000.

Assume further that the planners know that if they build the subway, they should maximize net benefits by charging the fare where the marginal benefits of the last subway ride equal the marginal cost, $.25. Since they do not know ridership at this low fare, a first reasonable thing for them to do would be to project on the basis of the two demand points they do have, as shown in Figure 4.3. The $.10 fare reduction seems to have caused a 40,000 increase in ridership. Extending this slope as if the demand function were linear, the number of riders is projected to be 200,000.

FIGURE 4.3 Benefits From a Subway

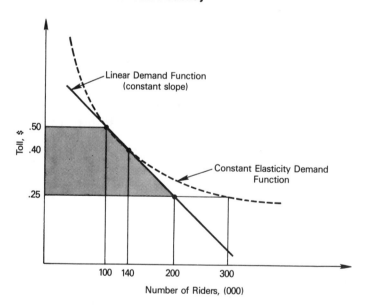

If the demand function is linear, each $.10 reduction in the toll raises ridership 40,000. The projected number of riders at a fare of $.25 is 200,000, and the consumer surplus gain is the shaded area, (.25)(100,000) + (.5)(.25)(100,000) = $37,500.

If the demand function has a constant elasticity of 1.5, the cut in toll to $.25 raises the number of riders to 300,000. The consumer surplus gain would be larger than in the linear case.

The consumer surplus from this change is the shaded area, equal to $.25*(100,000 + 200,000)/2 = \$37,500$. This consumer surplus is the sum of the pure price change effect at the old quantity $(\$.25*100,000 = \$25,000)$ and the expansion triangle $(.5*\$.25*100,000 = \$12,500)$. Note that some of this surplus is a pure gain and some represents a transfer to consumers from the bus company, which lost $.10*100,000 = \$10,000$ of profits.

Our investigation of natural monopolies in Chapter 3 left one question unanswered. The planners know that the fare that maximizes the net benefits of the subway is that where marginal benefits equals marginal cost. But they do not know whether it is sensible to build the subway in the first place. That is why they must do a benefit-cost analysis. Their answer is given by comparing the net benefits with the annual fixed costs of the subway. The tally is

Gain to consumers (riders) $37,500
Loss to producers (bus company) $10,000
Loss to taxpayers (fixed costs) $20,000
Net social benefits $7,500

Note that the marginal costs can be ignored in this calculation, because the toll already pays for these marginal costs. The only gain attributed to consumers was that received over and above paying the marginal cost of the subway ride.

This way of doing the analysis focuses on the gains and losses of different groups—consumers gain $37,500, producers lose $10,000, and taxpayers lose $20,000, making for net social benefits of $7,500. That same number can also be gotten by ignoring the gains and losses of different groups and simply focusing on real resource changes. Using this reasoning, 100,000 rides are taken more cheaply, for a saving equal to the marginal cost difference ($.15) times the number of rides taken more cheaply (100,000), for a total of $15,000. In addition, the expansion triangle, already evaluated at $12,500, gives the added benefit from the increase in number of rides. The annual cost of building the subway is $20,000. The sum is the same estimate of net benefits as before, $7,500. From an economic efficiency standpoint alone, there is not much to choose in one method over the other: probably the most reasonable advice is to do the analysis both ways to make sure the answer is the same. If it is not, something is wrong.

This latter calculation also illustrates the nature of a transfer. Consumers are better off by $37,500 overall, $27,500 of which represents real social gain but $10,000 of which represents a transfer from the owners of the bus company. When calculating the total gain of consumers, or any other group, the gross gain of $37,500 is relevant; when calculating the net social gain, all transfers should be netted out.

This example is, of course, very simple and only used to illustrate the basic ideas of benefit-cost analysis. When one actually does real world benefit-cost analyses, a host of complexities arise. We now cover a number of them. We begin by examining demand and supply functions more carefully, and then go on to a more careful examination of the market equilibration process.

INFERRING PROJECT BENEFITS

The previous example showed how we could infer the benefits of a project from the demand function for a good or service produced directly by the project (subway rides). It turns out that we can also use demand functions to measure benefits for a project that indirectly makes some good or service cheaper—a dam that supplies power more cheaply and lowers the cost of consumer goods, a road that lowers transportation costs, and so forth. But it can get complicated to see exactly how to use demand functions in this way. We now discuss some of the problems.

The Shape of the Demand Function

In the previous subway example we assumed that transportation planners knew two points on the demand function but had to extrapolate down to find how many riders there would be at a toll of $.25. They extrapolated along the linear demand function shown in Figure 4.3. But there could obviously be many demand functions going through the two points given, and the planners should really try many different ones to see how sensitive the results are to the assumed form of the demand function. Often demand functions can be estimated with more points than two by a statistical technique known as regression analysis. In that event as well, the analyst should fit regressions of several functional forms, to see how sensitive the results are to the assumed mathematical form of the demand function.

We do not carry out a full-blown analysis of all possibilities here, but we do show how the calculations would look with another common demand function. The linear function shown in Figure 4.3 assumes that the slope of the demand function is constant along its range; the other popular alternative is to assume that the elasticity, or percentage change in quantity caused by a percentage change in price, is constant along the demand function. The dashed line in Figure 4.2 plots a constant elasticity demand function. This constant elasticity (E) can be estimated by plugging in the formula:

(1) $E = (\Delta Q/Q) / (\Delta P/P)$

where Q refers to riders, P to the fare, and Δ represents the change. One could use either beginning or ending values for both Q and P, and the results would change accordingly. Since the choice is arbitrary, a reasonable compromise is to use the averages of the given points, 120,000 and $.45 respectively, and compute what is known as an arc elasticity:

(2) $E = (40,000/120,000) / (.10/.45) = 1.5$

This value is then plugged in to solve for ΔQ, the change in number of riders at a fare of $.25

(3) $1.5 = (\Delta Q/(.5*(100,000 + 100,000 + \Delta Q))) / (.25/.375)$

Adding the change $\Delta Q = 200,000$ to the initial level of 100,000 yields the number of riders at a toll of $.25 as 300,000, as shown in Figure 4.3.

It is apparent from the figure that the constant elasticity form means that as the price falls and ridership increases, the percentage, and not the absolute, change in the number of riders remains the same. This form then yields a larger consumer surplus gain than does the linear form. To compute exactly how much larger, it is necessary to use calculus: specifically, to find the area under the demand function between $Q = 100,000$ and $Q = 300,000$ by integration. The formula for this area A, analogous to the expansion triangle referred to earlier, is

(4) $A = \int_{100}^{300} f(Q)dQ - (.25)(200,000) = \$17,440$

which is an increase of $4,940 in both the expansion triangle and the net social benefits of the project. Exactly how to do this is shown in the first problem at the end of the chapter.

The problem of estimating consumer surplus gains when one is uncertain about functional forms has not attracted much attention, because there is not much one can say about it. It is obvious from Figure 4.3 that this could be an important problem: here this change alone raised the net social benefits from our prototype subway significantly. But at the same time the evaluator is often in the position of observing either two points on a demand function, or only points in a narrow range, with no clue as to whether to extrapolate on a linear basis, a constant elasticity basis, or some other basis. Economic theory cannot help—there really is no guidance as to what demand functions should look like over particular price and quantity ranges. The only sensible suggestion is that the evaluator should do the calculations in a variety of ways, comparing the results to see how sensitive they are to the assumptions, a technique known as sensitivity analysis. This technique will be proposed over and over in this book to deal with various difficulties. Sometimes it does not help much, but sometimes it does. In this case, for example, we are uncertain about how great net social benefits are, but either way they are positive and the subway looks like a good deal.

Shifts in the Demand Function

Even if we know the shape of the demand function, we have to worry about variables that might shift it. Referring to Figure 4.4, suppose the initial price of some good or service is P_0 and our project induces it to fall to P_1. Consumers would move along what is known as their ordinary demand function, yielding the consumer surplus of area $(A + B)$. That is all straightforward enough, but it turns out that this is not an exact measure of the gain from the price change if there are income effects.

The reason can be seen by decomposing the price reduction into its two components, the substitution effect and the income effect. As the price falls, consumers would buy more of the good even if their initial utility were not increased, because this good competes more favorably with other goods. This is known as the substitution effect. But they also gain income and utility, because the price reduction gives them more to spend on all goods, and they might consume more of this good because of this income effect as well. Consumption increases on the ordinary demand function because of both

FIGURE 4.4   Income and Substitution Effects

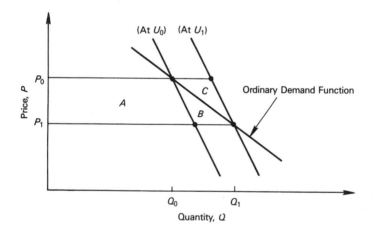

As the price falls from P_0 to P_1, consumers move along their Ordinary Demand Function from Q_0 to Q_1. Utility rises from U_0 to U_1, and if that rise in utility, or income, shifts demand, we can describe demand functions at the initial utility level, U_0, and the higher final utility level, U_1.

Area A is the gain in consumer welfare of this change measured at the new price level and old utility level, called the compensating variation.

Area $(A + B + C)$ is the gain in consumer welfare of this change measured at the old price level and new utility level, called the equivalent variation.

factors. But when measuring the utility gain to consumers from the price reduction—the goal in a benefit-cost analysis—the income effect must be excluded. To measure the true utility gain from the price fall, we need to hold utility constant and measure consumer surplus by comparison with that baseline.

This can be done in either of two ways, both of which make economic sense:

> The gain can be measured by finding the value of the price change at the initial utility level and the new price level, area A in the figure. This area is called the compensating variation, the sacrifice consumers would be willing to make to keep utility unchanged evaluated at this new price level.
>
> The gain can be measured by finding the value of the price change at the final utility level and the initial price level, area (A + B + C) in the figure. This area is called the equivalent variation, the sacrifice consumers would be willing to make to keep utility at its final level evaluated at the old price level.

Compared to the ordinary demand function, both measures remove income effects from the calculation. The reason for doing so is that as prices fall and real income rises, the income effect gives the change in consumption and consumer surplus from the derived change in income, indicating a form of double-counting. To measure the utility gain exactly, an experimenter might ask the consumer to pay the exact marginal valuation of the Q_0 unit into a kitty so that utility is held constant at U_0, the exact marginal valuation of the next unit, again keeping initial utility constant, and so forth until the experimenter has collected exactly area A into the kitty. Area A then measures exactly what the consumer would be willing to pay for the price change and still be at the same initial utility level, or the exact measure of consumer gain.

It may seem strange that there are two different exact measures of consumer change, but do not be alarmed. The reason is that there are two different utility levels. Once the price has fallen and the consumer is at U_1, the consumer is better off and consumes more of the good. Measured at this higher utility level, the value of the price reduction will then be greater. This means that when the price falls, the equivalent variation at the high utility level will exceed the compensating variation at the low utility level, and vice versa when the price rises.[1]

What should the evaluator do about all of this? First off, recognize that the whole problem comes about because of income effects. If alterations in the price of some goods do not change consumer incomes much, or if income changes do not affect consumption, consumer surplus could be measured exactly from the ordinary demand curve. Beyond that, when the problem does exist, as it will for goods that loom large in consumer budgets such as housing, income effects can be removed by either procedure.

Market Effects

We also have to inquire how the whole market works to measure benefits. For simplicity we assume away the previous issues—let us say demand functions are known to be linear and income effects are known to be absent. Even then, the exact measure of project benefits depends on two characteristics of the consumer market, whether costs are constant or increasing, and whether there are market imperfections.

The various cases are illustrated in Figures 4.5 and 4.6. Figure 4.5 shows the situation when there are no market imperfections—the demand function for the good measures the value of the good, and the supply function measures the true marginal social cost of producing the good.

Things are pretty straightforward if the marginal cost of supplying the good is constant, as shown in the left panel of Figure 4.5. Our project makes something cheaper—energy, transportation, or whatever; this lowers the supply function and generates the familiar shaded trapezoid in project benefits.

Now say the supply function is sloped upward, because it costs more at the margin to expand output. The project shifts the supply function from S to S', the market price falls from P_0 to P_1, and output rises from Q_0 to Q_1. Gains and losses from this change are as follows:

FIGURE 4.5   Value of Output, No Distortions

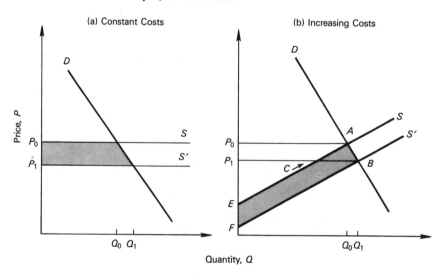

A project lowers the cost of providing a good or service, shifting down the supply function.
(a) If there are constant costs in the supplying industry, the supply function is shifted down and the shaded trapezoid represents project benefits.
(b) If costs are increasing, project benefits are given by the shaded area.

Consumers gain the consumer surplus trapezoid P_0ABP_1

Producers had a surplus of P_0AE before the change and get P_1BF after the change. Netting out the common triangle P_1CE, producers gain trapezoid $ECBF$ and lose trapezoid P_0ACP_1

The sum of the gain to consumers and producers from the change is the shaded trapezoid $EABF$, approximately the same as for the constant cost case but very slightly smaller, as is shown in the second problem at the end of the chapter.

In Figure 4.6 we then add market distortions. There could be lots of ways in which a market is distorted, and here we show only one. Suppose the good in question generates benefits to outsiders, called external benefits. Just as in the public goods examples in Chapters 2 and 3, these external benefits can be added to consumer demand to yield the higher social demand function D'. The difference between D' and D at any quantity represents the external benefits from the good.

In both panels of the Figure, market output rises from Q_0 to Q_1. All the external benefits up to Q_0 are not at issue—they were realized before the change and they still are. But new external benefits equal to the shaded parallelogram $ABCE$ are realized on the expanded output, and these new benefits must be counted in to get the social benefits from the project. That gives the shaded areas shown, the sum of benefits inside the market and new benefits outside the market.

FIGURE 4.6 Value of Output, Distortions

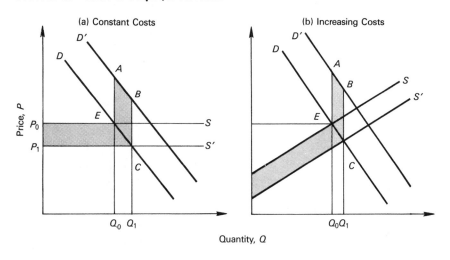

A project lowers the cost of providing a good or service in the presence of some market externality.

(a) If there are constant costs the trapezoid P_0ECP_1 gives the gain to consumers of the good or service and the parallelogram $ABCE$ the external benefits of the change in output. The net gain is the shaded area.

(b) If costs are increasing, project benefits are the sum of the net gains in the market and the external benefits, the shaded area.

INFERRING PROJECT COSTS

The previous section showed how we might estimate project benefits from demand functions for a good or service supplied more cheaply as a result of a government project. That is only part of the story. The project uses up resources as well, and we now turn to the question of measuring the social costs of supplying these resources from their own market. Again we consider both constant and increasing costs, with and without distortions in the relevant market.

Begin with the case of no distortions, shown for both constant and increasing costs in Figure 4.7. The simplest case is the constant cost case shown in the left panel. The previous market demand for the resource was given by the D schedule, and we assume the project shifts out this demand schedule to D'. Market output goes from Q_0 to Q_1, with the government buying the difference, Q_1-Q_0. But since costs and prices are constant, there is no change in the market price. The true social cost of the resources supplied is the shaded area, just the budget or taxpayer cost of the resource supplied (the price, P_0, times the quantity bought by the government, Q_1-Q_0). Since this price does not change, neither consumers nor producers gain nor lose

FIGURE 4.7   Cost of Resources, No Distortions

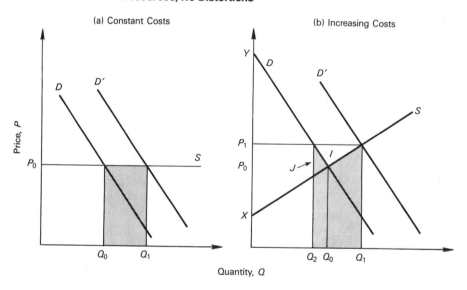

A project raises the demand for resources from D to D'. Market supply goes from Q_0 to Q_1.
(a) If costs are constant, the value of resources supplied is the shaded rectangle, exactly what the government pays.
(b) If costs are increasing, the value of resources supplied is the shaded area, less than what the government pays by the increasing cost effect, triangle I.

anything extra as a result of the added buying of the resource. A benefit-cost analyst can just look up how much the government entity paid for resources, and take that amount as the true social cost with no adjustment.

Things get more complicated in the increasing cost case shown in the right panel. Market output goes from Q_0 to Q_1, and the market price from P_0 to P_1, this time rising because of the increasing marginal cost over the interval. Gains and losses are as follows:

> Budget or taxpayer costs are given by the rectangle formed by the new price, P_1, and the amount bought by the government, Q_1–Q_2.
>
> The higher price leads to a loss in consumer surplus of the trapezoid from P_1 to P_0 out to the original demand function.
>
> The price increase leads to a gain in producer surplus equal to the trapezoid from P_1 to P_0 out to the supply function.

The difference between this gain in producer surplus and the loss in consumer surplus is the increasing cost effect, the triangle labelled *I*. Since *I* represents a net gain of producers in supplying the resource over and above the loss to other buyers, it must be deducted from the budget cost to get the social cost of supplying the resource, the shaded figure.

There is an alternative way to express the true social cost of supplying this resource. Note that the sideways triangle with the base equal to Y-X and the height equal to the initial output Q_0 is the surplus generated by the market for this resource—the difference between marginal benefits and marginal costs summed across all quantity levels. When the government raises demand for the resource, the price rises, the amount sold privately contracts to Q_2, and some of this initial surplus is lost—the shaded crowd-out triangle *J*. The social cost of supplying the resource is then the supply cost of supplying each unit the government buys from Q_2 to Q_1 (the area under the S function), plus the crowd-out triangle *J*.

Now suppose there are distortions, as shown in Figure 4.8. The true cost of supplying the resource is given by MC and the market supply is given by S. As before, any number of distortions might be imagined, but we examine here what are probably the most common, where the market supply function exceeds the true marginal cost of supplying the resource. There could be several causes of such a situation:

> There could be supply externalities, such as when the market supply of unemployed labor exceeds the true social cost of employing these resources.
>
> There could be monopolistic elements in the supply of such a resource, where again the resource can be supplied more cheaply than the market supply, with monopolistic sellers pocketing the difference.
>
> There could be an indirect tax levied in this market that is not justified by any externality, such as a salt tax in the old days or a telephone tax today.

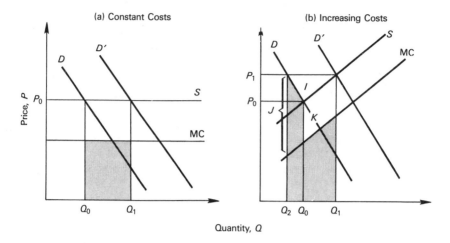

A project raises the demand for resources from D to D'. Market supply goes from Q_0 to Q_1.
There is a distortion such that $S > MC$.
(a) If costs are constant, the value of resources supplied is the shaded rectangle, less than what
the government pays by the distortion effect.
(b) If costs are increasing, the cost of resources supplied is the shaded area, the social cost of
supplying plus the lost surplus from crowding out.

FIGURE 4.8   Cost of Resources, Distortions

If the supply and marginal cost functions are flat, as with constant costs, the results are much the same as before. Budget costs are given by the market price, P_0, times the quantity, Q_1-Q_0. True social costs are given by the shaded area, MC times the same quantity. True social costs are less than budget costs by the difference between market supply and marginal costs, but there are no further complications.

The right panel in Figure 4.8 gives both complications at once. Now costs are rising and there are market distortions. The market price rises from P_0 to P_1 and quantity rises from Q_0 to Q_1. The true social cost, measured by the shaded area, can be derived in two different ways.

Most straightforward is just to add up the gains and losses of the relevant groups:

Taxpayers lose the rectangle formed by the new market price, P_1, and the quantity bought by the government, Q_1-Q_2.

Consumers lose the trapezoid formed by P_1 and P_0 and the initial demand function.

Producers gain surplus over and above this loss to consumers of triangle I. They also gain more monopoly profits on expanded sales of area K.

The true social cost is then the budget cost less area $(I+K)$.

The other way to express the true social cost is as the sum of two components. One is the true cost of supplying the government's output, given by the trapezoid formed by the MC line from Q_2 to Q_1. The other is the lost surplus in the market because of the crowding out effect, the shaded trapezoid J. The sum yields the same social cost as before.

This last case illustrates again the difference between a true social gain or loss and a transfer. When output expands in a market where the supply price exceeds marginal cost, taxpayers lose because they have to buy the expanded output at the high price, but sellers of the output gain. They sell at P_0 or P_1, and have costs that are lower. The difference between price and marginal cost then represents a transfer from taxpayers to sellers, and should be deducted in any calculation of the social cost of supplying the resources. Exactly how much should be deducted depends on the shape of all the functions, but the general principle holds: on efficiency grounds, transfers should be netted out.

Operationally, the analyst should be alert for these complications whenever additions to market supply cause price changes, and whenever there are distortions in a market. Cases where a government project can actually move a market enough to cause price changes may be relatively rare, but there could be significant distortions. Far and away the most common involves the "jobs" issue. Politicians often favor projects because they entail construction or other jobs in a legislative district. The spirit seems to run counter to that of benefit-cost analysis, which considers jobs as a use of labor and a cost, not a benefit. Much of the controversy can be resolved by recognizing that for certain types of labor the market and budget cost could overstate the true social cost. All that has to be done is to recognize that labor is a resource and use the analysis sketched out in Figures 4.7 and 4.8.

But before marking down the cost of labor, the analyst must keep several factors in mind. One is whether total employment in the area is truly expanded? If not, the budget costs of labor on this project really does reflect resource sacrifices somewhere else, and there is no reason to adjust this budget cost. Another question is whether the jobs are permanent, or are just for the construction phase. If the jobs are transitory, they should only reduce labor costs for a small portion of the total life of the project. A third question is whether the workers migrate from out of the district to take the jobs. If the jobs are filled by migrating workers, there could be no gain at all for local workers, and again there is no reason for adjusting budget costs. Whatever the case, the best way to deal with the jobs issue is by deducting amounts from the budget cost of hiring labor if there are distortions, as shown here, rather than just treating job creation as a separate consideration. And if there are uncertainties about how much to deduct, one should always do a sensitivity analysis to see whether the overall results depend on resolution of this issue.

MARKETS DO NOT CLEAR

The discussion of Adam Smith's invisible hand in Chapter 2 suggested two advantages of free markets. The first, most often cited, is that there is an automatic mechanism that insures that demanders' valuation of the last unit of output equals producers' cost of this same unit. The second, much less often cited, is that consumption is routed to those with the highest valuation and production is done by those with the lowest marginal costs. The second advantage hinges on the fact that the free market is assumed to clear, with neither excess demand nor excess supply at the going price. But what if markets do not clear?

The case can be examined with the aid of Figure 4.9. In the left panel we analyze a market in excess supply. The market would clear at price P_0, but a minimum price is imposed at P_1 that purports to help suppliers. There are

FIGURE 4.9   Markets Do Not Clear

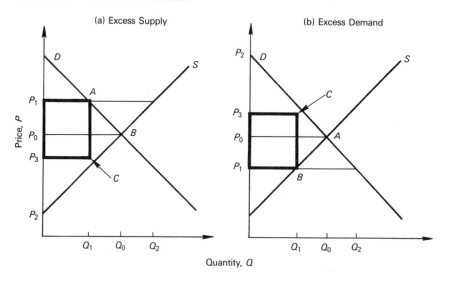

(a) A minimum price is imposed at P_1. Quantity demanded is at Q_1 and $Q_2 - Q_1$ resources are in excess supply. All suppliers with a supply price up to P_1 bid—the average supply price being P_3. This minimum price costs demanders the consumer surplus trapezoid P_1ABP_0. Suppliers lose P_0BP_2 but gain P_1ACP_3. Perhaps suppliers do not even gain from the minimum price.

(b) A ceiling price is imposed at P_1. Quantity supplied is at Q_1 and $Q_2 - Q_1$ units are in excess demand. All demanders with a marginal valuation down to P_1 bid for the units—the average valuation being P_3. The ceiling price costs suppliers the producer surplus trapezoid P_0ABP_1. Demanders lose P_2AP_0 but gain back P_3CBP_1. Perhaps demanders do not gain.

many illustrations of such policies. The classic one involves minimum wages to help low wage workers. Minimum prices have also been instituted for farm goods to help farmers and retail trade to help small stores. The well-known implication of a minimum price is that there could be excess supply, or for workers, unemployment, shown in the figure as the distance Q_2–Q_1.

First we ask how one might do a benefit-cost analysis of the minimum price policy itself. For demanders the situation is clear. As the price rises from the market clearing price P_0 to the set price P_1, demanders lose the usual consumer surplus trapezoid P_1ABP_0.

But for suppliers, the supposed beneficiaries of the minimum price, the situation is more complicated. Before the policy was instituted, suppliers gained the entire producer surplus triangle P_0BP_2. When the minimum price is introduced, three things happen, two of which are bad. The one good thing is that those who keep their jobs gain an increase in price. One of the bad things is that the number of jobs, or quantity units, is cut from Q_0 to Q_1. The second bad thing is that there is more competition for the fewer jobs. When the market cleared, only those with a supply price up to P_0 chose to supply their services. Now that the minimum price is imposed, those with a supply price up to P_1 are invited into the market and supply their services. Hence unemployment comes about from both demand and supply changes—more people are chasing fewer jobs.

From Figure 4.9 (a) it is impossible to tell who gets the jobs once the minimum price is imposed. All workers to the left of Q_2 would like to have the jobs, but there are only Q_1 jobs to go around. Unlike when the market clears, this market now cannot ration the jobs to those who want them most. For benefit-cost terms, a reasonable assumption might be that the jobs are allocated at random to all who want them, some with a low supply price and some with a high supply price. If jobs are allocated at random, we might expect that some average supply price up to Q_2, say P_3, might be the cost of working, and the gain of the Q_1 jobs measured by the outlined rectangle P_1ACP_3 in the new regime. The gain in the old regime without the minimum price was P_0BP_2. The change in suppliers' welfare from the minimum price is thus P_1ACP_3–P_0BP_2. Visually it seems that this gain would not even be positive in Figure 4.9 (a), though it could be—there are no theoretical predictions here. But it is certainly not obvious that a minimum price law will make suppliers better off—the price is higher, but the jobs are fewer and some of the people who will get these jobs will have a very low valuation of them. And, since the marginal conditions are not fulfilled, the minimum price law inevitably fails the Kaldor-Hicks efficiency test: demanders lose more than suppliers gain, and suppliers in total may not even gain.[2]

A second benefit-cost question that can be asked is the one addressed in the previous section. Suppose there exists unemployed labor because of the minimum wage law. The government initiates a project that puts a certain number of these workers to work. What is the social cost of this labor?

The question can be answered fairly easily with the aid of the same figure. Suppose the government does not hire all the unemployed workers. It demands X workers, where the total demanded $(Q_1 + X)$ is still less than the total supply Q_2 at this minimum wage rate. The budget cost of these new workers is P_1X. Since the previous job-holders were drawn at random from the existing supply, the new workers will be, too, and the social cost of the newly employed workers will be P_3X. The difference between P_1 and P_3 for each newly hired but previously unemployed worker is the amount that can be deducted from the labor cost of the project to account for the stimulation of jobs.

All of this can be transferred to the case of excess demand as well. Rather than fixing a minimum price and getting unemployment, suppose now that there is an attempt to provide some good more cheaply to households, so a maximum or ceiling price is imposed. The classic example of a maximum price law is rent control, but countries have also set ceiling prices for oil, natural gas, food products, and foreign currency. With a minimum price law the intended beneficiaries are the suppliers; for a price ceiling the intended beneficiaries are the demanders. But again, intended is not actual.

The analytics are shown in Figure 4.9 (b). A ceiling price of P_1 cuts quantity supplied to Q_1 and raises the number of demanders who want the goods, such as rental apartments. The excess demand for rental apartments is $Q_2–Q_1$, and the average valuation of those lucky enough to get the apartments under randomization is P_3. The loss to suppliers from the rent control law is the producer surplus trapezoid P_0ABP_1. Demanders gained P_2AP_0 before and P_3CBP_1 with the price ceiling, for a net change of $P_3CBP_1–P_2AP_0$. As before, this number is very likely not positive—it is not at all clear that the supposed beneficiaries of the rent control law will, in fact, gain. The net loss from the law is the loss to suppliers less the gain to demanders if the latter is positive; or the loss to suppliers plus the loss to demanders if the latter is negative. Rent control is bound to fail a Kaldor-Hicks efficiency test and may fail the test of making its supposed beneficiaries better off, just as did minimum wages.

And we could also ask how to value rent control apartments if an expanded supply was a by-product of another government investment. Just as the true social cost of minimum wage labor is the average supply price P_3, the true social value of added rent control units, say produced by some urban development project, is the average valuation of them, P_3 in Figure 4.9 (b). This is higher than the legal controlled rent because of the enforced scarcity.

MARKETS DO NOT EXIST

The previous cases may have seemed sufficiently complicated, but in a way they are the easy ones. Demand and supply schedules are given or assumed, market prices and quantities can be observed, and it remains only for the benefit-cost analyst to interpret properly these demand and supply schedules.

But many times in a benefit-cost study there will be changes in quantities for which there is no market. Projects may alter the risk of death, health or safety, they may waste or save time, or they may stimulate business in some area. Very often these kinds of changes comprise the main benefits of a project. What is the analyst to do then?

The simple answer is to try to find some allied market where the price or quantity change can be used to infer valuations for the missing market. Simple to say, but often hard to do. Some illustrations of how the task might be managed are given here. We start with what is probably the most controversial issue in benefit-cost analysis, valuing lives saved and lost, and then move on to some other applications of the technique.

Loss of Life

The most fundamental, and often most important, question in benefit-cost analysis is how to value lives saved or lost as a result of a program. Often policy actions involve changes in the risk of death—automobile seat belts save lives, cancer research saves lives, road improvements save lives, speed limits save lives, risky construction projects or coal mining risk lives. It does no good to argue that lives are so special that they should not even be dealt with in a benefit-cost analysis: although most of us think at least certain lives are pretty special, at the same time we realize that society does not have infinite resources to spend on medical research, and society does need fuel. Somehow gains and losses from these projects must be compared, and we are certainly better off trying to value lives sensitively and sensibly than we are just ignoring the question.

Furthermore, it is often felt that anybody who even tries to introduce valuation considerations in this area will inevitably end up undervaluing lives and mistakenly promoting risky projects. Such need not be the case at all, and recent research in this area seems to be arriving at implicit valuations that are very high, and hence do not promote risky projects.

Two general approaches have been used in valuing human lives, the discounted future earnings (DFE) approach and the required compensation (RC) approach. The DFE approach, often used in lawsuits, involves the simple addition of the future earnings of the deceased or the person who might become deceased. These earnings are discounted by the rate of interest (in a way described in Chapter 6) to adjust for the fact that earnings later are worth less than earnings now.

The assumption underlying such a calculation of DFE is to let the labor market value the worth of a person. The problem is that this is very definitely the wrong allied market. The earnings of the person represent the marginal product of that person's labor services to an employer. If the person is already retired, this method yields no value at all to his or her life. If the person is a minority member or a woman, the DFE approach imputes less value than to a white male of the same age and experience. And the method does not even count the value a person may place on his or her own life. Many people, even if they have low wages and DFEs, are quite reluctant to put their lives at risk.

The theoretical problem with the DFE standard is apparent from a close examination of what is gained and lost. The true gain is that some person gets to enjoy life longer. Hence that person, not that person's employer, should do the valuation. And it should be a valuation of that person's life, not just the person's labor services. Therefore a much better market valuation would be one where workers get to say how much compensation they require to subject themselves to risk of loss of life, precisely the approach of the RC standard.

The best such RC valuation comes from a different use of labor markets. Workers on some jobs have a very low statistical probability of dying on the job, while workers on other jobs have essentially no risk of dying on the job. Careful studies of relative wage rates that hold constant education, experience, region, and so forth have found that workers in the risky jobs get paid more, presumably because workers in these jobs are aware of their job risk and require some compensation for undergoing it. Working out the RC from these compensating wage differentials yields an RC value of a human life of from $2.5 million to $5 million in 1988 dollars, from five to ten times what one would get from a DFE standpoint.[3] This value is also higher than that implicit in all but two of 44 proposed, rejected, or adopted rules recently analyzed by the Office of Management and Budget.[4] Hence a careful use of the RC standard would already make society quite conservative about decisions that endanger lives.

But conservative enough? It depends on the details of the problem at hand. Suppose first that we have a risky construction project, so that the particular workers who will be at risk are the ones who bid up wages and in effect do the life valuation. There are three reasons why the RC standard, though much more conservative than the DFE standard, may not be conservative enough:

> Information—Do the workers know they are at risk? Do they have all the information they need to bid up wages?
> Bargaining power—Even if workers have the information, do they have enough alternative job possibilities that they can drive a hard enough bargain to bid up their wages an appropriate amount?
> Externalities—Do the workers incorporate the pain and suffering of friends and relatives some of whom may be economically dependent on these workers?

It should be hard to answer all of these questions in the affirmative; but if the answer to all is yes, at least in principle the government project will have to compensate the workers for their risk, this compensation will be automatically built into the costs of the project, and a comparison of project benefits and market costs will give a reasonable estimate of the net benefits of a project.

Needless to say, if the answer to all questions is not yes, there are external costs to the project over and above the market costs, and somehow or other these costs must be added in. If the project did not pass a benefit-cost test without the external costs added in, it certainly will not once they are added in. If it only barely passed it before, it probably will not now. It is only when project benefits are well above market costs that such a project merits careful consideration.

Before going on, there is one often confronted benefit-cost question that comes in at this point. We all know that drinking and driving do not mix, but the complicated public policy question is to what extent taxes should be imposed on the consumption of alcohol because of their resultant saving of lives? If the answer to the first and third questions regarding information and externalities is yes, the tax rate implied might be relatively low because the costs of drinking are already embodied in the demand function for alcohol. The only reason for a tax on liquor would be to reflect the cost to society in general of alcohol-induced accidents. But if the answer is no—that is, if drinkers are not well-informed about the risk of drinking or if they do not incorporate the pain and suffering of friends and relatives—there are large negative externalities to drinking and one can justify much higher tax rates.[5] As with the wage compensation, the question of how much to believe the market when lives are at stake depends very much on how much the people who subject themselves to risk are aware of what they are doing.

Obviously it becomes much harder to use market information when the lives at stake are not those of the workers making the valuation. The $2.5 to $5 million estimate of the value of a life is that based on the behavior of a few workers who are actually choosing between safe and risky jobs. Most people never do that. Should the implicit valuations of rather specialized workers be imputed to the population at large? There are many reasons why not:

Selection bias—Those who work risky jobs, even if they get compensation, probably have less aversion to risk than the average people who may be saved by cancer research or seat belts. Economists call this factor selection bias—people select themselves into occupations partly according to their taste for risk. The implication is that wages are not bid up as much as they would be by average people, and the value of a life that is imputed from these wages differentials even by the RC standard is understated.

Increasing marginal aversion to risk—RC values are estimated over a very small range where worker safety is very high, or the probability of death low. As shown by Figure 4.10, which plots a simple indifference curve between worker safety and all other goods (income), these RC values will very likely understate the true self-assessed valuation of risk when extrapolated to a range where

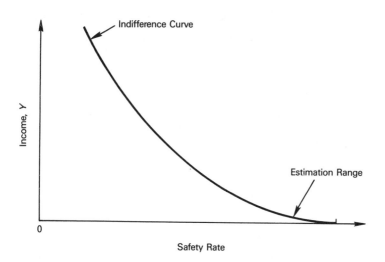

The indifference curve is that between worker safety and all other goods (income). Its slope is the marginal utility of safety over the marginal utility of other goods. Real world RC values are estimated from the estimation range, where jobs are very safe. Were safety rates lower, or the probability of death higher, the marginal utility of safety, or marginal aversion to risk, would also be higher, as shown by the fact that the slope of the indifference curve becomes more negative as we move left.

FIGURE 4.10   Increasing Marginal Aversion to Risk

worker safety is lower. A person may be willing to accept a change in death risk from .001 to .0011 for a certain compensation, but if the base risk is already .1, the very same worker may not be willing to accept any added risk whatever the compensation. And many programs, medical research in particular, deal with lives in this higher base risk range.

Age—The workers subjecting themselves to risk are generally young adults. Compared to children, they would have lower life valuations, other things being equal. Of course, compared to older members of the population, these young workers would have higher life valuations.

So there are lots of reasons why even the conservative RC standard may not sufficiently value lives. The direction of the biases do seem clear, however, and this standard might be used to give minimum values. If risks are on the cost side, and costs are just slightly below benefits, imposing more conservative valuations may be enough to tip the balance against the project—otherwise, probably not. The valuations should get still more conservative, depending on which lives are at risk and how the tastes of these people for risk might be expected to compare with those of the workers who determine relative wage levels. It should, of course, be stressed that because different projects put different people at risk, there is no inevitable presumption that all implicit life valuations should be the same.

Capital Values

Very often a project affects the capital or land values in an area. Polluting factories or noisy airports lower land values. There is no market in pollution or noise, but the change in capital values can sometimes be used as the allied market to fill in the gap. On the plus side, a new road or a dam may increase the business possibilities for land in a certain area, and this time drive up land prices. There is no market in expected business formations, but again an allied market.

The logic here is very simple. Suppose the value of land in an area (L) can be expressed as

(5) $L = f(N,P,T,Z)$

where N refers to noise, P to pollution, T to travel time to some central location, and Z to all other factors. An airport is going to be built near a particular community that will affect the first three independent variables. It will raise noise levels and lower land values, it will increase pollution and again lower land values, but it will reduce travel time to various places and raise land values. How should the airport be evaluated?

Statisticians can estimate what are known as hedonic regressions to give the relevant partial derivatives. For example, the partial derivative $\delta L/\delta N$ is the impact of one unit change in noise levels on land values. The net impact of the proposed airport (A) on land values in this community is then given by what is known as the total derivative

(6) $dL/dA = (\delta L/\delta N)(dN/dA) + (\delta L/\delta P)(dP/dA) + (\delta L/\delta T)/(dT/dA)$

The first bracketed expression in each term is from the regression, the impact of noise, pollution, and travel time on land values. The second bracketed term must be taken from physical information about the airport—usually an environmental impact statement will require this sort of information on what the airport is likely to do to these values in surrounding areas. The net impact of the airport on this community is then the sum of each change times the impact of each change on land values. It could obviously come out either as a plus or a minus, depending on whether the good things outweigh the bad things. That is just like benefit-cost analysis in general, and indeed equation (6) really is a benefit-cost analysis of the airport on the landowners of the community in question, with the partial derivatives from the hedonic regression answering the all-important valuation question. If the airport is a good thing, land values in the community will rise.

Having laid out the method, one can raise several questions about it. First, of course, is that as in the loss of life example previously discussed, our allied market has to work. If prospective buyers and sellers of land do not have the right information to alter land values appropriately, or if for any other reason it is impossible to infer proper valuations from land prices, the allied market approach to benefit-cost analysis will break down.

Second, it should be kept in mind that benefit-cost analysis through allied market capital values replaces all elements in the benefit-cost analysis. If there were expected to be atmospheric pollution that would cause an expected increase in cancer deaths, it would be double-counting to let pollution lower capital values through equation (6) and then tally the expected losses of lives in addition. Presumably these health risks are already counted in the regression, if the allied market is working in the first place, and they should not be double-counted. This difficulty means that it can be very tricky to use this method: the analyst has to know what the market is and is not already counting, and count everything once but not more than once.

Timing issues will be dealt with in the next chapter, but there is one important issue that comes up here. The presumption for most of this chapter is that benefits and costs of a project will recur every year. A subway will yield consumer surplus benefits every year it is in operation; a polluting airport will yield costs every year it is in operation. For the most part the analyst can just add up these recurrent values for any year, assuming, for example, that if the project is a loser in 1990, it is a loser in any future year. That is not quite right, as we will see in Chapter 6. But the important point for now is that the capital value changes are definitely not recurrent: expected pollution in all future years will alter land values now, once and for all. Hence the capital value changes can be viewed as summaries of the underlying real changes in all future years, much as the discounted present values we will discuss in the next chapter. Just as land value changes already do the valuation, they already do the future discounting.

Time Saving

Another missing market is that for people's time. Very often projects have as an important benefit the simple saving of time of commuters, weekend travelers, and so forth. This saving of time has probably been the most important benefit of airports, the interstate highway system, and perhaps even our subway. How should time savings be valued?

The natural allied market is the labor market. An hour saved is an hour that could be profitably used for production, which means that the hourly wage rate that makes firms indifferent between buying and not buying the last unit of labor should give the implicit marginal valuation of time saved, at least for small changes in time saved. Putting it another way, the value of a new hour created by some time saving innovation is the amount firms would have to be bribed to part with an hour from a productive worker—the wage rate. All we have to do is to figure out which wage rate. Unlike most prices that might be used to value output, wage rates vary tremendously by occupation, region, and so forth, so one should probably use some average.

But there is a more difficult conceptual problem involving the implicit assumption that all hours of time are perfect substitutes. The subway may save workers' time at the commuting hours, roughly the time that presumably would be saved were firms induced to give up the requisite amount of hours. Would this be the same as the value of vacation time saved by an interstate highway? Who can say?

One interesting attempt to solve this problem is described by Richard Layard.[6] In evaluating time saved for a third London airport, the analysts estimated the probability of using different modes of transportation as a function of the relative money prices, the relative commuting times, and other factors. Doing the analysis in this way lets travelers value money cost of commuting and its time saving simultaneously, in effect providing an internal translation of one into the other.

With all of these problems for each of these attempts to use allied markets, it is clear that they should be used rather carefully. Trying to use allied markets to fill in some missing values may be the best that can be done in a wide variety of cases, but the investigator should try to ensure that this allied market satisfies minimal assumptions for giving proper valuations. And as always, the investigator should use sensitivity analysis to deal with what can often be wide uncertainties in knowing how allied market outcomes should be interpreted.

UNCERTAINTY

To this point we have ignored any problems pertaining to uncertainty. Perhaps two people will die on average, but there is an equal chance that no people will die and that four people will die. What to do then? Should the investigator just average the potential outcomes, or do something more elaborate?

It turns out to depend on marginal utilities. Taking a less dramatic example, say that a project will yield a particular household different incomes with various probabilities.[7] The solid line of Figure 4.11 gives this household's utility of income over the relevant range. The slope of this line is the change in utility per unit change in income, or the marginal utility of income. As income rises, further changes in income are assumed to confer less utility, so that the marginal utility of income is declining as income rises. The logic underlying this slope is that as income rises, households satisfy progressively less pressing needs. When income is low, it is devoted to the necessities of life—food, clothing, shelter, and television sets. As income rises, more is spent on luxury goods such as theater tickets and textbooks.

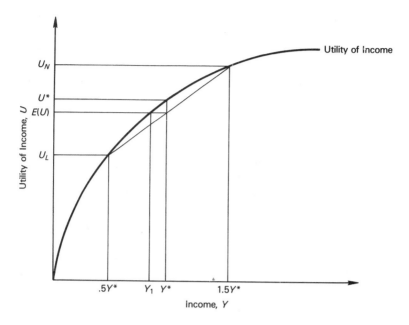

The utility of a certain income Y^* is U^*. The utility of a package that is $1.5Y^*$ half the time and $.5Y^*$ half the time is $E(U)$. Although income averages Y^*, utility of the package is less than utility of the certain income. Y_1 is the certain income that has the same utility as the uncertain package, hence the person should be willing to pay $Y^* - Y_1$, an insurance premium, to protect against uncertainty.

FIGURE 4.11   Marginal Utility of Uncertain Income Changes

These luxury goods may be tough to do without, but not as tough as the necessities.

We will conduct two experiments with this household. The first will be to give the household a certain income, Y^*, and observe that the utility of this certain income is U^*. The second experiment involves uncertainty. Say that household income still averages Y^*, but as a result of some project, it is now expected to be $1.5Y^*$ half the time and $.5Y^*$ half the time. The reason for this uncertainty could be almost anything—perhaps the time spent commuting on the subway will vary, perhaps its impact on capital values is uncertain, perhaps there are questions about losses to alternative suppliers. Is the package good for the household?

The utility for this uncertain package, $E(U)$, is the probability of each outcome times the utility of that outcome, or

(7) $E(U) = .5U_H + .5U_L$

Inspection shows that when the household is in luck, getting $1.5Y^*$, its utility rises less than it falls when the household has bad luck. Hence the utility of the uncertain package $E(U)$ is less than the utility of the certain package U^*. Uncertainty is undesirable to this household and the project that yields uncertainty is a loser.

The size of the loss can be expressed either in utility terms or in income terms. In utility terms the cost is $U^*-E(U)$, the utility loss of uncertainty. In income terms, generally more convenient because other magnitudes in the evaluation can also be put in these terms, the loss is Y^*-Y_1, where Y_1 represents the certain income that gives the same utility as the risky package. This loss, Y^*-Y_1, can be viewed as the Kaldor-Hicks compensation the family would require to make it indifferent between having the project and not, the income the household would sacrifice to avoid the uncertainty, or the annual insurance premium that would have to be paid to get an insurance company to assume the risk in the household's income.

The foregoing analysis suggests that in a wide variety of cases, uncertainty will not be a problem. Whenever a project alters gains and losses for a family over a fairly small income range, which is probably most of the time, the diminishing marginal utility factor can be ignored and the various outcomes simply averaged. As an illustration, one of the most widely publicized types of uncertainty involving public projects is that of cost overruns. But even if potential cost overruns are quite large, and quite unpredictable, the actual change in people's tax liabilities as a result of overruns is likely to be modest and not to cause changes in the marginal utility of income for the typical taxpayer. Moreover, it is possible to insure against risk—by buying insurance, holding a varied portfolio, and so forth—and simply including any changes in insurance premiums in the overall tally adequately counts for uncertainty.

But if there is great uncertainty and this uncertainty changes income or utility enough to matter, then simple averaging of outcomes generally will not suffice. Suppose that a commuter plans to take the subway to work every day, but one-third of the days the subway does not come. Then the utility of the subway to the workers is much less than two-thirds of the perfect certainty benefits. In such a case the utility would have to be discounted for the cost of the uncertainty.

SUMMARY

This chapter has discussed the main difficulties in assessing the benefits and costs of projects from an economic efficiency standpoint, using partial equilibrium analysis only. It first dealt with the cases where markets exist for the commodities being valued in a benefit-cost evaluation. Consumer gains and losses are measured by changes in consumer surplus, the difference between willingness-to-pay and price actually paid over the relevant quantity range. This consumer surplus gets tricky to measure if consumption changes as a result of the utility change itself or if there are market distortions, and the chapter showed how to measure the true surplus in that case. Producer gains and losses are similarly measured by changes in producer surplus, the difference between price received and production marginal cost over the relevant quantity range.

The chapter then showed how the marginal cost of resources to society could be estimated from marginal production costs. Some complications here involve externalities: the fact that the market price of resources could change as more or less are bought, and the fact that marginal costs are difficult to estimate if markets do not clear.

The chapter also suggested some techniques for assessing benefits and costs when markets do not exist at all. The general idea is to find some allied market where participants are expressing the market value of life uncertainty, expected changes in pollution and/or noise levels, or time saved. A final adjustment could often be necessary for an uncertain stream of benefits and costs.

NOTES

[1] A more complete discussion can be found in Lee S. Friedman, *Microeconomic Policy Analysis* (New York: McGraw-Hill, 1984), pg. 143–152. Friedman does reverse the sizes of the compensating and equivalent variations.

[2] Some other examples where consumer valuations cannot simply be read from demand or supply curves are given by Lee S. Friedman, *op. cit.,* pg 175–189.

[3] The lower value comes from Alan Dillingham, "The Influence of Risk Variable Definition on Value of Life Estimates," *Economic Inquiry,* April 1985, updated to 1988 prices. The higher value comes from Michael J. Moore and W. Kip Viscusi, "Doubling the Estimated Value of Life: Results Using New Occupational Data," *Journal of Policy Analysis and Management,* Spring 1988. More discussion can be found in Ann Fisher, Lauraine G. Chestnut, and Daniel M. Violette, "The Value of Reducing Risks of Death: A Note on New Evidence," *Journal of Policy Analysis and Management,* Winter 1989.

[4] John F. Morrall, "A Review of the Record," *Regulation,* November/December, 1986.

[5] Charles E. Phelps, "Death and Taxes: An Opportunity for Substitution," Public Policy Analysis Program Working Paper No. 8702, University of Rochester, May 1987. A nice discussion of the Phelps paper is in Aidan Vining and David L. Weimer, *Policy Analysis: Concepts and Practice* (Englewood Cliffs, NJ: Prentice Hall, 1988), Chapter 7.

[6] Richard Layard, *Cost-Benefit Analysis* (New York: Penguin, 1972). See in particular A. D. J. Flowerdew, "Choosing a Site for the Third London Airport: The Rosskill Commission's Approach."

[7] The analysis follows that originally proposed by Milton Friedman and L. J. Savage, "The Utility Analysis of Choices Involving Risk," *Journal of Political Economy,* August 1948.

PROBLEMS

1. The price of a weekly bridge toll pass has varied between 5 and 10 in the past. When $P = 10$, $Q = 5$, and when $P = 5$, $Q = 10$. Compute the formula for the inverse linear demand function connecting these two

points. Find the consumer surplus loss if the price is raised from 10 to 12; gain if the price is lowered from 5 to 3. Now compute the arc elasticity of a nonlinear constant elasticity demand curve between the points for $P = 10$ and $P = 5$.

2. The inverse demand function for a good is $P = 20-Q$. If costs are constant and the flat supply function is shifted down from $P = 10$ to $P = 9$, find the gains for consumers, producers, and society.

   Now say the initial supply is given by $P = 1 + Q$ and this function is shifted down to $P = Q$. Find the old and new price and quantity equilibrium. Now find the gains for consumers, producers, and society. What is the impact of altering the supply function? Any idea why?

3. The marginal cost (MC) of supplying a material used in the construction of a government project is $MC = .01Q$, where Q is quantity. Because of various market imperfections, the good is actually sold according to the supply curve $P = .02Q$, where P is price. The private inverse demand function for the good is $P = 6.0-.04Q$. The government will need 50 added units of Q at every P. Find

   a. The expression for the new inverse demand function
   b. The pre-government equilibrium
   c. The post-government equilibrium
   d. The budget cost of materials to the government
   e. The consumer surplus loss
   f. The producer surplus gain on old units
   g. The producer surplus gain on new units
   h. The net social cost of materials

4. Now you must hire labor to build the facility. The inverse demand for labor is $W = 92-L$, where W is the hourly wage rate and L is the number of hours demanded. The supply is given by $W = .02L$. There is a minimum wage of $2 per hour. Find

   a. The initial level of supply, demand, and unemployment in the market
   b. The budget and social cost of five more hours of work
   c. How would your answer change if there were an unemployment insurance system that paid workers $.50 an hour when they were unemployed?

5. A university town is considering a rent control law that would lower all rents in the town to $400 per month. Suppose all rentable properties in this town are alike, and are supplied according to $R = H$, where R is the monthly rent and H is the supply of apartments. Demand is given by $R = 1000-H$. Find

   a. The equilibrium without rent control
   b. Supply and demand with rent control
   c. The losses felt by landlords as a result of rent control
   d. The gains or losses felt by renters as a result of rent control
   e. Kaldor-Hicks net benefits of the proposed law

   The proposal is voted down, but the proponents are back with a new version. The demand function is to be interpreted as the demand of soon-to-be-rich graduate students. There are also plenty of poor people in the town who have a willingness to pay of $450 per month. They could not afford to rent before, but now can with the proposed ceiling of $400 a month. The new version of the law simply requires that half of all apartments go to these poor people, assumed to be easily distinguishable from the soon-to-be-rich graduate students. Find

    f.   The losses felt by landlords as a result of rent control
    g.   The gains or losses felt by graduate students
    h.   The gains or losses of the poor
    i.   The Kaldor-Hicks net benefits of the new law

6.   A worker typical in all respects works for a wage of $10,000 per year in a perfectly safe occupation. Another typical worker does the same job in a risky occupation with a known death probability of 1 in 1000 per year, receiving a wage of $10,200 per year. What value of a human life of a worker with these characteristics should the benefit-cost analyst use?

7.   Suppose that the utility of income schedule is given by $U = \sqrt{Y}$. A family starts off with a certain income of 100. A project is proposed that could raise the family's income to 144 with probability of one-half, or could lower it to 56 with probability of one-half. Find

    a.   The expected income of the family with the project
    b.   The expected gain or loss of the family with the project

FIVE
GENERAL EQUILIBRIUM BENEFITS AND COSTS

The discussion up to now has involved finding the gains or losses of a project in one market. But there are many cases where goods are such close substitutes that there will be substantial spillovers from one market to others. In such cases a partial equilibrium calculation of benefits and costs, such as we did in Chapter 4, may give a very poor approximation of the overall tally. Moreover, it becomes quite difficult analytically to measure benefits and costs market by market. To fill the gap, economists are increasingly using a technique called general equilibrium analysis to measure the net benefits of a policy change. In this chapter we go through a simple exercise to determine the conditions under which changes in other markets matter, and then we examine a simple general equilibrium analysis on both the consumption and production side.

THE IMPORTANCE OF OTHER MARKETS

It will be important to trace out the impacts of policy changes on other markets whenever two conditions are satisfied:

> Either demanders or suppliers have strong cross-substitution effects.
> There are either nonconstant costs or distortions in the affected markets.

Regarding the first condition, suppose a government project supplies cheaper power, transportation, or some other resource that lowers the cost of producing coffee. This lower coffee price reduces the demand for tea through demand-side substitution. The net social benefit or cost from this project could be poorly measured by conditions in the coffee market alone. Or, if it encourages farmers to grow more cocoa as well through supply-side adjustment, its impact could again be poorly measured.

The second condition is harder to see. To demonstrate it, we first take up the case where there are rising marginal costs in what will be called the secondary market, but no distortions. The left panel of Figure 5.1 shows the situation in what will be called the primary market, for the constant cost case. By reducing costs in the primary market, the government project shifts down the supply curve. The primary price falls from P_0 to P_1 and consumers of the primary good get a gain of area $(A + F + G)$.

Now we consider secondary markets. Suppose first that the secondary market is for a substitute good such as tea. When the price of the primary good falls, consumers consume more of it and less of the secondary good. The demand function for this secondary good depends positively on the price of the primary good. If area $(A + F + G)$ in the left panel measures the utility gain to consumers because of the primary price fall, and point Y in the right panel measures the change in demand because of this primary price fall with

FIGURE 5.1 Primary and Secondary Market Benefits, No Distortions

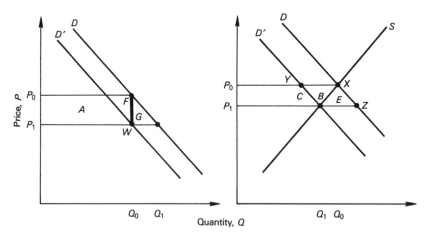

(a) The primary market price shift leads to a gain for consumers of area $(A + F + G)$.

(b) The primary price reduction reduces demand and price for a substitute good. Consumers switch from point X to Y with no change in utility. The gain for consumers is area C, the loss for producers is area $(B + C)$, and the net secondary loss is area B.

(c) The secondary price reduction reduces the demand for the primary good to D'. The final resting point is at W. The dark hatched line measures the general equilibrium demand that works in all changes in the secondary market. The net gain from the whole adjustment is area $(A + F)$.

no change in the secondary price, consumers switch from point X to point Y simply as a result of the primary price change. It can be shown that they move to point Y with no incremental change in utility.

What happens to utility in this secondary market? If there are no distortions, it depends on whether prices change. If not, either because the spillover effect is trivial or because the supply curve is flat in the secondary market, there will be no secondary market utility gain or loss. Quantity will move from X to Y with no change in consumer surplus in the secondary market. There can be no change in producer surplus in the secondary market because with flat supply curves, there is no producer surplus.

If, on the other hand, secondary market prices change because of increasing costs, the primary price change will lower prices in the secondary market. As the price falls to P_1, suppliers lose area $(C + B)$. Demanders have shifted to point Y with no change in utility beyond that already counted in the primary market, but then gain area C as the price falls to the new equilibrium at P_1. The net cost in the secondary market is then triangle B, and this loss must be deducted from area $(A + F + G)$ in the left panel to give the overall tally.

But we are not done yet. The fall in the secondary market price will feed back on the primary market and shift back the demand function to D' there. After this shift the primary market settles down to a final equilibrium at point W, on the shifted demand function. It has been shown that the proper measure of net benefits in this case is along the dark hatched line, area $(A + F)$. Under this assumption, area G equals area B—that is, area G is the amount that must be deducted from primary benefits because of secondary market price changes.[1]

Had the secondary good been a complement, say cream, everything would run in reverse. The lower primary price would raise the demand for the secondary good from D' to D, shifting consumers to point Z with no loss in utility. The market price would rise from P_1 to P_0. Producers would gain the surplus of area $(C + B)$, consumers would lose the surplus of area $(C + B + E)$, and the net secondary market loss would be triangle E. This result is perhaps surprising: under these conditions, whenever there is a price change in the secondary market, there is a loss of surplus that should be deducted from the gain in surplus in the primary market.

Things become even more complicated when there are distortions in the secondary market, such that the market supply price is above the true cost of supplying the good. The usual reason for such a distortion would be a commodity tax in the secondary market, but as before there are other imperfections that could also give the same result. If the secondary good is a substitute good with constant costs, as shown in Figure 5.2 (a), the result is different from before. Since costs are constant, the downward shift in demand entails no price change and no change in either producer or consumer surplus

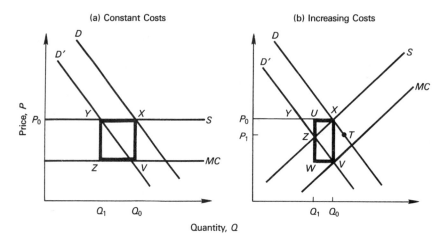

(a) When costs are constant, consumers switch from point X to Y with no loss in utility. There is no change in either producer or consumer surplus, but a loss in revenue or surplus of *YXVZ.*

(b) When costs are increasing, the price falls from P_0 to P_1 and quantity from Q_0 to Q_1. The net loss in the secondary market is triangle *YXZ* and rectangle *UXVW.*

FIGURE 5.2   Secondary Market Losses, Distortions

in the secondary market. But this time the fall in quantity in the secondary market does entail a loss in commodity tax revenue, which is labelled in the figure as a loss.

Why? There are two ways of seeing the point. The straightforward argument is that less revenue is available to the government, or to taxpayers. The deeper argument based on microeconomic theory is that since consumers' marginal valuation of the good exceeds the marginal cost of producing the good, as less of this good is produced, consumers lose more than producers gain. Either way, when there are secondary market distortions making the market supply exceed the marginal cost, there are secondary market losses if secondary output falls and gains if secondary output rises, even if secondary prices do not change. And as seems logical, everything is reversed if the distortion is that marginal cost exceeds market supply.

The right panel in Figure 5.2 (b) combines both sets of complications. Taking the case of substitutes, the primary price fall in the face of increasing costs entails a fall in both prices and output in the secondary market, from the Q_0, P_0 combination to the Q_1, P_1 combination. Producers lose the surplus in area P_0XZP_1. Consumers shift from point X to point Y with no utility change beyond that counted in the primary market, and then gain area P_0YZP_1 as the price falls. The tax loss is area *UXVW.* The net social loss in the secondary market is thus area *UXVW* + area *YXZ.*

And in the case of complements, both price and output rise up to the Q_0, P_0 combination. Producers gain area P_0XZP_1. Consumers lose area P_0XTP_1. If the tax is imposed at a constant amount per unit, the tax gain is just the same as the loss above, area $UXVW$. The net secondary market gain this time is area $UXVW$–area XTZ.

Although it might seem like this laborious procedure has adequately tracked down all secondary gains and losses, that is not so. The market for coffee affected the market for tea, and the market for tea affected that for coffee, and we worked that out. But it is logical to think that these changes in the markets for tea and coffee would affect still other markets, and we did not work those out. If we aim to do a careful benefit-cost analysis, it looks like we might have a mess on our hands.[2]

Fortunately there is a better way. Rather than laboriously working through all markets where relative prices might change (Figure 5.1) or where quantities might change in the presence of distortions (Figure 5.2), and then getting all the indirect effects of these changes, economists have developed a technique called general equilibrium analysis to deal with such questions. In the past fifteen years this technique has been successfully applied to questions of tariff policy by Alan Deardorff and Robert Stern, to questions of tax policy by John Shoven and John Whalley, and to benefit-cost questions.[3]

Although the actual calculations involved in doing a general equilibrium analysis can be quite elaborate, the basic idea is that of the general equilibrium demand function shown in Figure 5.1. The pre-policy change world is represented by a system of empirical equations giving demands and supplies for all relevant markets. This model is solved by the computer to yield the pre-policy set of consumer real incomes. Then the policy change, whether from tariffs, taxes, or some government project, is represented by shifting demand or supply equations appropriately. The model is re-solved by the computer, and a new set of consumer real incomes is computed. The gain or loss of each household from the policy change is just the change in real income from the change, sometimes even computed exactly to take in questions of compensating and equivalent variation discussed earlier. The Kaldor-Hicks net benefit from the policy change can then be computed in the usual way simply by summing these real income changes across households.

The technical skills necessary to build such a general equilibrium model would be beyond the ability of most readers of this book. But increasingly these models are being developed for use on personal computers, and it is not beyond the capability of most readers to use existing models. Moreover, there is no other way to answer certain benefit-cost questions. So we now take a look at two such models, one on the consumer side and one on the producer side.

A CONSUMPTION GENERAL EQUILIBRIUM MODEL
FOR TAX CHANGES IN THE UNITED KINGDOM

As in other advanced countries, the United Kingdom has a highly distortionary set of subsidies for housing. Under the U.K. personal income tax, those
who borrow to buy an asset that returns interest income can deduct the
interest on the borrowing and then pay tax on the interest. Those who borrow
to buy a house can still deduct the mortgage interest, but do not have to pay
any tax on the imputed return from the house—the fact that the homeowner
gets rent-free dwelling. This provision, common in most developed countries, subsidizes homeowners. The higher is their tax rate, the greater the
subsidy. In the United Kingdom this tax rate used to run as high as 90 percent
for upper-income groups, and it is now 60 percent. At the same time,
low-income groups receive subsidized rents on the expenditure side of the
budget.

It takes only a moment's reflection to see that the impact of these
housing subsidies are quite complicated to work out. Those who have high
incomes and high marginal tax rates and have bought recently at inflated
nominal interest rates can deduct a great deal of mortgage interest and
receive very large subsidies. Those with lower marginal rates who borrowed
at less inflated nominal interest rates receive less of a subsidy. Those who
paid off their mortgage or live in unsubsidized rental property receive no
subsidy at all. And those without a mortgage and in subsidized rental
property receive a subsidy that differs from the homeowner subsidy according to differences in the rental subsidy rate and the tax subsidy rate. One
cannot draw a simple diagram of this subsidy.

Suppose all public subsidies for housing were removed, so that the
effective market cost for housing in an owned unit was exactly the same as
the effective market cost for housing in a rental unit. One can imagine doing
a benefit-cost analysis of the question in theory, but be totally baffled by the
quantitative aspects. Not only would the analyst have to track down the
tangled set of subsidies just described, but there would be other complications as well:

> Housing costs form a large enough share of consumer budgets that one would
> have to deal with income effects (the demand complication discussed in Chap-
> ter 4).
>
> There are cross-substitution effects between housing and other consumer goods
> on the demand side, and between housing and other uses of land and capital
> on the supply side.
>
> There are further distortions, in particular a local property tax on housing.

To make a long story short, there is no way to do the benefit-cost
analysis other than with a general equilibrium analysis. That is exactly the
approach used by Mervyn King, who recently did do a general equilibrium

calculation of the net benefits from a removal of all housing subsidies in the United Kingdom.[4]

Even general equilibrium analyses have to be simplified somewhat, and King's basic simplification was to assume constant producer costs. Hence he did not get into the issues raised when the supply function in the secondary market is upward-sloping. He also aggregated all non-housing expenditures into spending on one composite good. But after making these simplifications, he did everything else with a great amount of detail.

He began with microdata on each of 5,895 households. The data gave him after-tax income, housing expenditures, rental expenditures, mortgage interest, and tax rates for each of these households in 1973. From these data he could compute the tax and rental subsidies for housing for each household. He could also remove these subsidies, and using a demand function that allowed for both income and substitution effects, he could compute a new set of after-tax incomes and housing expenditures. He could also measure the government's saving of revenue that would otherwise have gone into subsidizing housing. To keep the change revenue-neutral, he simply returned all of this revenue to households in proportion to their initial incomes.

Each household will gain the rebated revenues and lose the implicit value of the subsidy. Because the housing subsidies were distortionary, we would expect the overall Kaldor-Hicks summation of the net benefits of the change across all households to be positive, but particular households would gain or lose according to how much they benefited from the tax or rental subsidies. King spent a great deal of care in working out these gains or losses exactly, through explicit utility functions. A simplified description of how he did that is shown in Figure 5.3.

The top panel of the figure shows the indifference curve and budget line for a typical household, the bottom panel the housing demand function for the same household. Notice that the amount of housing consumed by the household, H, is the same in both panels, with this consumption being compared with that of all other goods, Y, in the top panel and the price of housing, P, in the bottom panel. This price of housing can be viewed as that existing initially, that is, the one that is influenced by the subsidy.

Since good Y is a composite of all other goods, its price can be set at unity, so that the slope of the budget line, normally the negative of the ratio of the housing price to other prices (as described in Chapter 2) is just $-P$. King did not assume this, but to simplify Figure 5.3 we can assume that as the household consumes more of the composite good Y, its marginal utility remains constant at unity. This means that the slope of the indifference curve, $-MU$, is just the marginal utility of housing. The slope of this indifference curve never reaches minus infinity even when H is very low, which in turn means that the indifference curve has a vertical intercept (with all people living in motels—this is an approximation!).

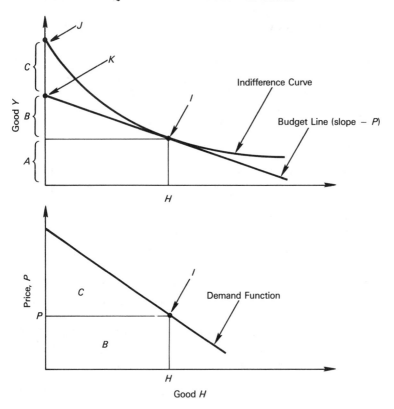

Point *I* represents the choice of the consumer, given income and prices. In the top panel income is depicted as line segments *B* + *A*. Point *K* means spending all income on good *Y*, and point *J* is on the same indifference curve as the final choice at point *I*. Hence line segments *B* + *C* show how much of good *Y* is necessary to compensate the consumers for not consuming good *H* at all.

In the bottom panel, note that amount spent on good *H*, line segment *B* in the top panel, is area *B* in the bottom panel. The total gain from consuming *H* over and above paying for it, line segment *C* in the top panel, is area *C* in the bottom panel.

FIGURE 5.3   Demand Functions and Utility Functions

There are three important points in the top panel:

Point *I* represents the initial position of the household, given income and the initial price of housing. As discussed in Chapter 2, this is the initial point of tangency of the household's indifference curve with the household's budget line.

Point *J* is on this same indifference curve, representing how much of the composite other good the household would have to be given to compensate it for the loss of all housing.

Point *K* is on the same budget line, showing consumption of the composite good if the household spent nothing on housing.

Point J is above point K because the household has declining marginal utility of housing: from the initial point, as housing is taken away the consumer needs to be compensated more than the pure saving of income—the indifference curve level of Y exceeds the budget line level of Y.

Putting all this in terms of consumer surplus, starting at point J our household is willing to give up line segment $(C + B)$ for the privilege of consuming H units of housing. B is what the household spends and C is the household's remaining utility gain, or consumer surplus. These same line segments are shown in the bottom panel as areas. The actual payment, area B, is the rectangle representing price times quantity. The remaining utility gain is the consumer surplus triangle, C. The difference between the top and bottom panels is that the top panel shows bottom panel areas as lines, and lines (such as P) as slopes.

Then King introduces the policy change that simultaneously alters the households income and relative price of housing, as shown in Figure 5.4. In the top panel income rises by the rebate, R, but the price of housing is simultaneously increased to P_1 by the withdrawal of the subsidy. This makes for a budget line with a higher intercept and a more negative slope, shifting the household to H_1. The difference between indifference curves valued in terms of the composite good is G, the net gain for the household from the total policy change. Were housing prices increased more for this household (that is, had the household faced a greater subsidy initially), this gain could easily have been negative. In the case shown, the slope of all indifference curves is MU, which depends only on the level of housing. Hence the indifference curves are parallel and the gain, G, is the same wherever it is measured. In more complex cases this gain will depend on whether it is measured at initial or final prices, as in the discussion in Chapter 4. Also, when the indifference curves are parallel, there is no change in housing consumption as income changes—hence the income effect is zero and the ordinary demand curve shown in the bottom panel can be used to measure consumer surplus loss. This loss of consumer surplus from the price increase is given by the shaded area, but the full change G, the rebate less this shaded area, cannot be shown in the demand panel.

Having computed the G for each household, King then adds them up across households to find the net Kaldor-Hicks benefit of the policy change. That comes to 17 percent of the revenue generated by the elimination of subsidies, or 0.5 percent of household income. Although this way of looking at things may suggest that gains are modest, 83 percent of households do gain from the measure, with the share of households gaining about 90 percent for those in the top quarter of the income distribution and about 65 percent in the bottom. This dispersion is largely due to the way the revenue was returned—were it returned equally to all households, a much higher share of low-income households would have gained and a smaller share of high-income households.

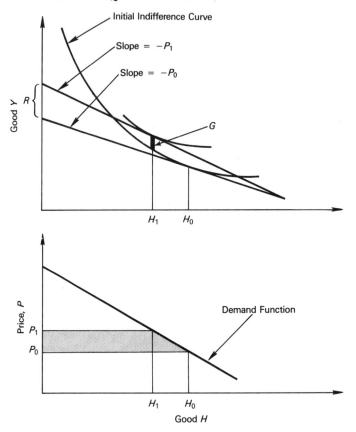

In the top panel the rise in price of housing to P_1 and the rebate (R) move the consumer to H_1, yielding a gain of G.

In the bottom panel, G is the rebate less the loss of consumer surplus on housing, with the latter shown by the shaded area.

FIGURE 5.4   Removal of a Housing Subsidy

A PRODUCTION GENERAL EQUILIBRIUM MODEL FOR AGRICULTURE IN SENEGAL

King's general equilibrium model made the simple production assumption of constant costs and worked out household utility changes carefully. The World Bank has generated a simple general equilibrium model that includes fairly simple consumption assumptions but tries to work out the agricultural production conditions quite carefully. The Bank has now applied this model to analyzing agricultural benefit-cost questions in Argentina, Brazil, Cyprus, Hungary, Indonesia, Korea, and Senegal. We will here examine one application to Senegal, done by Avishay Braverman and Jeffrey Hammer.[5]

Senegal is a poor country in West Africa where 77 percent of the work force is employed in agriculture (that same share is 2 percent in the United States). Agricultural products account for 70 percent of Senegal's export earnings, but government budget deficits related to agricultural pricing policy account for 2.6 percent of total output (0.8 percent in the United States).

The main subsistence crop in Senegal is millet. There are at least two promising ways to stimulate increases in the production of millet, hence cutting down on imports of rice and saving scarce foreign currency:

> Subsidies to groundnut farmers could be decreased, hence stimulating production of millet.
>
> Consumer price controls on rice could be removed, hence making imported rice more expensive to consumers and reducing the demand for it.

But it is not clear how much each policy should be pursued, whether one is better than the other, and in general who would gain and lose following any policy change when markets are so closely linked.

Braverman and Hammer try to answer the question with the aid of the World Bank's general equilibrium agricultural model. Their model contains demand functions for four consumer goods—rice, groundnut oil, millet, and maize. Of these, rice production is now penalized by the government and groundnut oil production is subsidized. There are five supply commodities—groundnuts, domestic rice, cotton, millet, and maize. The authors estimate separate supply functions for four different regions of the country, because of different growing conditions for the different crops. They estimate gains from policy changes in terms of the underlying utility functions, but only present results for real income changes.

The market clearing conditions of this model conform to actual conditions in Senegal. For the cash crops groundnuts and cotton, the entire crop is purchased from farmers at a government set price, companies process the materials, and export the total production of groundnut oil and fiber. Although farmers can also sell rice to the government at a set price, for the most part they do not and simply sell their domestically grown rice to domestic consumers. The government also imports rice, which it sells to consumers at a controlled price below the world price. Millet and maize are traded on free markets with no imports or exports, and with prices free to fluctuate to equate demand and supply.

The model was set to initial conditions for an average rainfall year, with price and income elasticities of demand for the consumer goods taken from the economic literature. Then some hypothetical policy changes were instituted in the price of groundnuts to farmers and rice to consumers, and real income gains or losses to farmers and consumers were computed.

The main results of the simulation are as follows:

A decline in the price received by producers of groundnuts reduces groundnut production and exports, the incomes of those forced to supply groundnuts, rice imports, and government budget deficits. There is a very slight net drop in foreign currency earnings—groundnut earnings decrease more than reductions in rice imports saved on foreign currency outlays. The real income of farmers generally decreases as a result of the change.

An increase in the consumer price of rice raises the profitability of millet and stimulates its production. Although the government budget deficit is reduced because of the higher yield of the tariff on rice, foreign exchange earnings fall because of the lost groundnut production. Real incomes fall substantially because of the lost consumer surplus on rice.

Hence both of the policy changes under investigation would appear to fail a test of economic efficiency. Braverman and Hammer also give some results that show that one using a partial equilibrium approach would greatly misstate the impacts of these policies.

SUMMARY

The chapter has shown how there could be secondary market effects of policy changes that depend on cross-elasticities of demand and supply. When marginal costs are increasing, changes in relative prices in these secondary markets signal added gains and losses. When there are market distortions, changes in quantity in these other markets signal added gains and losses.

But it is awfully tricky to estimate gains and losses market by market. To make the calculations manageable, economists have come up with a technique called computible general equilibrium analysis that deals with many markets simultaneously. One general equilibrium technique was used to measure the overall gain and distribution of gains from tax reform in the United Kingdom; another was used to assess the gains and/or losses from changes in agricultural price policy in Senegal.

NOTES

[1]The dark line is a general equilibrium demand function first used by Arnold C. Harberger, "The Measurement of Waste," *American Economic Review*, May 1964. It corresponds to a similar measure recommended by E. J. Mishan, *Introduction to Normative Economics*, Oxford University Press, 1981. See Frank S. Arnold, "Social Welfare Losses in a Multimarket Context," ICF Mimeo, 1983, for a useful paper comparing the two measures.

[2]One early statement of the dimensions of the mess can be found in Abram Bergson, "On Monopoly Welfare Losses," *American Economic Review*, December 1973.

[3]Alan V. Deardorff and Robert M. Stern, "An Economic Analysis of the Effects of the Tokyo Round of Multilateral Trade Negotiations on the United States and Other Major Industrialized Countries," MTN Studies, No 5 (Washington: US Government Printing Office, 1979). John B. Shoven and John Whalley, "A General Equilibrium Calculation of the Effects of

Differential Taxation of Income from Capital in the United States," *Journal of Public Economics,* June 1973.

[4]Mervyn A. King, "Welfare Analysis of Tax Reforms Using Household Data," *Journal of Public Economics,* July 1983.

[5]Avishay Braverman and Jeffrey S. Hammer, "Multimarket Analysis of Agricultural Pricing Policies in Senegal," *in* Inderjet Singh, Lyn Squire, and John A. Strauss (ed.), *Agricultural Household Models: Extensions, Applications, and Policy* (Baltimore: Johns Hopkins University Press, 1986).

PROBLEMS

1. A country grows rice and corn. The competitive supplies are given by

    $P_R = 2 + R$ where R is the quantity of rice and P_R the price;

    $P_C = C$, where C is the quantity of corn and P_C the price.

    The inverse demands are given by

    $P_R = 10 - R$

    $P_C = 10 - C + P_R$

    A new innovation shifts the supply of rice to $P_R = R$. Find
    a. The price and quantity for rice and corn before the innovation
    b. The price and quantity for rice and corn after the innovation
    c. The gains and losses to the producers and consumers of rice from the innovation
    d. The gains and losses to the producers and consumers of corn from the innovation
    e. The Kaldor-Hicks net benefits from the innovation
2. a. Use the same demand functions as in question 1, but now assume that there is an excise tax of 2 per unit on corn. Recompute the gains and losses to producers and consumers of corn and the Kaldor-Hicks net benefits from the innovation.
    b. Now say the inverse demand for rice is $P_R = 10 - R + P_C$. Have your answers of question 1 completely accounted for the Kaldor-Hicks net benefits? Why or why not?

        Considering questions 1 and 2 together, under what circumstances are there any indirect gains or losses in the corn market that force you to look at it as well. Under what circumstances do you have to consider changes that the corn market induces in other markets?

CHAPTER SIX
BENEFITS AND COSTS REALIZED AT DIFFERENT TIMES

One of the most basic problems in benefit-cost analysis is that resources are used or benefits are created at different times. Capital construction projects such as roads and subways must be built now at heavy cost, to generate benefits later. Other capital construction projects such as dams and drilling facilities entail environmental costs long after their economic benefits have lapsed. A life lost now entails costs for at least as long into the future as the person would have lived. For a wide range of projects, government decision makers and evaluators must know how to compare benefits received and costs borne now with benefits received and costs borne later. In this chapter we look into the matter.

There are two analytical difficulties in making the comparison:

Benefits and costs realized in different times are not comparable.
Some benefits and costs are recurrent, while some are realized only for a temporary period.

The general approach used to deal with both problems is to convert everything to common units, known as present values. Benefits and costs realized in different times can be converted to their present value by a process known as discounting, and then compared. Similarly, if benefits and costs are realized just once, or for a temporary period, they can again be converted to present values and compared with recurrent streams.

This chapter first explains how to compute present values, in general and in the presence of difficulties such as inflation and uncertainty. It then goes on to the more complicated question of how to compare public investment projects with other projects, distinguishing between projects that are financed by taxes and by government borrowing. An important element in this comparison is estimating something called the social rate of time preference: this chapter describes what this is and how it might be measured in economies that are closed and open to flows of international capital. This chapter is done entirely in terms of algebraic summations, as if all time periods were discrete. An appendix shows how these same notions can be dealt with in terms of calculus integrals and continuous time.

THE MECHANICS OF DISCOUNTING

The need for discounting can be seen from a common situation facing households. Suppose a household has a sum of $1,000. If the household spends it all today, it can obviously spend $1,000. If it deposits the money in a bank, earns interest at the rate of, say, 5 percent per year, and takes it out next year, it can spend $1,050 next year. Today's $1,000 is worth $1,050 next year. And $1,102.50 ($1,050 times 1.05) in two years' time. And so forth.

From this example, it must be true that a dollar now is worth more than a dollar later, because a dollar saved now can be converted to more dollars later. The same is true of a benefit or cost—this benefit or cost is worth more now than later, because the present benefit or cost can be saved and converted to more later. It might seem strange to think of benefits and costs being saved and converted, but if one recalls what the benefits and costs of Chapter 4 actually are, the logic follows perfectly. Consumer or producer surplus gains are nothing more than income these households would not have had otherwise. They are either in hand, in which case they can be saved, or in the form of expenses averted, in which case money would not have had to be borrowed. The same is true of government revenue gains or losses.

Benefits and costs realized at different times can be made comparable by expressing them in terms of present values—whenever a sum is realized, it is expressed as if it were received today. All one needs to make this conversion is to know the discount rate, or conversion rate. In the preceding example, the discount rate was just the going interest rate, 5 percent. Hence the present value of $1,000 today is just $1,000. The present value of $1,050 one year from today, which we have seen can be created by $1,000 today, is also $1,000. The present value of $1,102.50 two years from now, which also can be created by $1,000 today, is still $1,000. Generalizing, the present value of a benefit, B_t, in any future year t is just $B_t/(1 + r)^t$, where r is the discount rate.

This conversion shows how to solve the first of the problems just listed, the noncomparability of benefits and costs realized at different times. Just convert everything to present values, as if they were all received now. The same logic can also be used to solve the second problem, the fact that some benefits and costs are nonrecurrent. If a particular benefit is realized once in year t, its present value is $B_t/(1+r)^t$. If this same benefit is a recurrent stream received every year from now to eternity, the present value of this whole stream of benefits is

(1) $B_{PV} = B_0 + B_1/(1+r) + B_2/(1+r)^t + \ldots + B_T/(1+r)^T$

where B_{PV} refers to the present value of the whole stream of benefits, r is the discount rate over the whole time period, assumed for simplicity to be constant, and T is the final year in which any benefit is received. A condensed form of this expression is

(2) $B_{PV} = \sum\limits_{t=0}^{t=T} B_t/(1+r)^t$

With this conversion, the fundamental principle of benefit-cost analysis, given in Chapter 3, can now be restated:

> In any choice situation, select the policy alternative that produces the greatest present value of net benefits.

The logic is precisely the same as before, except now we are recognizing timing differences and working in our present value principle. This new version of the fundamental principle can be used to deal with gains and losses realized at different times, recurrent and nonrecurrent gains and losses, and any other complication.

To see how this formula can be applied, say that we have two projects, A and B. A yields \$1,050 one year from now, while B yields \$550 one year from now and \$540 two years from now. According to the revised fundamental principle, we accept the project with the highest present value of net benefits. That for A is \$1,000; that for B, using equation (2), is (\$550/1.05) + (\$540/1.1025) = \$1,014. In this case project B is more valuable, even though half of its benefits are received a year later than for A. The present value formula shows how to make the comparison.

It should be obvious that the present value of a stream of benefits depends very much on the discount rate used. In the preceding example the discount rate was 5 percent, and B had the higher present value. What if the discount rate were 10 percent? The present value of A falls to (\$1,050/1.10) = \$955. The present value of B falls to (\$550/1.10) + (\$540/1.21) = \$946. Now A

has the higher present value of benefits. Both present values have fallen, but because *B* involves more benefits farther in the future, and because these future benefits are now discounted at a higher rate, the present value of the *B* stream falls by more than the present value of the *A* stream.

In the preceding example the 5 percentage point change in the discount rate changed the present values by about 5 percent, an important change but hardly earthshaking. For long-lived investments the impact of a change in the discount rate would be much greater. As a benefit stream gets longer and longer, the influence of discount rates builds up, with the higher discount rates effectively making the future benefits count for much less than the lower discount rates. As the time horizon grows, the difference becomes greater and greater, and these greater differences are cumulated into a present value sum, the difference in which also gets greater and greater. Apparently small differences between discount rates can then translate to very large differences in present values for long-term projects.

A specific illustration of this point is given in Figure 6.1. There the present values of $1,000 received each year for *T* years is shown for different values of *r* and *T*. Note that for each of the four discount rates, *r* equaling 2.5 percent, 5 percent, 7.5 percent, and 10 percent respectively, the present value increases as more years of benefits (*T*) are added. But the rate of addition, given by the slope of each curve, is much less when the discount rate is high because the remote future benefits are more heavily discounted. In the limit, for projects that yield benefits forever, the

FIGURE 6.1   Present value of $1000 Received Every Year for *T* Years

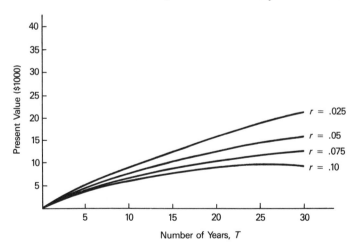

The formula used for all lines is

$$PV = \sum_{t=0}^{t=T} 1000/(1 + r)^t$$

As *r* rises, the influence of benefits far in the future falls and the present value falls.

stream with the lowest discount rate has a present value four times the stream with the highest discount rate.

A Simplifying Approximation

Expression (2) gives a useful way to summarize a great deal of information. At the same time, it requires the addition of several multiplicative terms and is rather cumbersome. Although there are present value tables and spread sheet programs for personal computers to ease this computational burden, it is still often useful to have a simplifying approximation to see quickly the order of magnitude of a stream of benefits.

A very simple approximation can be derived as follows. Suppose project benefits are at a constant level from $t = 1$ to $t = T$. Expression (2) becomes

$$(3)\ B_{PV} = B[1/(1 + r) + 1/(1 + r)^2 + \dots 1/(1 + r)^T]$$

Multiply (3) by $1/(1 + r)$

$$(4)\ B_{PV}/(1 + r) = B[1/(1 + r)^2 + 1/(1 + r)^3 + \dots 1/(1 + r)^{T + 1}]$$

Subtract (4) from (3)

$$(5)\ B_{PV}(1 + r - 1)/(1 + r) = B[1/(1 + r) - 1/(1 + r)^{T + 1}]$$

Cancel the $(1 + r)$ terms and divide through by r

$$(6)\ B_{PV} = (B/r)[1 - 1/(1 + r)^T]$$

Note that when T is very large

$$(7)\ B_{PV} = B/r$$

In other words, the present value of benefits equals the constant stream, B, divided by the discount rate, r, when T is very large. Rather than working out sums for periods that could be as long as, say, fifty years, the analyst can get pretty close simply by dividing the constant level of benefits by the discount rate. If the discount rate is 5 percent, or .05, the present value of a constant stream of benefits is twenty times the annual benefit. If the discount rate is 10 percent, ten times. And so forth.

This simple expression can be adjusted in various ways to make it more flexible. Suppose we are comparing the present value of a stream of benefits with that of a stream of costs, where each has a different profile. In one common case, there might be one time costs of C. The present value of net benefits, or benefits less costs, is then given by

(8) $B_{PV} = B/r - C$

In general, whenever benefit and cost streams, or different benefit streams, have different time profiles, they can be decomposed into their different components and the preceding simplification used.

A second type of complication refers to steady changes in the benefit stream. Instead of remaining constant forever, suppose benefits decay at a steady rate d beginning in year two. Working out the math in the same fashion as in equation (7) gives the present value of this decaying benefit stream as

(9) $B_{PV} = B/(r + d)$

The present value of the benefit stream is less than before, in an amount that depends on the decay rate and the discount rate.

Third, what if the benefits do not start for five years, but then are constant forever after that? Just eliminate the first four terms, do the math, and get the approximation. Or, what if benefits do not last forever but just twenty years, as in Figure 6.1? Just insert $T = 20$ into (6) and go ahead. These examples show how equation (7) can be used to approximate the present value of net benefits, or a benefit stream, in a wide variety of cases.

Inflation

It may seem simple enough to use these present value formulas, but some issues have caused enormous confusion and deserve special mention. One involves inflation, one involves risk, and one involves internal rates of return. We now examine each of these problem cases.

Suppose first there is general price inflation, such that all prices are forecast to rise at rate g forever. Two changes must be made in the preceding formulas. If benefits were expected to be B per year forever when prices were stable, they are now expected to rise at the rate of $(1 + g)$ forever. The constant B levels are said to be in real terms, and the benefits inflated by the expected rise in prices are said to be in nominal terms.

The other change involves interest rates. If prices are expected to rise at g percent forever, lenders will not lend without adding a premium to account for the fact that loans are to be repaid in depreciated dollars. Borrowers are willing to go along with this premium because they get to repay loans in cheaper dollars. According to what is known as Irving Fisher's law,[1] in such circumstances lenders and borrowers will reset the nominal, or money, interest rate (m) as follows

(10) $1 + m = (1 + r)(1 + g) = 1 + r + g + rg$

One can then make both changes in equation (3) to do the entire present value calculation in nominal terms

(11) $B_{PV} = B_0 + (B_1)(1 + g)/(1 + m) + (B_2)(1 + g)^2/(1 + m)^2 + \dots$
$$+ (B_T)(1 + g)^T/(1 + m)^T$$

Substituting (10) into (11) shows that both the numerators and denominators have a series of expressions in $(1 + g)^t$, all of which exactly cancel out. Once they cancel out, equation (11) in nominal terms is exactly the same as equation (2) in real terms. This leads to the important insight that it simply does not matter whether one puts all benefits and costs in nominal terms and uses the nominal discount rate, or in real terms and uses the real discount rate. Because the $(1 + g)$ expressions cancel out, the present value of the benefit stream is the same either way.

If it comes out the same either way, why all the confusion? Because one does have to be consistent. For years the official United States government discounting procedure has told evaluators to use real benefits, B, in the numerator and nominal discount rates in the denominator.[2] This is a case of mixing apples and oranges, and leads to incorrect present values for the benefit stream. But as long as the investigator is consistent, discounting real benefits with the real discount rate, r, or nominal benefits with the nominal discount rate, m, the answer will be correct.

The fact that real-on-real gives the same answer as nominal-on-nominal often spares the evaluator the necessity to forecast general rates of inflation. If, for example, one is evaluating a dam that yields a "stream" of real benefits, one can just compute the present value of that stream by using those real benefits and discounting by the real discount rate. It is completely unnecessary to forecast inflation. On the other hand, if the evaluator is computing the present value of a financial contract that has payments set in nominal terms, one can use the nominal stream of payments and discount by the nominal interest rate, again without an explicit forecast of inflation.

But there is one type of price change that will matter. Suppose a project generates a resource (such as oil or electricity) that is expected to change in relative price. The price for this particular resource is expected to rise at a rate of z percent more rapidly than all other prices. In such a case, the benefits in the numerator should be inflated in every period by the factor $(1 + z)$ if the real discount rate is used in the denominator, or by $(1 + z)(1 + g)$ if the nominal discount rate is used. The reason is that the project is producing a more valuable product every year, and the present value of benefits should be increased accordingly. Were relative prices expected to fall, the same equation should be used, this time making z negative and the present value less. Combining relative price appreciation at rate z and benefit decay at rate d, the general present value formula becomes

$$(12)\ B_{PV} = \sum_{t=0}^{t=T} B_t(1+z)^t(1-d)^t/(1+r)^t$$

Risk

Since capital markets add a risk premium onto rates of return to account for the fact that certain financial instruments are riskier than others, it is often alleged that benefit-cost analysts should do likewise. No, they should not.

Risk and uncertainty were already dealt with in Chapter 4. There it was argued that if a project yielded an uncertain stream of returns, with enough variance that households valued the gain from the good outcomes less than the losses from the bad outcomes, the utility of the package was less than that of a package with the same average return but no uncertainty. The appropriate correction is to find, and use in the benefit-cost analysis, the certainty equivalent income. Rather than averaging the incomes and finding the utility of that average, the investigator should find the utility of each outcome first, and then find the average of the utility outcomes. Or, the investigator should subtract from the average income the premium for an insurance policy that eliminates uncertainty.

If this were done, it is clear that counting for uncertainty also in the discount rate would be double counting. When one has already adjusted for uncertainty, there should be no more adjustment through discounting. Moreover, the only way uncertainty can be properly taken account of is by subtracting all insurance premia from the benefits before discounting. Any other procedure will distort present values.

Illustrating this point with the preceding example, suppose that the risk-free discount rate is 5 percent, the risk-adjusted discount rate observed for all financial instruments is 10 percent, project A returns $1,050 one year from now with perfect certainty, while project B returns $550 one year from now with perfect certainty but an average of $540 two years from now with some uncertainty. To buy an insurance policy that would eliminate the uncertainty in B in the second year would cost $10. Which project is to be preferred?

For project A nothing has changed. The benefit of $1,050 is certain, the risk-free discount rate is still 5 percent, and the present value is $1,000 just as before. For project B the first year's return is still $550, there is still no uncertainty, and the present value of this return is still $550/1.05 = $524. But the second year's return is $540 less the insurance premium, or $530/1.1025 = $481, making for a total present value for the uncertain B stream of $1,005. Project B still wins, but by less than before because we introduced uncertainty on this project but not project A.

What would have happened if we had instead accounted for risk by using the risky interest rate of 10 percent? The numbers were already given, a present value of \$955 for A and \$946 for B, with A now becoming the project with the higher present value. Here is a case where dealing incorrectly with risk actually distorts project choices. Although mistakes on this issue will not usually matter as much, there is no point in making mistakes. In general, there is no way that alterations in the discount rate can account for benefit or cost uncertainty, because uncertainty will generally have different impacts on different streams of returns. Because this is so, the proper approach is to deal with uncertainty at its source in expressing project benefits and costs in certainty equivalent terms, and then to discount those certainty equivalent amounts with the risk-free discount rate.

Internal Rates of Return

The preceding equations inserted a real discount rate, r, to compute present values. Sometimes analysts have followed the procedure in reverse, finding what is known as the internal rate of return that makes the present value of net benefits of a project equal to zero.

To see the difference in the two techniques, suppose a project yields net benefits for three years. The present value formula is

(13) $B_{PV} = B_0 + B_1/(1 + r) + B_2/(1 + r)^2$

The recommended approach is simply to insert the B's and r, compute the present value of benefits, and apply the fundamental principle.

The alternative approach is to find the internal rate of return (i) by setting the present value of net benefits equal to zero

(14) $0 = B_0 + B_1/(1 + i) + B_2/(1 + i)^2$

It will generally be true that a high i means a good project—one that would have a positive present value if discounted at r. But the internal rate of return is not always a good guide. As can be seen in problem 5 at the end of the chapter, (14) is a quadratic equation which will have two solution values for i, both of which could make sense, and make the internal rate of return impossible to use. Moreover, there is no general answer to the question of whether it is better to have very high internal rates of return for a short time or lower internal rates of return for a long time. The only way to answer such a question is to compute a present value for both streams and compare.

As with the benefit-cost ratio discussed in Chapter 3, the internal rate of return often gives correct information about a project, but sometimes not. It is either redundant or wrong. The most sensible policy seems then not even to compute it, but rather to focus on the net benefits of a project, which is always the proper indicator.

THE OPTIMAL DISCOUNTING RULE

We now turn from the mechanical question of how to compute present values to the economic question of how to choose among public investment projects. The answer involves discount rates, but the issue is more complicated than just choosing the right discount rate and filling in the formula. It is necessary to understand what will be called the optimal discounting rule.

To explain the logic of the rule, imagine that we know whether a proposed public investment project will subtract resources from consumption or investment. If we were sure that a public investment project displaced private investment, the rule would be quite straightforward. Since both the public and the private project create a stream of benefits over time, there is no reason for favoring one or the other. Private investors make their decisions by discounting streams of returns by the existing real interest rate, r, so any benefits of a public project should also be discounted by r. This logic works whatever determines r—the macroeconomic policies of a country, its tax policies, whatever. The public project should earn more than the private project it displaces.

But when the project displaces consumption, things get much more complicated. There is an argument for using an easier standard to screen the public investment if in the absence of this project, society is underinvesting for the future. If it is underinvesting, there is a form of external benefit to greater public investment that can be encouraged by applying an easier standard. This raises the question, one long debated by economists, of whether society is underinvesting.

Does Society Underinvest?

Superficially, it would seem that the answer is yes. If a particular generation devotes resources to consumption, only that generation enjoys the resources. If the same resources were devoted to investment, the fruits of the resources would be enjoyed by future generations as well. Since future generations have no voice in the initial decision of whether to consume or invest; they have no way to express their potential enjoyment, and there could be said to be an external benefit to greater investment.

But there are several links between the present and the future that mitigate this externality. One is capital markets. Suppose the world were running out of oil. It would be known in advance that oil is a dwindling resource, and that fact would drive up its price, in effect spreading the burden of the future scarcity to the present.

Another important link between the present and the future is bequests. A large share of private wealth in the United States wealth is generated by transfers from one generation to another.[3] The scale of these transfers suggests that intergenerational altruism is a motivating force in the behavior of households. If households really do care about their future heirs, they might save and invest enough to provide for them. And one could even construct a self-interest rationale, whereby the older generation agrees to save for the young, provided that the young takes care of the old in its retirement.

The ABFK Rule

If society does underinvest, the discounting rule for projects that displace consumption, and hence raise the aggregate amount of investment, should be less stringent than for projects that displace investment. This feature is recognized by defining a new discount rate, called the social rate of time preference (r^*). This social discount rate is less than the existing real interest rate (r) for societies that are underinvesting. The question of how this rate is to be used for discounting has been worked out more or less independently by Kenneth Arrow, David Bradford, Martin Feldstein, and Mordecai Kurz.[4] Their rule features two steps:

All resources should be valued in terms of consumption units.
All consumption gains and losses should be discounted at r^*.

To see how the rule works in two very simple cases, say that a project generates consumption benefits of B per year indefinitely and is known to be created entirely out of resources that would otherwise have been devoted to the present year's consumption. The present value of these resources is C. Applying the first step of the ABFK rule, the resource cost of the project in terms of consumption units is also C. Applying the second step of the ABFK rule, along with equation (7), the present value of benefits is B/r^*. The net present value of the project in consumption units is then

(15) $B_{PV} = B/r^* - C$

If this net present value is positive, or if $B > r^*C$, the project yields net social gains.

Now suppose that the project displaces private investment of the same resource value C. To make things easy, assume that this private investment yields a real rate of return of r forever, giving an annual sacrifice of consumption goods of rC indefinitely.

The cost in terms of consumption goods of this reduced investment is the present value of this stream evaluated at r^*, or rC/r^*. The gains are the same as before, B/r^*. The net present value of the project becomes

$$(16) \ B_{PV} = B/r^* - rC/r^*$$

If this net present value is positive, the project yields gains. Canceling the r^* terms, this time the condition for the project to yield gains is that $B > rC$. But note that since r is greater than r^*, the ABFK rule requires public investment projects to pass a more difficult test when they displace investment goods (16) than when they displace consumption goods (15). The reason, to repeat, is that since society is underinvesting, projects that displace consumption divert resources from consumption to investment and are subsidized accordingly.

These applications were given to illustrate how the ABFK rule deals differently with projects that displace consumption and investment. Especially in the latter case, things are likely to be much more complicated in practice. If a private investment depreciates, it will pay a higher return to cover the depreciation, but for a shorter time. The discounting equation will look different from (16), but the principle of converting the sacrifice to consumption goods and then discounting still holds.

Beyond that, the analyst will not usually know whether a project will displace consumption or investment. But the analyst should know whether a public investment project is to be financed by higher taxes or higher borrowing. Spending proposals voted on by local districts must by law specify the way the project is to be financed, and since most other governmental projects are proposed within the context of an overall budget, the analyst can usually determine what goes up or down if the project goes forward.

In the United States from 90 to 95 percent of output is devoted to public or private consumption, so a reasonable presumption might be that any tax that reduces output to finance public investment also reduces consumption. It might appear that investments financed by an increase in property taxes will lower investment, but if the supply of capital is highly elastic to a community, as we will see it probably is, even property taxes can be shown to fall mainly on labor, and on consumption. Moreover, recent work by Roger Gordon and Joel Slemrod suggests that capital taxes are actually negative at the federal level.[5] In view of these considerations, it seems reasonable to assume that tax-financed public investment projects reduce consumption, and to use the version of the ABFK rule shown by equation (15).

When a project is financed by added borrowing, there are two ways to determine its burden in terms of consumption and investment. One involves a phenomenon known to macroeconomists as "crowding out." To simplify a complex story, higher government borrowing for whatever purpose will, in the long run, subtract resources largely, and perhaps entirely, from private investment, hence suggesting the version of the ABFK rule shown by equation (16) for bond-financed public investment projects.[6]

A more precise way to deal with the question focuses on interest payments. When a government borrows more, the cost comes in the form of higher interest payments. Other things being equal, taxes will have to rise, and consumption goods to fall, to cover these interest payments. The sacrifice of consumption units to pay for the project can then be expressed as vC, where v is the long-term borrowing rate for the government. The present value of benefits is still B/r^*, the present value of consumption goods sacrificed is vC/r^*, and the ABFK test is in effect whether $B > vC$. For bond-financed state and local public investments in the United States, v is usually slightly less than r and the test is easier than that in equation (16), because state and local interest is not taxable. For bond-financed federal government investments, the borrowing rate is approximately r, and the rule is essentially the same as that given by equation (16). For governments threatened with bankruptcy, or for developing countries where there is a large outstanding stock of debt, the borrowing rate might be above r and the ABFK test might be more stringent than that given by equation (16).

THE SOCIAL RATE OF TIME PREFERENCE

The ABFK rule shows how to deal with projects that are financed by taxes or borrowing, but we still have not said how to measure the social rate of time preference r^*. Since any difference between this social rate and the existing real interest rate hinges on the notion that an economy might be underinvesting, the only sensible approach seems to compute it as if the economy were not underinvesting. Here we show how to do this, both for a closed economy and an economy open to international capital flows.

The Social Rate of Time Preference in a Closed Economy

The salient fact about a closed economy is that national saving must equal national investment. If the two differ, foreign borrowing or lending cannot fill the gap: interest rates must change to equate the two.

Suppose such an economy increases its national saving. The higher saving gradually forces down interest rates and encourages more private investment. This in turn gradually increases the capital stock and output levels. The rise in capital gradually lowers the return to capital because of the law of diminishing returns. In the long run there must be equilibration of capital markets at the point where potential investors are indifferent between borrowing to invest and not borrowing, or where the marginal product of capital equals the real interest rate. Hence in the long run a higher saving economy will also be a higher investment economy; it will have more capital, higher output, and lower real interest rates.

The mechanics for such an economy are shown in Figure 6.2. On the horizontal axis is capital per worker, k. On the vertical axis is output per worker, y. The top line gives the production function, $y = f(k)$. The slope of this production function at any point shows the increment to output per unit change in capital, or the marginal product of capital. In equilibrium, profit maximizing investors will go to where the marginal product of capital equals the interest rate, r. Hence in equilibrium the slope of the production function is the real interest rate. This slope is declining as the capital stock increases because of the law of diminishing returns: the more capital there is, the less additions to the capital stock raise output.

Assume the number of workers is growing at rate n, either because of population growth or technological improvements that release labor. To equip these n new workers at the prevailing capital-labor ratio, k, requires new net investment per worker of nk. Because saving equals investment in this closed economy, actual net investment per worker is the national share output devoted to capital formation, s, times output per worker, y. If actual net investment, sy, exceeds that required to maintain the capital-labor ratio, nk, k will rise. If sy is less than nk, k will fall. In general, k will stabilize where

FIGURE 6.2   The Social Rate of Time Preference in a Closed Economy

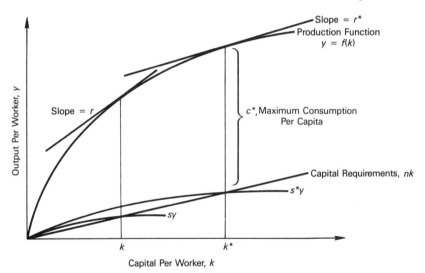

(a) When society devotes s percent of output to capital formation, capital formation is sy, the equilibrium capital stock is k, and the marginal product of capital, or real interest rate, is r.

(b) When society devotes s^* percent of output to capital formation, capital formation is s^*y, the equilibrium capital stock is k^*, and the real interest rate is r^*. This situation is called the Golden Rule because consumption per capita, c^*, is maximized. r^* is the interest rate at this optimal position.

(17) $sy = nk$

the equilibrium growth position for this economy. Such a point is shown in Figure 6.2 at saving rate s. The capital-labor ratio for such a saving rate settles down at k, output is read from the production function, and the interest rate, equal to the marginal product of capital, is read from the slope of the production function at k. At this point output and capital per worker are stable, but since the number of workers is growing at rate n, real output and the capital stock are also growing at rate n. This growth rate n is the permanent growth rate for the economy.

This exercise shows what would happen in equilibrium for a particular national saving or investment rate. If this rate were to be increased, say to s^*, the new workers would be equipped with more capital, the capital-labor ratio would rise to k^*, and the interest rate would fall to r^*. At this higher saving equilibrium, the level of output per capita (y) would be higher but the equilibrium growth rate would still be n.

Should such a higher saving policy be followed? There is no objective answer to the question because all saving withdraws resources from present-day consumption to increase the capital stock and output in the future. In these terms saving is like a transfer of consumption goods from the present to the future, and more saving represents more of a transfer. In view of economists' unwillingness to make interpersonal value judgments, there is no way to say whether such a move is desirable.

But there is a way to say whether such a move raises aggregate consumption, or has positive net benefits in terms of the consumption goods of all generations. Aggregate equilibrium consumption per worker is shown in Figure 6.2 by the difference between output, y, and nk at any k. It is clear from the figure that this distance is maximized when the slope of the production function, r, equals the slope of the nk line, n. This position maximizes the level of per worker consumption for all time, and would be the one suggested by the fundamental principle of benefit-cost analysis if the welfare of all generations were tallied up. Each and every generation does not gain from the higher saving—the present generation must save more and sacrifice consumption goods—but all generations together do gain. For this reason, this consumption-maximizing position is sometimes called the Golden Rule position: each generation is doing (saving) unto others (future generations) what it would have others (past generations) do unto it. The Golden Rule position is characterized in the figure by a saving rate of s^*, a capital-labor ratio of k^*, and an interest rate of $r^* = n$.

In this sense, an economy with a saving-investment rate of less than s^* could be said to be undersaving or underinvesting. It also follows, of course, that an economy saving at a rate higher than s^* is oversaving, in the sense that the marginal product of capital is so low that long-run consumption per worker actually falls as the saving rate increases.

The connection with the social rate of time preference should now be apparent. If the economy is initially saving at rate s, the going interest rate is r, which exceeds the Golden Rule interest rate. If public investment displaces private investment, the relevant discount rate should be r, just as argued previously. If public investment displaces consumption, and hence raises the economy's saving rate, capital-labor ratio, and consumption in the long run, the public investment should be evaluated by the discount rate at the optimal saving position, $r^* = n$. In that sense, n might be used as the social rate of time preference for an undersaving economy. Note of course that if the economy is not undersaving, the going interest rate will already be the social rate of time preference, $r = n$.

This analysis is very simple and glosses over many real world complications. But it does show at least one way to define undersaving or underinvesting economies, and how one might calculate a social rate of time preference for such economies.

The Social Rate of Time Preference in an Open Economy

The previous model for determining the social rate of time preference relied on the fact that national saving equaled investment. That is an increasingly unrealistic description of today's economies. There is a thriving international capital market that supplies capital elastically to national economies. If an economy reduces saving, interest rates may not rise and investment may not fall because foreign funds can be borrowed to fill the gap between investment and saving. Similarly, if a country increases its saving, it can lend abroad. In either case the national interest rate will closely follow world interest rates.

Figure 6.3 shows the analytics in the extreme case where a country's real interest rate always equals the world real interest rate, and is determined by the world real interest rate. This is called the small open economy case by macroeconomists. The vertical axis now shows income per worker instead of output per worker, because it is possible to earn income on foreign lending. The horizontal axis now shows wealth per worker (w) instead of capital per worker, because wealth now includes claims on foreigners.

The closed economy production function of Figure 6.2 is supplanted by the open economy income function. If national wealth is zero—our citizens own nothing at all—output would have been zero in the closed economy case because there would be no capital, and capital is necessary to produce output. In the open economy case the country simply borrows capital from abroad and earns the labor income from this capital. Hence the intercept of the income function, the labor income that can be earned even if wealth is zero and all capital is rented, is y_0.

As wealth rises in a closed economy, more and more capital is combined with the same labor force and the closed economy faces the law of diminish-

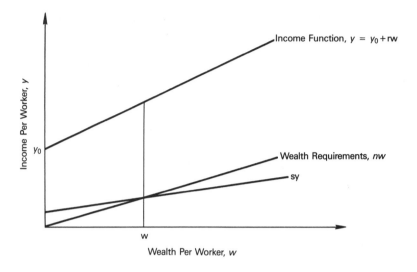

(a) When society saves *s* percent of income, equilibrium wealth is *w*. As *s*
increases, *w* will increase, *y* will increase, and consumption per worker will
increase indefinitely, as long as the fixed slope of the income line (*r*) exceeds
the slope of the wealth requirements line (*n*).

FIGURE 6.3   The Social Rate of Time Preference in an Open Economy

ing returns. This does not happen in a small open economy, because as wealth
rises, citizens simply invest abroad. The country is by assumption too small
to saturate the whole world with capital, so a constant world real interest rate
r is returned on this foreign lending. The value of income for any *w* is thus
$y_0 + rw$, and the slope of the income function is fixed at *r*.

With these changes the rest of the analysis follows. For any pre-chosen
saving rate we draw the *sy* function, and the equilibrium is where $sy = nw$,
using the same logic as before. If the slope of the income function, *r*, exceeds
the slope of the *nw* line, *n*, the country can continually raise long-run consumption per worker by saving more. This is unlike the closed economy case,
because there the reward for greater saving is limited by the law of diminishing returns.

In the closed economy case one could at least define underinvestment
and a social rate of time preference with reference to this long-run optimal
position. There is no way to do that in this open economy case. The country
can save more and more, raising long-run consumption all the time, with no
limit. The poor present generation can contribute to the rich future generations without anybody, or any consideration, ever saying "enough."

So it becomes difficult to define an underinvesting economy and a social
rate of time preference for a small open economy. Such a country can borrow
and lend at *r*, *r* cannot be changed, and *r* itself becomes a logical, and perhaps
the only, candidate for the social rate of time preference.

What to do?

How does one distill a discount policy out of this mess? We can put everything in terms of consumption units, as directed, but we hit an impasse when we have to choose a social rate of time preference.

Since it matters whether a country should be treated as a closed economy or a small open economy, a first question is which model is appropriate. For the U.S. federal government, the answer is probably neither. The United States is clearly no longer a closed economy, but since it can and does affect world real interest rates, it is not a small open economy either. The best answer seems to be that the U.S. economy and the U.S. federal government should be treated as a hybrid case: the analyst should either use brackets or take the social rate of time preference as some average of the closed economy rate, n, and a logical choice for the small open economy rate, r.

There can be no general guidance for what these values are because both r and n change over time. In either case the relevant rates should not be past rates but those forecast for the future: this is when the public investment will be yielding returns. In 1988 the consensus forecast of the long-term nominal interest rate (m) expected for the next few years was about 8 percent and the consensus forecast of the long-term inflation rate (g) was about 4 percent.[7] Plugging into equation (10), we get $r = 4$ percent. Presumably, real interest rates of about this level were being used by private investors at the time.

Private investors do not have to worry about social rates of time preference but government decision makers do. Again, the 1988 consensus for the anticipated long-term growth rate of real output and capital, n, a likely candidate for the social rate of time preference in a closed economy, was 2.5 percent. Roughly averaging this closed economy rate with the open economy rate of 4 percent gives a social rate of time preference of perhaps 3.5 percent. Were this social rate to be used in discounting, there would be a very modest stimulus for federal government public investment projects that displace private consumption.

Although the conceptual arguments would differ for U.S. state and local governments, the actual numbers do not differ by much. As previously pointed out, the U.S. government may be large enough to affect world interest rates, but no state or local government is. Hence we are back to the small open economy case, where the most likely candidate for the social rate of time preference is just r, about 4 percent in 1988. To plug into the ABFK rule, state and local decision makers can just use this rate for tax-financed public investment projects but still have to measure the relative interest factor, v, for bond-financed public investments.

Just as no U.S. state or local government is large enough to influence world real interest rates, most foreign countries are not either. Hence for these governments as well, the appropriate social rate of time preference seems likely to be the standard r. The actual number may not be the same as in the

United States because of tax differences, expectations about exchange rate changes, and a host of other considerations. And again there would be a v factor that would come into play for bond-financed public investments.

These comments were written to give as clear guidance as possible, but it should be obvious that there is a great deal of uncertainty all the way through the argument. There is uncertainty about whether a country is underinvesting in the closed economy case, and what the social rate of time preference might be in that case. There is no objective definition of underinvesting or for the social rate of time preference in the open economy case. To preserve the opportunity cost logic, all relevant rates have to be forecast as private investors are forecasting. And all these rates change over time. On the other side we know that relatively small changes yield big changes in expected present values for long-lived investments. In view of all this, it seems that a minimum requirement would be to compute the present value of benefits for tax-financed projects with various social rates of time preference, perhaps using values for r of 2 percent, 4 percent, and 6 percent (and corresponding v factors for bond-financed projects). In this way, the analyst not only knows how the numbers come out for different assumptions, but also how much difference is made by the assumptions.

SUMMARY

This chapter first showed how otherwise noncomparable benefits and costs can be made comparable by expressing everything in present value terms. The fundamental principle of benefit-cost analysis is now to be interpreted as pertaining to expected present values, rather than contemporaneous gains and losses.

It went on to show how to compute present values in a variety of situations. The present value of a stream of benefits or costs is the expected value in each year, discounted by the interest rate compounded over that time. This present value is independent of general price inflation, which means that the calculation can be done in either real or nominal terms. But it is not independent of specific price inflation, which raises the present value. Risk should be dealt with by converting gains and losses to certainty equivalent terms before discounting, rather than by altering discount rates.

The general rule for evaluating public investment projects is to convert all gains and losses to consumption terms, and then discount by the social rate of time preference. This rule imposes a more stringent test on public investment projects that displace investment (are bond-financed) than it does on projects that displace consumption (are tax-financed) when a society is underinvesting. The social rate of time preference would be below the real interest rate in economies that under save and are not open to international capital flows, and about the real interest rate for economies that are open to international capital flows.

NOTES

[1]Irving Fisher, *The Theory of Interest* (New York: Macmillan, 1930), Chapter 19. Although Fisher's law should be amended when a country has an income tax with the deductibility of nominal interest, it explains actual rate movements reasonably well. See Thomas J. Sargent, "Interest Rates and Expected Inflation: A Selective Summary of Recent Research," *Explorations in Economic Research*, Summer 1976.

[2]The official procedure for all projects up to 1972, and for water projects still, is to discount real benefits with the nominal interest rate. Since 1972 the government claims to compare real benefits with a real discount factor for nonwater projects, but it uses an unduly high real discount rate of 10 percent.

[3]The share of net wealth due to bequests is at least 15 percent and perhaps higher. But there is a stirring empirical argument about how much higher. The issue is discussed in Franco Modigliani, "The Role of Intergenerational Transfers and Life Cycle Saving in the Accumulation of Wealth," *The Journal of Economic Perspectives*, Spring 1988.

[4]Kenneth J. Arrow, "Discounting and Public Investment Criteria," *in* Allen V. Kneese and Stephen C. Smith (ed.), *Water Research* (Baltimore: Johns Hopkins University Press, 1967); Arrow and Mordecai Kurz, *Public Investment, the Rate of Return, and Optimal Fiscal Policy* (Baltimore: Johns Hopkins University Press, 1970); David F. Bradford, "Constraints on Government Investment Opportunities and the Choice of Discount Rate," *American Economic Review*, December 1975; and Martin S. Feldstein, "The Inadequacy of Weighted Discount Rates," *in* Richard E. Layard (ed.) *Cost-Benefit Analysis* (New York: Penguin, 1972), Reading 13.

[5]Roger H. Gordon and Joel Slemrod, "Do We Collect Any Revenue from Taxing Capital Income?" *in* Lawrence H. Summers (ed.), *Tax Policy and the Economy* (Cambridge, MA: MIT Press, 1988).

[6]Macroeconomists who have worked out the investment-saving analysis realize that bond-financed increases in public investment spending will drive up interest rates and crowd out private investment entirely, unless interest-sensitive consumption shares some of the burden. Empirically consumption seems to be so little sensitive to the interest rate that it will probably not share any of the burden—see Phillip Howrey and Saul Hymans, "The Measurement and Determination of Loanable-Funds Saving, *Brookings Papers on Economic Activity*, 3:1978.

[7]A convenient way to find annual forecasts of inflation, interest rates, and real growth rates is from the Congressional Budget Office. It makes semiannual budget projections using consensus private forecasts of these rates. For the numbers in the text, see *The Economic and Budget Outlook: Fiscal Years 1989–1993*, February 1988.

PROBLEMS

1. You are comparing two projects, both of which cost $100 in year zero (right now). Project *A* returns $114 in year one and nothing in year two. Project *B* returns $125.40 in year two and nothing in year one. Which is the best project when $r = .06$? Which should be done according to the amended fundamental principle? Answer the same questions for $r = .11$ and $r = .15$.

2. You have a project that pays a stream of benefits equalling $100 per year, beginning next year and lasting forever. What is the present value

of this stream if the discount rate is .10? .05? .03 with a benefit decay rate of .04 starting in year two.

If the stream is in real dollars, the real discount rate is .04, and the expected rate of general price inflation is .06, find the present value of the stream. Now do the same when the price of the good produced by the stream is anticipated to rise .01 per year beginning in year two, but no general price inflation is expected.

3. Suppose your benefit stream started at 10 in year one (one year from now) and lasted for three years. The discount rate is .02. Find the present value. Now for ten years. Now forever. Now with a decay to 9 in year two, and a continuation of the stream and that decay rate forever. Now with a decay to 9 in year two and a continuation of 9 forever. Now with 10 for three years, a drop to 5 in year four, and a continuation at 5 forever.

4. The discount rate is .05. Project A costs 5 in year zero and returns 10.50 in year one. Project B is a lottery with a one-half chance of winning. If you win, you get 8. If you lose, you get nothing. How much will you pay for a lottery ticket if you are neither risk-averse nor risk-loving (say you are risk-neutral)? Would you prefer A or a free lottery ticket?

Now say that A entails certain costs of 5 in year zero but a one-half chance of 10.50 in year one and a one-half chance of 0 in year one. You are risk-averse and offered A for free. Do you want it?

Now you are offered a new option for A. You can guarantee winning, and getting 10.50 in year one if you just buy insurance in year zero. You still have to pay the certain cost of 5 in year zero. How much are you willing to pay for the insurance?

5. Refer to equation (14) in the text. Suppose net benefits are 10, -22, and 12 in the three years. Solve for the internal rate of return (i). Suppose the going interest rate (r) is .07. Based on internal rate considerations, do you want the project? Is there another way to choose? Do you want it?

6. Say that a closed economy's production function is given by $y = \sqrt{k}$ where y is output per worker and k is capital per worker. The trend growth of the labor force is .05 per year and the saving rate is .2. Find the equilibrium capital-labor ratio and level of output per capita. What happens to levels of labor, capital, and output over time? What discount rate is used by private investors? What is the social rate of time preference? What is the discounting rule for tax-financed projects? For bond-financed projects?

Now suppose the economy is open to international capital flows, with a fixed real interest rate of .06. Find the social rate of time preference and give the rules for discounting tax- and bond-financed projects.

APPENDIX
CONTINUOUS DISCOUNTING

The present value equations in the text apply the compound interest formula from year to year—that is, $1000 grows to $1050 next year and to $1102.50 in the following year. Most people have learned that when a bank is quoting interest rates, it matters how often interest is compounded, annually, semi-annually, or what. How often is interest compounded in the discrete time formulas given in the text? Here we go through the case of continuous discounting to see how we have to adjust our discrete time equations.

Suppose we begin with a principal of $1 at an interest rate of r per year. If interest were compounded annually, this $1 would grow to $\$1(1 + r)$ in one year. If it were compounded semiannually, it would grow to $\$1(1 + r/2)^2$ in a year. If triannually, $\$1(1 + r/3)^3$. In general, $V = (1 + r/m)^m$, where V is the value after one year and m is the number of discounting periods during the year. And if done for t years, $V = [(1 + r/m)^{m/r}]^{rt}$.

It can be shown that as m approaches infinity, the expression in the brackets approaches the base of the natural logarithim, e. Hence the future value, V, of $1 is e^{rt}. And the discounted present value of V is e^{-rt}. So the discounted present value (B_t) of some fixed amount B_0 received at time t is

(1) $B_t = B_0 e^{-rt}$

As an illustration, say $t = 1$. Then $B_1/B_0 = e^{-r}$, which is approximately $1-r$.

Values for the discounted present value of a fixed sum B_0 are shown in Figure 6A.1. These values decline over time because they are discounted by progressively higher amounts as t increases, just as in the discrete case in the text.

For the most part, we have worked not with discounted present values of a particular future amount, but with the discounted present value of a whole stream of benefits. Suppose we want to measure the discounted present value of this stream from year zero to year T, the shaded area in the figure. That is measured by integrating the B_t expression between 0 and T

$$(2) \quad B_{PV} = \int_0^T B_0 e^{-rt} dt = (B_0/r)(1 - e^{-rT})$$

For very large T, e^{-rT} approaches zero and $B_{PV} = B_0/r$, just the expression used in the text. Since the expressions are identical, this means that the annual interest rates quoted for the discrete, or discontinuous, time cases in the text are those yielded by continuous discounting. The analyst can equally well use the discrete approximation given by equation (2) in the text or equation (1) in this appendix. Without going through them, it can also be shown that all the propositions used in the text about inflation and decay rates also hold in continuous time.

FIGURE 6A.1   The Present Value of a Continuously Discounted Benefit Stream

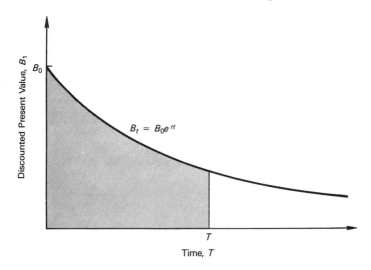

$B_t = B_0 e^{-rt}$ gives the discounted present value of a fixed benefit, B_0, at any time t. The shaded area is the present value of the stream from $t = 0$ to $t = T$.

$B_{PV} = \int_0^T B_0 e^{-rt} dt = \dfrac{B_0}{r}(1 - e^{-rT})$ which approaches $\dfrac{B_0}{r}$ as T approaches infinity.

SEVEN
THE GAINS AND LOSSES OF DIFFERENT GROUPS

To this point we have stuck to the Kaldor-Hicks standard in our evaluation of public programs. A program is judged to be a success if it yields positive net gains, or if the gainers could compensate the losers and still be better off. Since we have not required the gainers to pay this compensation, however, there will be gainers and losers and we have avoided the difficult question of examining who actually gains and loses. Who these gainers and losers are, and how much they gain or lose are questions that simply do not matter under the Kaldor-Hicks standard.

In real life, of course, one can think of many instances where it does matter who gains and loses from a project. One extreme example is people living outside a jurisdiction. For almost any government project there will be some living outside the jurisdiction who are affected positively or negatively by a project. Taxpayers inside the jurisdiction would have every right to ignore these gains or losses, or to give them less weight, in making public decisions. A second extreme example, one that raises more difficult ethical questions, involves the rights of criminals. In most states convicted felons lose their right to vote, implying that society is giving their gains or losses less weight in public decisions.[1]

But the importance of particular gains and losses seems to be greatest as regards distributional questions. In Chapter 2 we argued that governments have a valad rationale for pursuing the goal of redistributive equity. Society might go out of its way to alter the distribution of income, actually sacrificing some economic efficiency to raise low-income living standards. If low-income living standards are raised by direct transfers, the sacrifice might be as represented by Arthur Okun's leaky bucket: a society will accept the fact that some income will leak out as it is transferred from high- to low-income groups. If the redistribution is regional—projects are undertaken to raise incomes in some regional area—the sacrifice might be in the form of location of projects in areas other than the one that is optimal from an efficiency standpoint alone.

There is another way to make the sacrifice, and this forms the main business of this chapter. Suppose that instead of doing simple Kaldor-Hicks evaluations of all projects, decision makers were prepared to modify the evaluation to give an extra weight to the gains or losses of low-income groups. As compared with the Kaldor-Hicks rule, this weighted net benefit calculation would be implicitly accepting some efficiency sacrifice—a different set of projects would pass a weighted net benefit test than a strict economic efficiency test. But the efficiency sacrifice should not be too large—it is bounded on the other side by that implicit in the cheapest alternative way of raising low incomes. Although the hard-nosed rules of economic efficiency might be relaxed to allow some projects that raise low incomes, they should not be relaxed so much that society raises low incomes inefficiently.

This reasoning suggests that instead of the usual two-way classification into programs that do and do not pass the economic efficiency test, we should now classify programs that raise low incomes into three groups:

Group A—Those that pass the test for economic efficiency

Group B—Those that fail the test for economic efficiency, but are more efficient than any other program in raising low incomes

Group C—Those that fail the test for economic efficiency, and are less efficient than some other program in raising low incomes

There would be a strong argument for doing the projects in group A from both an efficiency and an equity standpoint. If the other program in question is feasible from political and administrative standpoint, there would be very little justification for doing projects in group C. And those in group B raise the traditional efficiency-equity quandary—how should one goal be traded off against the other?

In this chapter we consider these issues. We show how distributional gains and losses can be brought into the benefit-cost calculation and explain the three-way classification. This classification requires some new information about programs, and we show how this new information might be compiled. We then show how this classification technique can be applied to the question of whether the minimum wage should have been increased in 1988?

DISTRIBUTIONAL WEIGHTS

The logic of the three way classification can be demonstrated by generalizing the previous net benefits calculation to add terms expressing the social value of various gains and losses. To see how this is done, the general formula for determining the weighted benefits of some program is

$$(1)\ NB = \sum_{i=1}^{m} w_i \Delta Y_i$$

where NB refers to the weighted net benefits of the program, m is the number of groups in society, ΔY_i refers to the income change, or gain or loss, of the ith group, and w_i to some weight, or social value, applied to this income change. A Kaldor-Hicks evaluation abstracts from social judgments of the desirability of gains and losses, sets all weights at one, and simply adds up all gains (positive ΔY_i) and losses (negative ΔY_i). Under these circumstances a positive NB implies the existence of gains in excess of losses.

But if a community did not want to count fully the gains or losses of outsiders or of criminals, it might attach weights of less than one, perhaps of zero, to these gains or losses. If it did want to raise low incomes, it might attach weights of more than one to these gains or losses.

Whenever weights different from one are attached to income changes, programs that do not pass a strict economic efficiency test may pass the modified test. Hence any deviation from weights that are one across the board introduces potential economic inefficiency into program decisions. To take one example, suppose high-income groups lose $60 from some program and low-income groups gain $50. A strict efficiency calculation would find net benefits equal to -$10 and judge the program a loser on efficiency grounds. If a weight of 2 were attached to the low-income gains, the weighted benefits of low-income groups would equal $100 and the program would be judged a success by the modified standard. But we should remember that on efficiency grounds the program really is a loser, and the modification is just another way of saying that society is prepared to tolerate some inefficiency for the sake of improving the distribution of income.

Society might have some tolerance for this sort of economic inefficiency, but as Arnold Harberger has argued, this tolerance should not be unlimited.[2] If there were some costless way of raising the income of the same recipients and charging the same taxpayers, that form of redistribution should clearly be preferred to accepting inefficient programs. In general, the strict efficiency rule should only be modified when there is no alternative program that effects the same transfer of gains and losses more efficiently. In Harberger's view, using weighted benefits is not a particularly illuminating way to make the program choice; he would prefer simply to find the cheapest way to raise low incomes a certain amount.

The notion of which program is the cheapest alternative form of redistribution is an elusive one. For each project that raises low incomes but barely fails the economic efficiency test, this suggests unleashing a group of analysts to try to find a way to do the same job more cheaply. As with the notion of actually paying Pareto compensation in Chapter 3, were such alternative programs instituted every time a low-income-raising program failed the test of economic efficiency, both the tax code and the array of public programs would get impossibly cluttered.

As an alternative means of proceeding, most analysts have decided that as a practical matter, the relevant standard of comparison for programs that raise low incomes is a general broad-based transfer program financed by a general broad-based tax. This typically means a slight rise in the personal income tax rate, with the revenue being redistributed across the board in the form of higher transfers. Such a marginal change in the tax-transfer system will raise low incomes, because those of lower incomes gain more from the transfers than they lose from the higher tax rates. It will also be a somewhat costly way to raise low incomes, because both the higher transfers and the higher tax rates will distort behavior. This is a clear and objective way of comparing this transfer inefficiency with inefficiency through modification of the strict Kaldor-Hicks rule for making program decisions, but it should be understood to be only a pragmatic compromise with Harberger's standard of finding *the* best alternative way of raising low incomes.

If the marginal distortions from greater transfers, or the leaks in Okun's bucket, are small, society should just redistribute directly, make program decisions on strict efficiency grounds, and not use any weighted benefit calculations. Should they be large, society is already forced to tolerate economic inefficiency to raise low incomes, and it should be prepared to accept some projects that raise low incomes, even if they fail a strict economic efficiency test.

The point can be seen by simplifying equation (1). Suppose there are only two groups, poor people gaining ΔY_p from some project, and the nonpoor, everybody else, gaining ΔY_n. The weight applied to the income of the nonpoor is one, and that applied to the income of the poor is w_p. We can define this weight w_p as that required to make a project pass the modified net benefits test by setting $NB = 0$.

(2) $0 = NB = w_p \Delta Y_p + \Delta Y_n$

To illustrate how this expression can be used in the preceding example, ΔY_n is -\$60, ΔY_p is \$50, and the w_p necessary to bring NB up to zero is 1.2. In this case the project fails the Kaldor-Hicks economic efficiency test and the weight required to get NB up to zero is greater than one. Conversely, had the project passed an economic efficiency test, the weight required to make $NB = 0$ would be less than one. If, for example, ΔY_p were 60 and ΔY_n were -50, w_p would have been .83.

Equation (2) can be expressed in terms of the gain of poor people by moving ΔY_n to the other side and dividing through by w_p

(3) $\Delta Y_p = -\Delta Y_n / w_p$

At the same time, we know that if society transferred income to poor people through a marginal change in some taxed transfer program, the expression for the rise in poor incomes would be

(4) $\Delta Y_p = -(1-c)\Delta Y_n$

where c is Okun's leaky bucket ratio and $(1-c)$ is thus the loss of nonpoor income that stays in the bucket and makes the poor better off. If, for example, the nonpoor were forced to give up \$40 to raise poor incomes by \$30, $(1-c)$ would be .75 and c would be .25–one-fourth of all income given up by the nonpoor leaks out in the form of economic inefficiency and never even raises poor incomes.

Putting these two expressions side-by-side shows how the two types of inefficiency can be compared. Equating (3) and (4) and canceling $-\Delta Y_n$ gives

(5) $w_p^* = 1/(1-c)$

where w_p^* is now the required weight that also makes the program just as efficient as transfers in raising low incomes. If c, the leaky bucket coefficient, is zero, w_p^* is one. Saying this another way, direct redistribution is costless $(c = 0)$, and society should only do Kaldor-Hicks evaluations and not weight gains unduly $(w_p^* = 1)$. But as direct redistribution gets more inefficient, c increases, $(1-c)$ falls, and w_p^* rises—society is prepared to tolerate more program inefficiency for the sake of raising the incomes of the poor.

From these relationships we can construct the three-way classification previously described. When w_p is less than one, the program passes the Kaldor-Hicks economic efficiency test and falls into group A. When w_p is greater than one, the program fails the economic efficiency test, but could still be more efficient at raising low incomes than a change in direct transfers. But when w_p is greater than $w_p^* = 1/(1-c)$, the program is not even as efficient as direct transfers in raising low incomes and falls into group C. In this latter case, we will say that the program fails the transfer efficiency test.

This classification is shown graphically in Figure 7.1. The horizontal axis gives the leaky bucket coefficient, c, and the vertical axis gives w_p, the required weight to make $NB = 0$. If, for example, w_p is less than one, the program actually passes the economic efficiency test. This type of program fits in group A and is shown in the figure as area A. The economic efficiency boundary that separates efficient programs in group A from other programs is thus drawn as a horizontal line at $w_p = 1$.

Moving up, as w_p is above one, it can be seen from (2) that the project is no longer economically efficient. It is necessary to inflate the gains to poor people to make $NB = 0$. But from equation (5) we can see that as long as w_p is less than w_p^*, the project is still more efficient than direct transfers in raising low incomes. The line where $w_p^* = 1/(1-c)$ thus becomes the transfer efficiency boundary. The programs of group B fail the economic efficiency test and are above the economic efficiency boundary, but they pass the transfer efficiency test and are below this transfer efficiency boundary.

And for the most inefficient projects of all, w_p is greater than w_p^*. These projects are not economically efficient because w_p is greater than one, and

FIGURE 7.1 Sorting the Programs

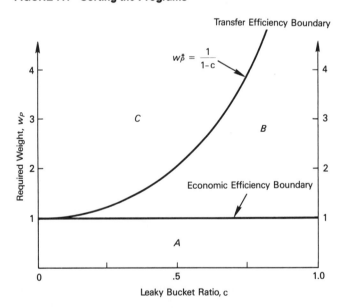

Group A programs pass the economic efficiency test
Group B programs fail the economic efficiency test but pass the transfer efficiency test
Group C programs fail the economic efficiency test and the transfer efficiency test

they are not as efficient as direct transfers in raising low incomes because w_p is greater than w_p*. They pass neither the economic efficiency nor the transfer efficiency test, they are above both boundaries, and are shown in the figure as group C.

HOW TO USE THE CLASSIFICATION SCHEME

The first step in sorting programs into these three classes is to measure all the ΔY_i. These are nothing but the gains and losses of different groups, which form the basic raw material for doing any benefit-cost study. The analytical steps in measuring these gains or losses are just those recounted in Chapters 4 and 5—one must compute surpluses, changes in other markets, and so forth. It should also be understood that all the ΔY_i used here are also present values discounted at the social rate of time preference, as suggested in Chapter 6.

Before one tries to classify programs, it should always be remembered that benefit-cost analysis is nothing more or less than a way of presenting information about programs to policy makers. This information on ΔY_i is key, because it says who gains and loses from a program and how much they gain or lose. Whatever fancy steps are taken later on, the analyst should keep firmly in mind always to present and highlight this basic information. Never give the results of a weighted benefit-cost (or any other) calculation without showing in clear terms who gains and loses how much.

Estimating the Weights

The approach suggested in the previous section involves plugging the ΔY_i into an equation like (2) to find the w_p necessary to have a program pass a modified net benefits test. There may also be occasions where the analyst simply wants to compute plausible weights from other information, and plug these into an equation like (1) to get overall distributionally-weighted net benefits.

There are at least two ways to proceed. One, suggested by Burton Weisbrod, is to infer these weights from other policy actions.[3] The main such action in the United States is the income tax—here policy makers do indeed confront the question of how much of a gain in their income taxpayers of various incomes should pay to the tax collector. If a nonpoor person should pay \$.30 of every dollar and a poor person \$.15, in some sense society is saying that at the margin these sacrifices represent equal pain. Alternatively, the \$.15 sacrifice of the poor person is as painful as the \$.30 sacrifice of the nonpoor person, and w_p equals 2. In general, this reasoning suggests that $w_i = t_n/t_i$ where t_i refers to the marginal tax rates facing taxpayers at various low-income levels.

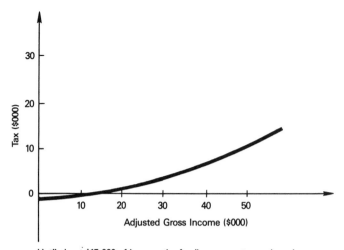

Until about $15,000 of income the family pays no tax and receives an earned income tax credit. That phases out at a 10% rate. From an income of about $15,000 to about $30,000, the marginal tax rate is 15%. Above this level the marginal tax rate is from 28% to 33%.

FIGURE 7.2   U.S. Income Tax Schedule, 1988 (Family of Four, Working Head)

Figure 7.2, which gives the new structure of marginal tax rates after the landmark tax revision of 1986, shows how such a scheme would work out for the United States. Those with a working head of household and family incomes up to about $15,000 a year for a family of four do not pay any tax and receive an earned income tax credit. That phases out at the rate of 10 percent (for every dollar's increase in earned income, the credit drops ten cents). Those with family incomes between about $15,000 and about $30,000 a year pay a marginal tax rate of 15 percent. Those over $30,000 pay a marginal rate that varies between 28 percent and 33 percent. Using the preceding formula, the weight would be 3 for those in the bottom group, roughly the poverty population, and 2 for those in the middle group.

Of course, there are problems in interpreting too much from the tax code. That code is a highly complicated document that tries to satisfy many goals. Evening the pain of marginal tax losses is certainly one of the important goals, but it is not the only one, and an analyst could get into a bizarre position in trying to interpret the tax code too literally. As one illustration, as part of a delicate compromise on treating capital gains as ordinary income for tax purposes—these gains are largely received by the very rich and were formerly taxed at favorable rates—the very highest marginal tax rate is 28 percent, below the 33 percent marginal rate faced by most upper-middle-class taxpayers. Does this mean that a benefit-cost analyst should attach a weight greater than one to gains received by the super rich? Presumably not.

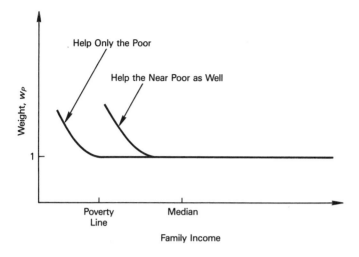

The weight schedule on the left has $w_P > 1$ only for the poor.

The weight schedule on the right has $w_P > 1$ for the near poor as well.

FIGURE 7.3   Bracketing the Weights

A second approach involves postulating plausible mathematical relationships between the weights and family income.[4] Without going into the details, one could specify weighting relationships like those given in Figure 7.3. In the relationship shown on the left, weights are in excess of one but gradually declining toward one for families with incomes below the poverty line. For all families with incomes above the poverty line, weights are one. In the relationship shown on the right, higher weights are used for all families in poverty and slightly above the poverty level. The two approaches are each defensible, and seem to bracket the preferences most taxpayers might have toward helping the poor—either help only the poor (the strict approach) or help those with somewhat higher incomes as well.

How Big Is the Leak?

To get a full classification of programs into the three groups, and in particular to locate the transfer efficiency boundary w_p^*, we also need to know how efficient direct transfers are at raising low incomes. How big is the leak in the leaky bucket?

We first show how the leaky bucket coefficient can be calculated in principle by adapting a model used by Richard Layard.[5] As shown in Figure 7.4, suppose that all workers operate on the pre-tax supply schedule S. Half of the workers have low skills and face the demand schedule D_L. The other

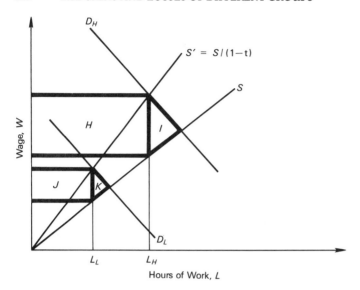

Tax revenues raised from the low income market are J and the dead weight loss is K. Half of the total loss $(J + K)$ is assumed to be borne by low-income workers and the rest by nonpoor employers.

Tax revenues raised from the high-income market are H and the dead weight loss is I. All of this loss is assumed to be borne by nonpoor workers and nonpoor employers.

Total revenues are $H + J$, and each group receives back $.5(H + J)$.

$$\Delta Y_P = - .5 (J + K) + .5 (H + J) = + .5 H - .5K$$
$$\Delta Y_n = - .5 (J + K) - I - H + .5 (H + J) = - .5H - .5K - I$$

FIGURE 7.4. Calculating a Leaky Bucket Ratio

half have high skills and face the demand schedule D_H. In pre-tax equilibrium the highly skilled workers would end up working more hours for a higher wage, because of demand considerations only. We could also complicate things to include different supply schedules and unequally sized groups. While such complications would make the analysis more cumbersome, they would not make it much more enlightening about leaky buckets.

The broad-based transfer program used as a comparison standard is one that assesses a proportional tax rate t on all labor incomes and then gives all of the revenue back to the two groups—half to those of low skills and half to those of high skills. The supply curve shifts up to $S' = S/(1-t)$ because of the tax, and we get the new equilibria at L_L and L_H in the figure.

Taking first the situation for low-skilled groups, the tax revenue raised by this proportional tax is shown by rectangle J. As was seen in Chapter 4, workers suffer a loss of producer surplus and employers a loss of consumer surplus that is greater than J by the triangle K, the dead weight loss or excess burden from this tax. There will be such a dead weight loss whenever both the demand and the supply functions are sloped, so that the equilibrium quantity changes as a result of the distortionary tax. All of this is true for the highly skilled groups as well—the tax revenue is rectangle H and the dead weight loss triangle I. The only difference is that because the proportional tax is imposed on more hours and a higher wage in the high skill market, the areas are much greater. Total tax revenue raised by the proportional tax is area $(H + J)$.

We first calculate ΔY_p for this direct transfer program. Low-income workers lose the producer surplus, and employers of low-income workers lose the surplus under the demand schedule. We make the arbitrary assumption that these employers of low-income workers are nonpoor, and that their losses are half of the total loss $(J + K)$. Low-income workers then lose the producer surplus of $.5(J + K)$ and gain back $.5(H + J)$ from the redistribution

$$(6) \ \Delta Y_p = -.5(J + K) + .5(H + J) = .5H - .5K$$

Nonpoor employers lose the surplus under the demand curve from the low-income market, the entire surplus in the high-income market (assuming both workers and employers are high income) and gain back the redistribution

$$(7) \ \Delta Y_n = -.5(J + K) - H - I + .5(H + J) = -.5H - .5K - I$$

Comparing (6) and (7), we see that our transfer program is just sending $.5H$ from the nonpoor to the poor, with the two dead weight loss triangles, I and K, leaking out of the bucket. We can see this same point another way by summing ΔY_p from (6) and ΔY_n from (7) to get the overall Kaldor-Hicks efficiency loss for the program. It is just area $(I + K)$, the sum of the dead weight loss triangles. This calculation is also written out in Table 7.1.

Equation (4) gave the definition of the leaky bucket ratio, c. Manipulating that equation, substituting in from (6) and (7) and canceling the .5 terms

$$(8) \ (1 - c) = \Delta Y_p / -\Delta Y_n = (H - K)/(H + K + 2I)$$

It can be seen that when the dead weight loss triangles I and K are zero, the right side of (8) equals one, c is zero, and there is no leak in the bucket. As the dead weight triangles grow, the numerator on the right side declines, the denominator rises, the fraction falls, and the leaky bucket coefficient rises.

The final step in the argument is to express these areas in terms of each other. Two parameters are used:

z gives the size of the triangle in each market compared to the rectangle.
x gives the relative size of low compared to high incomes.

TABLE 7.1   Gains, Losses, and Leaky Bucket Ratios from a Transfer Program

ΔY_p (from Figure 7.4) = .5H–.5K
ΔY_n (from Figure 7.4) = –.5H–.5K–I
Kaldor-Hicks gain = $\Delta Y_p + \Delta Y_n = -K-I$
   Program fails the economic efficiency test

$$(1 - c) = \frac{\Delta Y_p}{-\Delta Y_n} = \frac{.5(H - K)}{.5(H + K + 2I)} = \frac{H - K}{H + K + 2I}$$

Let $z = \dfrac{I}{H} = \dfrac{K}{J}$ (triangle–rectangle ratio)

$x = \dfrac{J}{H}$ (relative income ratio)

$$(1 - c) = \frac{H(1 - zx)}{H(1 + zx + 2z)} = \frac{1 - zx}{1 + zx + 2z}$$

x	z	1–c	c	w_p^*
.1	0	1	0	1
.1	.2	.69	.31	1.45
.1	.4	.52	.48	1.92
.2	0	1	0	1
.2	.2	.67	.33	1.50
.2	.4	.49	.51	2.04

Table 7.1 works out the gory details, and gives some sample calculations for $x = .1$ and $.2$ and $z = .2$ and $.4$, reasonable sample values taken from the economic literature. When z is zero, the dead weight loss triangles disappear, the leaky bucket coefficient c is zero, and the weight that makes one indifferent between accepting inefficiency in the program decision and in the transfer program is zero, because there is no transfer inefficiency. But as z and x grow, c rises, and $w_p^* = 1/(1-c)$ rises as well.

These simple and obviously rough calculations do illustrate some important points:

When there are no dead weight loss triangles, there is no transfer inefficiency, and no rationale for doing other than a straight efficiency evaluation.

As the triangle-rectangle ratio, z, grows, the leaky bucket coefficient c does as well. Typically c is greater than z.

The relative income parameter x does not seem to matter much.

One can have relatively modest triangle-rectangle ratios and still justify weights up to 2.

It may seem like this analysis is complex enough, but it has been oversimplified in several important ways. One added complication involves the fact that the leaky bucket coefficient depends on the size of the dead weight loss triangles. One side of these triangles depends directly on the tax rate; the other side depends on the change in hours of work which in turn depends on the tax rate. This means that the dead weight loss from a marginal tax change on top of an existing tax is likely to be highly nonlinear, or that the leak in the bucket will depend in a complex way on the pre-existing level of tax rates. As with the general equilibrium calculations described back in Chapter 5, such complications begin to exceed the capabilities of simple geometric or algebraic analyses.

But it is possible to use the computer to work out complications of this sort. One example is a recent study by Edgar Browning and William Johnson.[6] Their calculation is quite similar in spirit to the general equilibrium simulation done by King and described in Chapter 5. Whereas he simulated the removal of a distortionary tax with constant production costs, Browning and Johnson assume constant market wages and simulate the introduction of an incremental transfer program. The Browning-Johnson simulation is based on microdata for 1976, and they graft on labor supply elasticities from the economic literature to compute the gains and losses of individual families. Since they use microdata, they must aggregate into groups before computing a leaky bucket coefficient, and while they compute many for many different assumed elasticities, their basic estimate is a high leaky bucket coefficient of .71. Their estimate is high because they are grafting a transfer program onto a set of tax rates from 1976 that are already much higher than those prevalent in 1988, and, as mentioned, transfer inefficiencies could be compounded at high tax rates. Were they using 1988 tax rates, their estimate of c would be some amount lower, perhaps ranging around .5. Whatever the particular number, their conclusion is the same as that of the simple analysis previously used; even modest labor supply distortions can lead to sizable transfer inefficiencies and justify deviations from the strict Kaldor-Hicks standard.

A REAL WORLD EXAMPLE—MINIMUM WAGES

One of the most controversial programs alleged to raise low incomes is the minimum wage. Passing rises in this minimum has always been one of the key political objectives of organized labor. But with the Republican Administration of the 1980s labor was not able to get a higher minimum passed through 1987, and for 1988 the question of whether to raise it became a focus of major legislative controversy. The minimum had been set at $3.35 an hour in 1980 when it was 45 percent of average hourly earnings. After seven years of erosion through inflation, by 1988 it had fallen to 37 percent of average hourly earnings, lower than at any time since the late 1940s. The Democratic Congress was generally in favor of boosting it substantially, President Reagan was opposed, and one Republican Congressman, Thomas Petri, was pushing an increase in the earned income tax credit as an alternative.

The minimum wage was discussed in Chapter 4 from an economic efficiency standpoint. Since it introduces a distortion into the labor market, the minimum wage will never pass a Kaldor-Hicks efficiency test—it will never qualify for group A. It could qualify for group B, but that depends on the facts of the case. The higher wage will clearly benefit those low-wage workers who keep their jobs, but there is one demand problem and one supply problem. The demand problem is that the higher wage will reduce employment demand by an amount that depends on the elasticity of demand for low-wage labor. The supply problem is that the higher minimum will tempt new workers into the market, increase the competition for the now-scarce jobs, and require some rationing mechanism that does not necessarily give jobs to those who most value them. With the minimum wage there is also another empirical issue that should be kept in mind: there turns out to be a surprisingly loose relationship between low-wages and low-family incomes. The majority of minimum wage workers are not from low-income families, but rather low-wage teenagers and secondary workers in nonpoor families. Any evaluation of rises in the minimum wage from an income distribution standpoint should thus try to compare all of these considerations in computing income changes for poor and nonpoor families.

The basic facts of minimum wages for 1987 are taken from a Congressional Budget Office study and are shown in Figure 7.5.[7] The highest minimum wage that was said to be acceptable to the President was $4.35 an hour. 3.06 million workers made just the minimum wage of $3.35 and another 8.69 million made from $3.35 to $4.35 an hour, making for a total of 11.75 million workers earning from $3.35 to $4.35. This number is shown as total employment at the present minimum. All of these workers keeping their jobs were assumed to get a raise, the $3.35 workers of 30 percent and those above $3.35 of an average of 9 percent (they were heavily concentrated toward the upper end of the wage distribution). Applying labor demand elasticities from the literature to these percentage increases gave hypothetical employment at a minimum of $4.35 of 11.39 million workers, a .36 million reduction, also shown in the figure.

Were the minimum to go from $3.35 to $4.35, low-wage workers would gain area A in the figure. If there were no labor supply elasticity, the .36 million losing jobs would lose area D. If labor supply were upward sloping, the loss to the low-wage workers losing jobs would be less than D, but as previously mentioned, the higher minimum would also tempt new workers into the market and cause some extra rationing inefficiency. It is hard to assess these offsetting forces without a much more elaborate study, so they have been assumed away by making supply inelastic over this range.

Regarding the connection between low wages and low-family incomes, only 17 percent of the $3.35 workers were from poor families and another 13 percent in families with incomes between 100 and 150 percent of the poverty line. For the class above $3.35, the numbers were 15 percent and 11 percent,

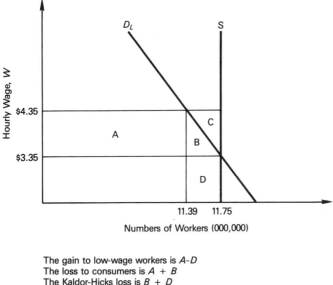

The gain to low-wage workers is *A-D*
The loss to consumers is *A + B*
The Kaldor-Hicks loss is *B + D*

Low-wage poor workers gain	$ 5.6 billion
Low-wage nonpoor workers gain	$15.5 billion
Nonpoor consumers gain	− $24.1 billion
Kaldor-Hicks gain	− $3.0 billion
Program does not pass efficiency test	

$$w_p \Delta Y_p = -\Delta Y_n$$

$$w_p = (24.1 - 15.5)/5.6 = 1.54$$

FIGURE 7.5   The Minimum Wage in 1987

respectively. Hence while increases in the minimum will raise some poor incomes, most of the gains or losses will be felt by the nonpoor.

Using these family income breakdowns, the figure shows that the gain to low-wage workers from raising the minimum, assuming all workers work full-time, would be $21.1 billion, of which $5.6 billion would be realized by those with family incomes 150 percent of the poverty line or less and the remaining $15.5 billion by nonpoor workers. But the minimum wage would also raise labor costs and ultimately cost consumers of low-wage goods by area $(A + B)$, $24.1 billion, here assumed all to be borne by the nonpoor. The net Kaldor-Hicks loss is $3 billion, showing as expected that the minimum wage increase fails the economic efficiency test.

The w_p necessary to make $NB = 0$ can be derived by solving equation (2) in the way shown in the figure. This weight comes out to be 1.54. Whether this w_p puts the minimum wage increase in group *B* or group *C* then depends on the relevant value of the leaky bucket coefficient for transfer programs. As can be seen from Figure 7.6, if the leaky bucket coefficient is greater than

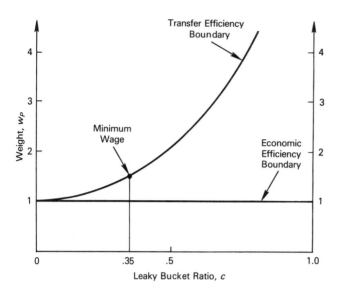

Minimum wage has an implied $w_P = 1.54$.
If $c > .35$, minimum wage is more efficient than transfers program at raising low incomes.

If $c < .35$, minimum wage is less efficient than transfer program at raising low incomes.

FIGURE 7.6   The Minimum Wage

.35, so that w_p is less than w_p^*, the minimum wage increase is more efficient than transfers at raising low incomes and qualifies for group B. If c is less than .35, the minimum wage increase is a less efficient way of raising low incomes than transfers and falls into group C.

The straight Browning-Johnson leaky bucket coefficient was .71, suggesting the minimum wage is much more efficient than transfers at raising low incomes. Were their study redone with the lower overall tax rates of 1987, their leaky bucket coefficient would be lower, perhaps .5. And in the case at hand, the actual comparison was between the minimum wage and an increase in the earned income tax credit. As previously stated, that gives low-wage poor workers a wage subsidy, and thus increases incentives to work for some workers. As the earned income tax credit is phased out, the effective marginal tax rate on workers is increased, so there are other workers for whom a higher earned income tax credit represents a disincentive to work. Whether rise in the earned income tax credit then raises or lowers work incentives cannot be ascertained without more information. But it probably could be said that compared with the general transfer program used by Browning and Johnson, the tax credit has at least ambiguous effects on incentives to work—for some, the incentives are greater, for some, the incentives are worse. The effective leaky bucket coefficient to this alternative way of raising low incomes is thus probably less than .5, and perhaps less than .35.

The bottom line is that it is hard to tell whether the minimum wage increase satisfies the transfer efficiency test or not. It clearly fails the test of economic efficiency, and it is as inefficient as a transfer program with a leaky bucket ratio of .35. This would seem like a reasonably inefficient way to raise low incomes: the only thing that gives one pause is that studies of other ways of raising low incomes also report significant inefficiencies.[8]

SUMMARY

The chapter has considered programs where there are clear gainers and losers. A strict efficiency program test is blind to such considerations, but any benefit-cost analysis useful in actual political decisions must go into them. A first obvious point is that the analyst should always display these gains and losses so that decision makers know what is involved. Beyond that, rather than simply adding up all benefits and costs received by all groups, a modified benefit-cost procedure might weigh some gains and losses, such as those received outside the jurisdiction, less heavily, and some, such as those received by low-income groups, more heavily.

It should be recognized that whenever one departs from strict Kaldor-Hicks neutrality, one is altering benefit-cost decisions so that some inefficiencies will be tolerated for the sake of raising low incomes. This leads to a three-way classification of programs that raise low incomes into those that pass an economic efficiency test; those that fail an economic efficiency test but are more efficient than transfers at raising low incomes; and those that fail an efficiency test and also are less efficient than transfers at raising low incomes. The first group of programs can be defended on both efficiency and equity grounds, the third group on neither, and the second group raises the age-old tradeoff between efficiency and equity.

This chapter then showed how one might compute both the weight on low-income gains required to have a program pass a net benefits test and a measure of the inefficiency of transfer programs. In the specific case of the minimum wage, raising the minimum wage in 1988 was found to lead to Kaldor-Hicks losses and fail the economic efficiency test. It was about as inefficient at raising low incomes as a transfer program where one-third of the taxpayer losses were dissipated and did not even raise low incomes. This seems like a high degree of transfer inefficiency, but it turns out that other studies of transfer programs report similar inefficiencies. Hence a minimum wage increase seems roughly on the borderline between programs that are more and less efficient ways of raising low incomes than a general increase in transfers.

NOTES

[1]These issues of "standing" are discussed by Dale Whittington and Duncan Macrae, Jr., "The Issue of Standing in Cost-Benefit Analysis," *Journal of Policy Analysis and Management,* Summer 1986.

[2]Arnold C. Harberger, "On the Use of Distributional Weights in Social Cost-Benefit Analysis," *Journal of Political Economy,* April 1978. See also his "Reply to Layard and Squire," *Journal of Political Economy,* October 1980.

[3]Burton Weisbrod, "Deriving an Implicit Set of Governmental Weights for Income Classes," in Samuel B. Chase (ed.), *Problems in Public Expenditure Analysis* (Washington: The Brookings Institution, 1968).

[4]Edward M. Gramlich and Michael J. Wolkoff, "A Procedure for Evaluating Income Distribution Policies," *Journal of Human Resources,* Summer 1979.

[5]Richard E. Layard, "On the Use of Distributional Weights in Social Cost-Benefit Analysis," *Journal of Political Economy,* October 1980.

[6]Edgar K. Browning and William R. Johnson, "The Trade-Off between Equality and Efficiency," *Journal of Political Economy,* April 1984.

[7]Congressional Budget Office, "The Minimum Wage: Its Relationship to Incomes and Poverty," Staff Working Paper, June 1986.

[8]It was just as hard to make a clear verdict when I first looked at minimum wages. See Edward M. Gramlich, "The Impact of Minimum Wages on Other Wages, Employment, and Family Incomes," *Brookings Papers on Economic Activity,* 2:1976.

PROBLEMS

1   Say we have two projects that yield the following net gains to high- and low-income groups:

	ΔY_p	ΔY_n
Project *A*	0.5	1.1
Project *B*	1.0	0.2

Compute net benefits by the Kaldor-Hicks standard. Which project is preferable? If the income tax is used to determine the weight for low-income gains, and high-income groups face a marginal tax rate of .2 and low-income groups of .15, which project is preferable? What about when marginal tax rates are .6 and .2, respectively? What w_p makes society indifferent between the two projects?

2   Let's go back to Chapter 4, problem 5. The supply of rentable properties is $R = H$, and the demand is $R = 1000 - H$. The rent control law places a rent ceiling of $400 per month. Bring yourself up to speed by working out the pre- and post-rent control solutions for R and H, the losses of landlords (assumed now to be high-income), and the gains or losses of renters. If all renters are low-income, is there a w_p that makes the rent control law a winner?

Now take the modification where all renters on the given demand function are assumed to be students with high permanent incomes and for whom there is no political desire to introduce subsidies. The amendment requires that half of all rented apartments go to low-income families with a willingness-to-pay of $450 a month. Find the losses felt by high-income landlords as a result of rent control, the gains or losses felt by high-income students, the gains or losses of the poor, Kaldor-Hicks net benefits of the new law, the w_p required to make modified net benefits equal to zero, and the transfer leaky bucket coefficient that makes you indifferent between this version of rent control and higher transfer to help the poor.

3   The AFL-CIO is pushing a minimum wage of $5 per hour. The demand for the hours of low-wage workers is given by $W = 10-L$, and the supply is fixed at $L = 8$. Labor economists estimate that this amount of labor will be supplied even if the wage were to fall to zero, and that all consumption of products made by low-wage workers is done by high-income families.

   a.   Find the labor market equilibrium with and without the higher minimum wage. Find the gains and losses to workers and employers from the higher minimum. Compute Kaldor-Hicks gains or losses, the w_p required to make weighted net benefits equal zero if all low-wage workers were also from low-income families, and the w_p required to make weighted net benefits equal zero if half of the low-wage workers were also from low-income families.

   b.   The labor economists locate a glitch in their analysis. It turns out that the supply of labor is really given by $W = .25L$. Repeat all the computations in 4a with the new supply function.

4   The supply function for all labor is $W = L$. Half of the workers in the town are low-skilled and poor and half are high-skilled and nonpoor. The low-skilled workers face an inverse demand function of $W = 10-L$; the high-skilled workers face an inverse demand function of $W = 30-L$. All production is either consumed by high income workers or sold on the world market. The new mayor, worried very much about low incomes, proposes a proportional tax on all incomes that would raise the supply function to $W = 1.5L$. The proceeds of this tax would be given equally to all workers.

Find the pre- and post-tax equilibrium for the low- and high-skill market. Find the loss in producer surplus, the loss in consumer surplus, and the tax revenue raised in each market. Assuming low-wage employers are themselves of high income, find the gains or losses of low- and high-income groups once the tax proceeds are redistributed. Find the Kaldor-Hicks gain or loss from the redistribution program, the leaky bucket coefficient, and the value of w_p^*.

EIGHT
PHYSICAL INVESTMENT
AND THE ENVIRONMENT

The logic of benefit-cost analysis was first developed for physical investment projects. The early benefit-cost documents used by the government in the 1930s and 1950s involved physical investment projects, as did the first major studies by academic economists such as John Krutilla and Otto Eckstein.[1] The field has been an active one ever since, with many physical investment evaluations being done on many different types of investment projects in many different countries.

Physical investment projects raise most of the standard issues covered so far in this book—valuation of resources, uncertainty, discounting, and dealing with gains and losses of different groups. They also raise a relatively new environmental question, and this question will be the particular concern of this chapter. Unlike many other benefit-cost issues, where it might sometimes seem that the stakes are rather small, environmental issues can often attain significant proportions. When deciding to build a dam that will kill an endangered species or a power plant that will generate long-lived nuclear contaminants, public sector decision makers are often being asked to make very fundamental choices. To a large degree, these choices may not be the stuff of economics, that marginalist discipline. But as with the questions of valuing human lives and assessing distributional changes, there are some techniques and styles of reasoning that can still help focus the analysis on the fundamentals, and we will be looking carefully at these.

This chapter begins by discussing some methods of measuring the gains and losses of a project in a particular year. Then it reviews the time discounting question, introducing the possibility of a three-way choice: given the information at hand, a project may not make sense to do, may make sense to do now, or make sense to do later. It goes on to examine some of these issues for a specific development project, the Tellico Dam in Tennessee.

ESTIMATING GAINS AND LOSSES AT THE TIME

The prototype physical investment project produces some valuable resource—oil, some other raw material, flood control, or power. The value of this resource is typically measured by the degree to which it shifts down supply curves for all the producers that use the resource. As was discussed in Chapters 4 and 5, these gains represent the primary market gains. But in producing the resource, two kinds of costs are incurred. There are the usual costs of developing and operating the project, building the dam or whatever. In addition, environmental costs are incurred as valuable land is occupied or depleted. In some cases, such as when coal is strip mined, it is possible to restore the land to its initial state once the production period is over—here the timing of the social and environmental costs of producing the resource roughly matches the timing of the use of the resource. In other cases, such as a power plant producing long-lived nuclear contaminants, the environmental costs persist long after the production period is over.

Project Benefits

Both the size and the distribution of project benefits depend on the degree to which the project shifts down relevant supply functions and on the size of the project. The points are illustrated for the constant cost case in our prototype project in Figure 8.1. If the project has a large enough capacity to shift the supply function for the whole market down from P_0 to P_1, the gain is the entire consumer surplus gain, P_0ABP_1. If the market for the good is competitive, this gain will be passed through by producers and accrue to consumers of the good.

If, on the other hand, the project has a capacity limited to Q_2, it will not be large enough to affect the marginal equation of supply and demand and to reduce consumer prices. In this case, the gain is limited to the rectangle, P_0CDP_1. Moreover, since this smaller capacity project does not reduce prices, the entire gain accrues to the producers that are able to take advantage of the cheap supply without lowering prices.

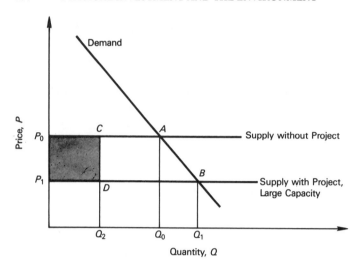

If capacity is large, the primary benefit is the entire consumer surplus gain, P_0ABP_1, with the gain accruing to consumers.

If capacity is limited to Q_2, the primary benefit is the rectangle, P_0CDP_1, with the gain accruing to suppliers.

FIGURE 8.1   Cost Reducing Physical Investment

We will discuss how these project benefits change over time more systematically later, but for now it is easy to see that whether benefits rise or fall, and at what rate, depends on how the parallel and vertical lines change. On the capacity side, the limit amount Q_2 could gradually rise as new deposits of the resource are found, or fall as deposits are depleted. On the price side, both the price with and without the resource could change over time. If without the project producers take advantage of another resource that also can be depleted, the no-project price P_0, sometimes called the backstop price, can rise over time and project benefits increase. If without the project producers can rely on supplies and a technology that is not getting more expensive over time, but our resource is gradually getting more costly to mine, the with-project price P_1 can rise relative to the backstop price and project benefits fall.

Environmental Costs

The main cost from our prototype project is that valuable wilderness lands are despoiled or depleted. The evaluator can only go so far in measuring these costs because some—such as the loss of an endangered species or a breathtaking view—cannot easily be quantified. But it is still possible to get what might be thought of as a lower-bound estimate of costs through what is known as the travel cost method, developed by Marion Clawson and Jack

Knetsch.[2] We will focus on this travel cost method, but with the usual caveat that the fact that some costs cannot be quantified does not mean they should be ignored. It is often helpful to have lower-bound estimates, but only if they are understood to be lower-bound estimates and not full estimates of all the costs of a project.

The travel cost method is based on the fact that while the actual out-of-pocket cost of using a wilderness area may be very low, the travel cost for people to get to the area typically will not be. The demand for using the area, for camping, fishing, hunting, birding, or whatever, can then be inferred from patterns of use given the out-of-pocket and travel costs. The basic assumption being made is that consumers respond to changes in travel cost in just the same way that consumers of any other good respond to changes in its price.

To conduct a complete travel cost survey of the consumer value of one wilderness area, visitors to the area must be counted and surveyed as to place of origin. The travel cost of users is measured, and the demand function comparing full cost to quantity of use, such as in person-days, is plotted. If the area is destroyed or lost, the lost surplus is the area below this common demand curve and above the price for each consumer.

Often it will not be possible to conduct a full survey of users of one area. The travel cost method can still be used to estimate a demand function for the area being valued if similar data are available for similar areas. Suppose there is a similar wilderness area that is a certain distance nearer to or farther away from the area that is being valued. The demand function for that comparison area is estimated in the same way, and the price and surplus loss for users of the area being valued by adjusting the price for differences in average travel time.

A few of these possibilities are demonstrated in Figure 8.2. Suppose the demand function for a comparison wilderness area were estimated as shown, and the average traveler to this comparison area faced the full daily price—travel cost, user fees, and so forth—of P_0. The estimated use at this daily price is Q_0 person-days. If this area itself were lost because of some physical investment project, the loss would be the area of the surplus triangle ACP_0. This area in turn equals the number of lost person-days, Q_0, times the average loss for each person-day, $.5(A-P_0)$.

Now suppose we were using this comparison area to estimate the demand function for another area we were trying to value, alike in all respects except that it was more remote from major population centers. We might be able to calculate that this greater remoteness raises the full daily price of using the more remote area by the average traveler from P_0 to P_1, and cuts the number of users to Q_1 person-days because of the greater remoteness (higher cost of getting there). If this area were sacrificed to a development project, the loss would be the area of the smaller surplus triangle, ABP_1.

Often what is lost is not an entire wilderness area, but just some part of it. There may be oil drilling in one corner of the area, or a dam that reduces

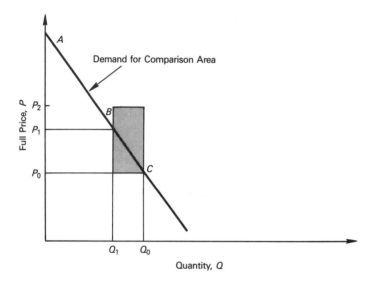

If the comparison area itself were totally lost, and consumers faced a price of P_0 and used Q_0, the lost surplus would be the area of the triangle ACP_0.

If a more remote wilderness area were lost, and consumers faced a price of P_1 and used Q_1, the lost surplus would be the area of the smaller triangle ABP_1.

If use of the area were constricted from Q_0 to Q_1, with the price remaining at P_0, the loss would be the area of the shaded rectangle—the average valuation of all using the area when the price is P_0 times the number that can no longer use the area.

FIGURE 8.2   Estimating the Value of Lost Wilderness Resources

the number of days per year of whitewater canoeing. Suppose we had this situation, where the average price of using a particular area remained at P_0, but instead of supplying Q_0 person-days of wilderness recreation, the area could only supply Q_1. This would be a case of markets not clearing, exactly like that analyzed in Chapter 4. We know the average valuation of a person using the wilderness at price P_0 is some average like P_2. The number of users rationed out by the new constriction is Q_0–Q_1. The loss is then the area of the shaded rectangle, the number of lost users times average loss per user. One can make a similar modification if the demand function for a comparison area were being used to measure use restrictions in a more remote area.

Just as the benefits of the project rise or fall depending on how the relevant vertical and horizontal lines shift over time, so it is also with the environmental costs. If the demand function shifts out because income or population is growing in the region that supplies users of this wilderness area, the lost surplus will too. If travel costs rise, the lost surplus may fall. If use restrictions rise, the lost surplus will rise.

THE THREE-WAY CHOICE

We now examine these time factors more systematically, using a simple version of a model worked out by Richard Porter.[3] We begin by modifying the general time discounting formula for the present value of project benefits given in Chapter 6, so that we can bring out some new aspects. Assume first that project benefits are net of any development costs, which in effect are smoothed out over time. These benefits can be represented by B_t, where B refers to the benefits net of costs and t refers to the year. The project benefits might rise and fall over time, and they might also experience relative price appreciation or depreciation of the sort discussed in Chapter 6. We combine all these factors into a net rate of relative benefit appreciation of z. We also assume that the project can be started at any arbitrary date S, where the benefits last for T years after this starting date. Using the subtraction method described in Chapter 6, the general formula for the present value of benefits, B_{PV}, is

$$(1)\ B_{PV} = \frac{B}{r-z}\left(\frac{1+z}{1+r}\right)^{s}\left(1-\left(\frac{1+z}{1+r}\right)^{t}\right)$$

We now do some calculations with this formula. In Chapter 6 we focused on the formula when benefits lasted for a long time. If $r > z$, and as T approaches infinity, project benefits approach

$$(2)\ B_{PV} = \frac{B}{r-z}\left(\frac{1+z}{1+r}\right)^{s}$$

It can be seen that project benefits also approach infinity as z approaches r, that is, when the benefit appreciation term approaches the discount rate. The reason, of course, is that if there is an infinite supply of a resource to exploit (T is infinity), and if the relative price of this resource is rising over time at a rate at least as high as the discount rate, there is no limit to the value of the project.

On the other side, we do some calculations for small values of T. If $T = 1$, we can substitute into (1) to find project benefits of

$$(3)\ B_{PV} = \frac{B}{1+r}\left(\frac{1+z}{1+r}\right)^{s}$$

If $T = 2$, we can perform similar calculations, this time noting that r^2 and z^2 will be very close to zero for small decimal values normally taken on by discount rates and relative price appreciation rates. Using this approximation, project benefits equal

$$(4)\ B_{PV}=\frac{2B}{1+2r}\left(\frac{1+z}{1+r}\right)^s$$

In general, for small values of T, the formula given in (1) can be approximated by

$$(5)\ B_{PV}=\frac{TB}{1+Tr}\left(\frac{1+z}{1+r}\right)^s$$

On the cost side, we have considered development costs such as building and operating a facility as a negative component of the project benefits, so we do not have to count them further. But we do want to focus on environmental costs. They too start in year S, the year the facility is being developed, and they are assumed to rise at rate n per year. The general expression is

$$(6)\ E_{PV}=\frac{E}{r-n}\left(\frac{1+n}{1+r}\right)^s\left(1-\left(\frac{1+n}{1+r}\right)^T\right)$$

As T approaches infinity and as the growth rate n approaches the discount rate, environmental costs approach infinity. The project generally would not be done regardless of the initial level of environmental benefits—these do not even have to be quantified. The only exception to this statement would be when project benefits are also infinite—that case we leave for the philosophers to work out. It may seem unreasonable to assume that the environmental costs of a project last forever and rise at rate n forever, but there are some real world instances. Certain types of nuclear wastes, for example, have half lives of hundreds of thousands of years, probably as close to infinity as one gets in benefit-cost analysis, and their costs may plausibly rise at the rate of growth of the whole economy, which in turn may be close to the discount rate in some cases, as we saw in Chapter 6. It would not, thankfully, be normal to have infinite present values of environmental costs, but it would not be unknown either.

For this analysis we will assume that environmental costs last just as long as project benefits. If oil is drilled in an area, there is less hiking and fishing while the oil wells are active, but once the wells stop producing, the area can be restored to its pre-development status. Such will not always be the case, but increasingly governments are requiring restorative measures as part of a license for developing a resource, and it is certainly worthwhile to look at such a situation. More complex cases where the time span of environmental costs exceeds that of project benefits can be worked out, but we will not do that here. Under this assumption, and using the simplifications described above, the present value of net benefits of a project started in date S, lasting for a small number of years (T), with full restoration at that time and the costs of that built into benefits or costs, can be given by

$$(7) \quad NB_{PV} = \frac{TB}{1 + tr}\left(\frac{1+z}{1+r}\right)^S - \frac{TE}{1 + Tr}\left(\frac{1+n}{1+r}\right)^S$$

Now to the three-way choice. The two-way choice described up to now is to build the project if the present value of net benefits is positive. That test determines whether the project is a present value winner or not. But if this project lasts only a finite time, one can also ask whether it is better to build the project now or later. Basically the answer to the latter question is given by comparing the present value of benefits now, when $S = 0$, with those in one year, when $S = 1$. If they are higher later, the fundamental principle of benefit-cost analysis—choose the option that maximizes the present value of net benefits—suggests that it is better to wait.

Mathematically, the first test can be conducted by evaluating (7) at $S = 0$ and seeing whether the sum is positive

$$(8) \quad NB_{PV} = \frac{T(B - E)}{1 + Tr} \underset{<}{\overset{>}{\gtrless}} 0$$

Since the postponement question is not of much interest for projects that are present value losers, we will assume that this test is passed, or that $B > E$. The next test is conducted by using calculus to differentiate (7) with respect to S, and then evaluating this derivative at $S = 0$. The result is

$$(9) \quad \frac{\partial NB}{\partial S} = \frac{T}{1 + Tr}[(z - r)B - (n - r)E]$$

Notice that if (9) is positive, the fundamental principle says to wait and realize higher benefits later on. In general, things will only come out this way if relative price appreciation is expected: otherwise, the fact that future benefits are discounted encourages development now. This also means that following the methodology of Chapter 7, we can set the derivative equal to zero to find the rate of relative price appreciation necessary to make postponement worthwhile, z^*. The expression is

$$(10) \quad z^* = r\left(\frac{B - E}{B}\right) + \frac{E}{B}n$$

and is plotted as the Postponement Boundary on Figure 8.3.

We can notice several properties of this postponement boundary:

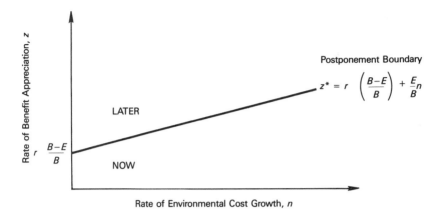

Assume that a project passes a net benefits test, so that $B > E$. If the expected rate of benefit appreciation, z, exceeds z^*, on the Postponement Boundary, it makes sense to delay development. If the expected rate of benefit appreciation falls short of z^*, it makes sense to develop now.

FIGURE 8.3   To Develop Now or Later?

The postponement question is only interesting when there are positive net benefits expected from development. In this model that means that $B > E$, so that the postponement boundary has a positive intercept.

The postponement question is only relevant when there is a finite amount of the resource to be developed. For infinitely lasting resources, such as hydroelectric power, if net benefits are positive now, there is nothing to be gained by waiting.

The rate of relative price appreciation necessary to make postponement worthwhile depends positively on the rate of growth of environmental costs. The reason is that the higher environmental costs are expected to be in the future, the more it makes sense to develop a project now.

The rate of relative price appreciation necessary to make postponement worthwhile depends negatively on the discount rate. The reason is the same one discussed in Chapter 6. The lower the discount rate, the more future-oriented is society, and the more is society inclined to conserve resources.

From an economic standpoint, there may not be too many instances where the prevailing rate of price appreciation exceeds the real interest rate for a long period of time. The upshot of many models of exploitation of finite resources is that the rate of return on these resources is the rate of relative price appreciation, so conditions of capital market equilibrium would drive this expected rate of price appreciation close to the discount rate for most times and resources, and tend to make developers indifferent between developing now and developing later.[4] But there may also be times and places where prices are out of equilibrium, or where one developer thinks she knows better than the market what will happen, that will encourage post-ponement.

From an environmentalist standpoint, this new role of the discount rate eliminates what had been an inconsistency in the argument about benefit-cost analysis. In the old days when environmental costs were ignored, environmentalists trying to kill projects would argue for high discount rates, on the grounds that higher discount rates would reduce the present value of net benefits and make projects fail the benefit-cost test. But it can be seen in Figure 8.3 that now that environmental costs are considered, high discount rates make it more likely that worthwhile projects will be developed now. Hence this new postponement option puts environmentalists in what should be a more comfortable position of arguing for low discount rates, on the grounds that delay, or resource conservation, makes good sense.

Finally, a word about operational procedures. It would be possible, but rather silly, to use the above apparatus to decide now when a project should be begun—that is, to find the optimal value of the starting date S. The reason why it is not necessary to carry things that far is that there is no reason the calculations given here cannot be done year by year. We do the two tests for $S = 0$, and if the results say do not develop, we do not develop. Next year we can do it all again, taking into account any new information that might have been accumulated about expected rates of price change, discount rates, or the growth of environmental costs. New estimates are made and both tests are redone. In such a way we can follow sequential decision-making over time.

THE TELLICO DAM

We now review a specific physical investment project that raises many of these issues, the Tellico Dam on the Little Tennessee River. This is an old project that took more than forty years between the initial proposal and the completion of the dam. Although the project involves a renewable resource—hydroelectric power—so it was never rational to consider postponement explicitly, the project does illustrate how the calculation of net benefits can change over time as relative prices and scarcities change, and in this case with conceptual improvements in benefit-cost methodology. The Tellico Dam is also noteworthy because it was the first project to be seriously challenged under the Endangered Species Act.

The lower 33 miles of the Little Tennessee River were considered among the best trout fishing areas in the southeast. But back in 1936, when the Tennessee Valley Authority (TVA) first proposed the Tellico Dam, the government was more worried about poor farmers and unemployed workers than fishermen. The TVA proposed a dam and canal arrangement that would create jobs, bring power and flood control to the area, and replace the wild fishing stream with a lake and reservoir. The dam would also have flooded the ancestral burial grounds of the Cherokee Indians.[5]

Essentially nothing was done about the TVA proposal for almost thirty years. But in the intervening time the TVA did undertake extensive development in the area. Between the time the project was first proposed in the 1930s and was later reconsidered in the 1970s, the TVA constructed more than twenty such reservoirs within 100 miles of the Tellico site. This development in effect raised the social value of the remaining wild river and lowered that of lakes and reservoirs.

The project was again proposed by the TVA in 1963, funded by Congress in 1966, with land purchase and construction started in 1967. But then came another series of delays. The first was the National Environmental Policy Act of 1969, which held up construction until the TVA could come up with an environmental impact statement (now required on all such projects). The second was when zoologists discovered a unique species of snail darter (a small minnow) in this stretch of the Little Tennessee. The Endangered Species Act of 1973 had recently been passed, and the spawning area of the snail darter would have been threatened by the damming of the river. The snail darter flap endangered the Endangered Species Act more than anything else, but eventually a compromise was struck under which a specially created Endangered Species Committee (ESC, dubbed the God Committee) would arbitrate such disputes. It did so in early 1979, and the committee ruled against the dam. But Tennessee congressmen were able to enact an override on an appropriations bill, and the dam was finally completed in 1980. The ironic postscript to the whole episode was that while it was thought that closing the dam would kill off the snail darter, more were later discovered, and the snail darter lives on.

The empirical estimates of benefits and costs "evolved" just as much as the politics of the dam. Table 8.1 shows these numbers and how they changed over time. The numbers are taken from various reports over the years, updated to 1978 dollars. Midpoints are used whenever ranges are given. The numbers are shown as presented in the documents, in terms of annual benefits (B) and annualized capital costs ($(r+d)C$). These are the present values discussed earlier spread out over the years by multiplying both sides of the equation by $(r + d)$. Expressing things in this annualized form gives the interest and depreciation expense necessary to cover the initial capital cost C.

Four sets of numbers are shown in the table. Comparisons between these numbers illustrate many of the dos and don'ts discussed in the preceding pages. The first set of numbers comes from the original TVA estimate of benefits and costs in 1968. The second is from the second TVA estimate in 1978, changed to respond to some conceptual criticisms of the first estimate and also altered because of changed conditions. The third set is a reanalysis by the staff of the ESC, also in 1978. The fourth set is not strictly comparable. By 1978 the dam had been partially built but not closed. This set of numbers

TABLE 8.1   Annual Benefits and Costs of the Tellico Dam and Reservoir (Millions of 1978 Dollars)

	ORIGINAL 1968 TVA ESTIMATE	REVISED 1978 TVA ESTIMATE	ENDANGERED SPECIES COMMITTEE ESTIMATE	PARTIAL DEVELOPMENT
Total Benefits (B)	16.53	6.85	6.50	3.10
Land Enhancement	1.62	.34	—	—
Flood Control	1.13	1.04	1.04	—
Navigation	.89	.31	.10	—
Power	.89	2.70	2.70	—
Recreation	3.70	2.30	2.50	3.10
Water Supply	.16	.05	.05	—
Agriculture	—	.11	.11	—
Employment	8.14	—	—	—
Total Costs $(r + d)C$	5.02	3.19	7.22	4.29
Dam	5.02	3.19	3.19	2.26
Land	—	—	4.03	2.03
Net Benefits $(B-(r+d)C)$	11.51	3.66	-.72	-1.19

Source: General Accounting Office, *The Tennessee Valley Authority's Tellico Dam Project: Costs, Alternatives, and Benefits* (Washington, GPO, 1977); Staff Report to Endangered Species Committee, *Tellico Dam and Reservoir* (Washington, GPO, 1977). Midpoints are used whenever ranges are shown, and all numbers are converted to 1978 dollars.

is the ESC evaluation of the gains and losses from tearing down part of the dam, retaining the wild river and snail darter spawning area, and just completing the ancillary development.

The original TVA estimate of benefits and costs made in 1968 shows net benefits being very high ($11.51 million), but many of its estimates are dubious. The most important question mark involves the value of jobs created. The estimate of employment gains was a gross estimate of jobs created by the project times annual wages, with no adjustment for any opportunity costs. As was discussed in Chapter 4, there are two things wrong with including the entire $8.14 as an employment gain:

> Although there may have been permanent job gains back in the 1930s, by the late 1960s unemployment was very low nationally, in this part of Tennessee, and for the trades likely to be hired by the project. By this time the project would have undoubtedly drawn most of its labor from other useful purposes, there would not have been many permanent employment gains, and not much justification for crediting the project for jobs created.

> Even if there were employment gains, one should count not the gross wages, but only the gain in surplus for the employees. It is unlikely that these workers could have made this entire amount more than they would have made somewhere else.

In all subsequent analyses these supposed job gains were omitted, even by the TVA.

A second discrepancy between this and later evaluations was for land enhancement. This represented the supposed gain in annualized capital values from the newly created lakefront property, but again as discussed in Chapter 4, involved double counting because many of the direct recreational benefits from the lake were also counted. In subsequent evaluations this item was first scaled back by the TVA, and then omitted entirely by the ESC.

The recreation benefits were estimated using the travel cost method previously discussed. They were reduced between the first and second TVA evaluations because of the greater supply of similar lakes in this region of Tennessee—in effect, the demand function for the Tellico Lake was assumed to be shifted back. In the fourth estimate where the dam would not be closed, these recreational gains went back up because of the travel cost value for wild river trout fishermen in one of the few remaining wild rivers.

A final item that was greatly scaled down in subsequent evaluations was for navigation, reflecting the supposed cost reductions from the increased barge traffic in the canal that was to be built around the dam. Between the time of the initial and subsequent TVA evaluations barge traffic declined, and by the time of the later estimate most firms that might have located in the area would not have even used barge traffic. In any event, the item only reflected the gains from barge traffic without counting losses that might have been felt by rail and trucking firms.

There was one item where the initial TVA evaluation seemed to underestimate benefits from the project. When the initial evaluation was done energy prices were very low, and not much gain was attributed to the power from the dam. By the late 1970s energy prices had risen sharply, and much greater values were used for the added electricity. By this time, ten years later, energy prices are back down again, and smaller values would be used.

On the cost side, the initial TVA evaluation had a high cost of building the dam. This was lowered in the 1978 evaluations because the dam had been partially completed by that time. The smaller cost for the partial development option reflects the fact that under this option, it was slightly cheaper to tear out part of the dam and finish the ancillary development than to complete and operate the dam.

The TVA did not count any cost for the land used up because of the flooding from the dam, reasoning that this land had already been purchased and was therefore costless. This reasoning misunderstands the idea of opportunity costs. Although the land was purchased, it still existed and could have been leased or sold for some other purpose, such as farming, had it not been flooded by the dam. Hence the ESC staff did include an estimate of the opportunity cost of the flooded land, both for closing the dam and a lower estimate for leaving the dam partially completed but not closed.

There was also some dispute about what number to use for the opportunity cost of land. The present value of the land lost to the dam was about $40 million in 1978. This present value was annualized to $4.03 million by applying the official government nominal discount rate, at the time 10 percent, to the $40 million. This 10 percent nominal rate was the same one criticized in Chapter 6, because it should not be used to discount real values. Everything else in this evaluation was in real terms, and the discount rate should have been as well. Hence the ESC estimate was much too high—a better estimate would have used a real discount rate of about 3 percent and an annualized land cost of closing the dam of about $1.2 million ($40 million times .03) and of partial development of about $.6 million.

Comparing the two columns on the right of Table 8.1, we see that in 1978 the ESC itself was facing a choice of closing the dam and suffering an annual loss of net benefits of $.72 million or of the partial development option, which entailed losses of $1.19 million. The first of these losses did not include any valuation for the snail darter and the loss of the Cherokee burial grounds. In the face of these numbers, the ESC did vote against closing the dam and for the partial development option. In effect, the ESC put an annual value of at least $.47 million on the snail darter and the Cherokee burial grounds. This difference was quite small, less than 7 percent of the annual cost remaining in 1978.

Had real discount rates been used, the choice would have been between positive annual net benefits of $2.1 million were the dam closed and $0.2 million under the partial development option. Closing the dam looks slightly better relative to not closing it in this case, because more land is affected by the high discount rate if the dam is closed. But the difference made by closing the dam is still surprisingly small. And the positive net benefits from closing the dam are nothing to write home about because the calculation was done after about $2 million of annualized construction expenses were incurred, viewed as bygones, and ignored.

As was previously mentioned, the Tellico project involves a renewable resource, so it was never sensible to consider delay in developing the resource—net benefits were either positive or negative as forecast at date x. But it is still interesting, and sobering, to see how the numbers can change over time as job conditions change, the relative supply of lakes and rivers change, the relative price of electricity changes, and, although never explicitly considered, whether the snail darter is viewed as endangered or not.

Although it is sobering that political muscle overrode analysis in the end, it can hardly be surprising that when decisions become highly charged politically, politics usually wins out. And now that the snail darter has miraculously been saved, through no fault of the government's, the final decision is at least arguably correct—given the bygone capital cost, and depending on the value one might place on the Cherokee burial grounds, closing the dam might actually have yielded positive net benefits.

SUMMARY

This chapter has looked at the methodology of evaluating physical investment projects that entail long-run environmental costs. One has to get initial benefits and costs right, as always, but in these cases an extra premium is placed on knowing how these benefits and costs change over time, because they will be changing for a long time.

The first important new insight is that sometimes, when the growth rate of environmental costs is high relative to the real discount rate, one does not even have to measure initial benefits and costs to make an efficiency decision about a physical investment project—environmental costs are infinite, and that is the end of the story from an efficiency standpoint.

The second new insight is that other times, when the project exploits a finite resource and when the expected rate of price change of project benefits is high relative to the real discount rate, it makes sense to delay even projects that pass the efficiency test. True, they pass it, but the net present value of the project is even greater if development is delayed. These two insights dramatically alter the role of the discount rate in physical investment benefit-cost analyses. A low discount rate, implying a great weight on future interests, makes it harder for a project to pass the benefit-cost test on both environmental and conservationist grounds.

The chapter also looked at one particular project, the Tellico Dam in Tennessee. The project was initially seen to have very large net benefits, but because of changes in relative prices and scarcities over time, it now has very slight net benefits—so slight, in fact, that the Endangered Species Committee actually voted against closing a partially built dam (though that decision was later overridden politically).

NOTES

[1]John Krutilla and Otto Eckstein, *Multiple Purpose River Development* (Baltimore: Johns Hopkins University Press, 1958); and also Eckstein, *Water Resource Development: The Economics of Project Evaluation* (Cambridge: Harvard University Press, 1958). A later book that reviews a number of such studies is Krutilla and Anthony C. Fisher, *The Economics of Natural Environments: Studies in the Valuation of Commodity and Amenity Resources* (Baltimore: Johns Hopkins University Press, 1975). One that introduces some new issues relevant to developing countries is Partha Dasgupta, Stephen Marglin, and Amartya Sen, *Guidelines for Project Evaluation* (New York: United Nations Industrial Development Organization, 1972).

[2]Marion Clawson and Jack Knetsch, *Economics of Outdoor Recreation* (Baltimore: Johns Hopkins University Press, 1966); and Jack Knetsch, "Economics of Including Recreation as a Purpose of Eastern Water Projects," *Journal of Farm Economics*, December 1964.

[3]Richard C. Porter, "The Optimal Timing of an Exhaustible, Reversible Wilderness Development Project," *Land Economics*, August 1983.

[4]A number of such models are discussed by Tom Teitenberg, *Environmental and Natural Resource Economics*, 2nd edition, (Glenview IL: Scott, Foresman and Company, 1988).

[5]Much of the following material comes from the Staff Report to the Endangered Species Committee, *Tellico Dam and Reservoir* (Washington: Government Printing Office (GPO), 1979).

Also useful were the TVA, *Alternatives for Completing the Tellico Project* (Washington: GPO, 1978) and the General Accounting Office, *The TVA's Tellico Dam Project: Costs, Alternatives, and Benefits* (Washington: GPO, 1977).

PROBLEMS

1. Suppose that the cost of a dam is $1000, all paid in the initial year, and the consumer surplus benefits start a year later at $200. The discount rate is 5 percent. Compute the present value of net benefits of the dam when the consumer surplus decays at the rate of zero, 5 percent, and 10 percent, respectively.

   Now suppose that the benefit decay rate is set at 5 percent but that there are environmental costs of $20 a year beginning in the year of operation. Compute the net present value if these environmental costs also decay at 5 percent a year, if they are constant at $20 a year forever, if they rise at 5 percent a year.

2. A different dam will flood a good hunting area. Evaluators have found a similar area for which the demand function is $P = 100-Q$, where P is the daily price paid by users and Q is the number of daily users. The cost of maintaining trails in the perhaps soon-to-be-flooded area is $5 per day per user. Since the soon-to-be-flooded area is farther from an interstate highway than the comparison area, it costs hunters an added $2 a day to get there. Find the cost of flooding the area.

3 a. There is a small pool of oil in a remote wilderness area in a northern state. Geologists expect it to yield a net profit of $50 at today's prices for five years, and then fizzle out. Economists think the relative price of oil will rise at 4 percent a year as far as the eye can see, and that the overall price level will rise by another 3 percent a year forever. The government has agreed to use 3 percent as the proper real discount rate. Environmentalists argue convincingly that if the oil is drilled, there is a risk of killing off the last remaining wolverines in the state. A careful assessment of naturalists' enjoyment of these wolverines sets the value at $5 in the initial year and growing at 1 percent a year forever. Should the oil be drilled? Why or why not?

   b. Suppose you did not drill the oil. Geologists give you the further data that 5 barrels of oil can be drilled for each of five years, at an initial cost of $1 per barrel and an initial price of $11 per barrel. All prices and costs are expected to rise at 4 percent a year indefinitely. The nominal discount rate is 7 percent. The situation on wolverines is the same as before. Should the oil be drilled? Why or why not?

   c. You cannot find a job and you go to work as the benefit-cost analyst for an oil company. Is there any relative price assumption for the next five years that makes it economic to drill now?

NINE
HUMAN INVESTMENT

Chapter 8 examined cases where the government actually built a physical structure such as a dam or a drilling rig. A different form of investment is also a common feature of governmental policy in modern societies—investment in the population directly. Under these "human investment" projects, the nation invests resources and the time of its citizens now in the expectation that these citizens will be more productive later on. The outstanding example of a human investment program is public education, but health programs, job training, and subsidies for higher education and day care can also be thought of in this light.

Human investment programs can be justified on many grounds. Public education was one of the first responsibilities taken on by state and local governments in the United States, partly because there were public goods efficiencies from having government educate people and partly to give those who otherwise would have gone without a chance at the rewards of high incomes. Although very little controversy surrounds the notion of having the government support education and other types of human investment programs, there are a series of marginal questions that involve benefit-cost analysis—should the government do a little more of this program or a little less of that? Hence it makes sense to develop a methodology for measuring the gains and losses from human investment programs.

Both individuals and collective bodies make human investment decisions. Every time an individual decides for or against attending college one more year, he or she is weighing the benefits of continued education—higher lifetime incomes plus any increase in appreciation of cultural offerings—against the costs—the time cost of attending college plus the tuition expense. Governments can go through similar calculations to determine whether human investment programs should be expanded or contracted, this time being careful to distinguish overall social gains from internal transfers.

This chapter first tries to determine exactly what should and should not be considered a gain or a loss from a human investment program, from an individual's standpoint and from society's standpoint. It goes on to show how these gains and losses can be inferred statistically from the types of data that are likely to be available. It discusses some new advances in social experimentation, where the government actually creates the data to do the evaluation. Finally, it examines two specific human investment evaluations—that of an attempt to put welfare recipients to work in California and that of an early childhood education project in Michigan.

BENEFITS AND COSTS

Table 9.1 catalogues the benefits and costs for a typical human investment program. The table shows entries for the individuals directly benefiting from the human investment program (participants), for all others in society, and for the sum of the two columns. In this way it distinguishes the individual benefits and costs that reflect overall social gains and losses from those that reflect internal transfers. Since human investment programs typically make an investment now and derive a return later on, all entries in a table such as 9.1 should be in present value terms.

TABLE 9.1 Benefits and Costs of a Human Investment Program (Present-Value Terms)

	INDIVIDUAL	OTHERS	SOCIETY
Benefits			
1. Gain in after-tax earnings	X		X
2. Gain in taxes paid		X	X
3. Nonmonetary satisfaction	X		X
Costs			
4. Tuition	X		X
5. Scholarships		X	X
6. Higher living expenses	X		X
7. After-tax earnings foregone	X		X
8. Taxes foregone		X	X
9. Transfer payments foregone	X	–X	

The first two rows in the table record the present value of future income gains of the program participants. These individuals are assumed to be paid what they are worth in the marketplace—hence if their income rises, their marginal product does also, and that represents a social benefit of the human investment program. But participants do not reap all of the benefits of their greater productivity: since they pay higher income taxes on their higher income, participants gain the after-tax earnings (row 1) and others in society gain the present value of future tax increases (row 2).

The next item in the third row reflects the fact that education or human investment is valued not solely for its impact on income. Education may enable participants to get jobs they like, even if those jobs do not pay any more than the jobs they would have had without the training. In this sense the participants are clearly better off, and since nobody is worse off, society gains as well, even though the form of the payment is in terms of enjoyment rather than dollars. One could make a similar argument if education opened up cultural horizons for participants, and although nothing is entered in the column for others, it would not be stretching things to say that others also gain in a nonmonetary sense from the greater education of the program participants. Although this item is quite difficult to quantify, we can again use our bracketing technique of doing everything else before worrying about row 3. Perhaps the human investment will have positive net benefits even without valuing this item.

On the cost side, the most obvious cost is the explicit amount paid for education—tuition by the participants in row 4 and scholarships by others in row 5. These payments together cover the training institution's resource cost of providing the education. To this is added the higher living expenses, if any, incurred when participants live away from home in row 6.

The next two items refer not to explicit costs but to opportunity costs. When participants attend educational institutions, they may have to give up their job or at least not work as many hours. They sacrifice current earnings to get an education, and these current earnings reductions are sacrifices in income to the participants and consumption goods to society just as much as the explicit out-of-pocket costs. Hence rows 7 and 8 count as costs the foregone earnings and taxes on these foregone earnings, just as was counted on the plus side in rows 1 and 2.

Row 9 is the only internal transfer on the list. When recipients of training earn more, they may receive fewer transfer payments for welfare, unemployment insurance, or whatever. These transfer reductions represent at the same time a loss to the program participants but a gain to those who no longer make the transfers.

Two other items might have been included in Table 9.1. On the cost side, if the educational institution is operating at full capacity, adding one more student pushes the institution along a rising supply curve and raises average costs for all other students. A cost entry should be added to the table to reflect this change. Similarly on the demand side, if the occupations for which these participants are being trained are crowded, more students will push down the wages of all graduates, effectively generating losses for nonparticipants.

As a final comment in interpreting Table 9.1, it might be felt that because we have labeled the third column social benefits and costs, we should always look at it when evaluating human investment programs done for social reasons. Not so. In computing these social benefits and costs, we have simply summed the participant gains and losses with all other gains and losses, just as we did when using the Kaldor-Hicks efficiency standard for evaluating programs. Should a program be done for income distribution reasons, we may want to weigh the gains and losses of the participants, such as disadvantaged workers, more heavily than those for others in society. In this case we should redefine social benefits and costs to be a weighted average of the student net benefits and those of others, with the weights being the distributional weights discussed in Chapter 7.

A METHODOLOGICAL FRAMEWORK

Of the items in Table 9.1, data on tuition and scholarships can typically be collected from program information in a straightforward manner, and data on nonmonetary satisfaction are typically rather hard to come by. What distinguishes a good evaluation of a human investment program from one that is not so good is in how it measures the various income gains and losses.

The various issues can be illustrated with a framework drawn from a statistical technique called multiple regression analysis. Let us say that we can express the postprogram income of participants as

(1) $Y_i = a_0 + a_1 X_i + a_2 Z_i + u_i$

where the i subscript refers to the ith individual, Y_i is the postprogram income of this individual, X_i is a variable indicating whether the individual was in the program being evaluated, and Z_i represents a set of observable but independent characteristics of the individual (age, sex, ability measure, race, and so forth). The a's are known as regression coefficients, or partial derivatives, that tell how much a unit change in either X_i or Z_i will alter the individual's postprogram income. The first of these coefficients, a_0, is an intercept that says what income will be if all X_i and Z_i variables are set at zero. The term u_i represents what is known as a residual. It can be thought of as the combined influence on income of all unobservable characteristics. The regression coefficients are computed such that over a group of individuals the residual is random with an average of zero—it is intended to measure deviations from the regression line fit to data for all individuals.

The easiest way to interpret X_i is to view it as a binary variable that takes on a value of one when the ith individual is in the human investment program and zero when not. Hence if we change X_i by one unit by putting somebody in a human investment program, income changes by a_1, and a_1 becomes the impact of the program on the participant's income. The regression computes a_1 simultaneously with the other coefficients, so in effect it holds constant all observable Z values when arriving at the program estimate.

This point can be seen in another way. Suppose we did a random experiment with our program, where we had 100 individuals in our program and 100 individuals not. We call the first group the treatment group and the second group the control group. The selection of individuals into treatment and control group should be done at random—by picking random numbers, lottery, or whatever—and with a group as large as 100 we could be sure that the average residual would be zero for each group. We could also be sure that the average Z value for each group would be the same, though as long as we can measure Z, this latter requirement is unnecessary. We then put the 100 participants through our human investment program, wait a decent interval, and observe the income of all 200 treatment and control subjects.

When it comes time to do the evaluation, we can express earnings for the average member of the treatment group as

(2) $Y^T = a_0 + a_1 + a_2 Z^T$

Note that we have simplified things to include just one Z variable, we have used the proposition that the average residual is zero, and we have dropped the i subscript because we are no longer referring to any one student but now the group average. Since $a_1 = 1$ for each member of this treatment group by assumption, we can simply add this coefficient to the intercept.

Going through precisely the same operation for the control group gives

(3) $Y^C = a_0 + a_2 Z^C$

The only change is that since $a_1 = 0$ for each member of this control group by assumption, that term drops out.

The impact of the program on income can then be derived by comparing the mean of income for all treatment subjects with the mean of income for all control subjects by subtracting equation (3) from equation (2)

(4) $Y^T - Y^C = a_1 + a_2 (Z^T - Z^C)$

If the mean Z score for each group is the same, the difference in income means, positive or negative, is just the impact of the program, a_1. If the Z scores are different, the analyst just runs the regression given in (1) and all coefficients are estimated. Either way, the impact of the program corrected for all intervening Z variables and estimated without statistical bias is just a_1.

To take a concrete example, suppose these 200 subjects differed by height, and height mattered in determining later income. We would hope that as we randomized selection into the treatment and control groups, the average height of each group would be the same. But even if it were not, we could run the regression of (1) where we use statistics to explain income with two independent variables, the subject's height and whether the subject was in our program. The computer would estimate regression coefficients which would satisfy expression (4). The difference in treatment and control group income would then be the program effect plus a measured term that corrects for height differences between the two groups.

POTENTIAL PITFALLS

There are, of course, a number of pitfalls in conducting such evaluations. We now discuss some of the more common ones.

Indicators of Program Performance

A first problem involves the indicator of program performance. We have said that the evaluator should be interested in the coefficient a_1, the impact of the program on future earnings. But there are some famous cases where confusion arose because other indicators were used. One was in the case of the Coleman Report, a massive survey of educational attainment under the leadership of James Coleman in the mid 1960s. Another was in the case of a report on variations in income by a team of social scientists under the leadership of Christopher Jencks in the early 1970s.[1]

Both of these reports focused on V_x, the proportion of the variance of the outcome measure, Y, explained by the human investment program variable, X. This proportion can be shown to equal

$$(5) V_x = [a_1^2 S_X^2 / S_Y^2][1 - R_{XZ}^2]$$

where S_X^2 is the variance of X, S_Y^2 is the variance of Y, and R_{XZ} the correlation coefficient between the two independent variables X and Z.

Examining (5), it can be seen that there are three reasons why the proportion of variance explained by X alone could be small, only one of which implies that the human investment program might fail a benefit-cost test:

The impact of X on Y, a_1, could be close to zero. This is the case where the human investment program would seem to fail a benefit-cost test.

There could be much less variance in X than Y, because income variance is increased by occupation, region, luck, or whatever. In this case the human investment program might well pass a benefit-cost test but have its influence swamped by all the other factors that cause incomes to vary.

There could be such a high correlation between X and Z that R_{XZ} would be close to one and V_x close to zero. In this case also the human investment program might well pass a benefit-cost test, but the impact of the program might be so highly correlated with the impact of the other independent variable Z that it would be hard to discern the separate impact of the program.

The problem faced by the Jencks group was to explain variations in income (the Y variable) with educational attainment (the X variable) and other factors (the set of Z variables). Their principal finding was that the share of variation in income explained by educational attainment, V_x, was very small. The explanation for the finding was the second one given;—the variation in income is so enormous because of occupational differences, regional differences, luck, or whatever, that the share of the variance due to educational attainment alone is small. It may be that educational attainment would not pass a benefit-cost test in the Jencks data, but we would never know from looking at V_x.

The problem faced by the Coleman group was to explain educational test scores (their Y variable) with school district spending (the X variable) and community income levels (the Z variable). Whereas for the Jencks group, the factor making it difficult to observe the impact of X was the fact that the variance of Y was large relative to that of X; for the Coleman group the difficulty was that X and Z were highly correlated, making it difficult to tell whether school spending (X) or community income (Z) was responsible for the variation in test scores. Again it could be that school district spending on schools would fail a benefit-cost test, but again we could not tell from looking at V_x.

Scholars are still analyzing both sets of data, and there are enduring puzzles about how education works and how powerful it is in influencing income or any other outcome measure. There are in addition a whole raft of empirical measurement problems to go along with these conceptual problems. But the relevant point here is that from a benefit-cost standpoint (not the only concern of either report, to be sure) the focus should be on a_1, the simple impact of the human investment program on the relevant outcome measure, not on V_x. Human investment spending might have a strong enough impact on the outcome measure that it satisfies a benefit-cost test, even though its independent variance is sufficiently low or its correlation with other variables is sufficiently high that human investment does not explain much variance in test scores by itself. To go back to the point raised in Chapter 1, an evaluation should only require a program to have benefits that outweigh costs (large a_1), not to be a panacea (cause a large V_x in the face of all other factors that make for changes in the outcome variable).

Implementation Problems

Social scientists are now becoming more cognizant of the fact that just because a program is legislated, that by no means insures that it will work properly. There are any number of bureaucratic, institutional, and organizational reasons why programs do not operate or are not being implemented as planned.

The big quandary for evaluators is not to identify poor implementation of a program but to know what to do about it. One approach would be to say that since a program is not being implemented properly at certain sites, the subjects at these sites should not be included in the treatment group for the data analysis. In this way the evaluation does not penalize the program for the fact that it was not implemented properly at these sites. The alternative approach would be to consider the implementation of a program part and parcel of the whole program, to include the subjects from these poor implementation sites in the treatment, and to measure program effectiveness from the entire data set. In this case the program is penalized for the fact that it was not implemented properly—programs can now fail a benefit-cost test either because they are not effective or because they are not well implemented.

Convincing arguments between these two approaches can be marshalled on either side. Why penalize a good program because of a few jokers at the Peoria site? Or, why do you think a national program will be well implemented when the Peoria version could not be? One sensible compromise might be for the evaluators to wait a decent interval for program managers to get the bugs out of the program before subjecting it to a formal analysis. Another is to do the evaluation twice, with the subjects from the poor site in and out, to see how much impact the implementation issue has on the overall results. Perhaps the choice will not matter much, or perhaps the program will pass a benefit-cost test even if data from the poor sites are included.

Measurement Problems

A related issue refers to the measurement of the X, Y, and Z variables. Often these variables cannot be measured very precisely. In the standard human investment case, we may not have good measures for participant income at the conclusion of the training program (Y), for income or some other characteristic at the start of the training program (Z), or even for the amount spent on the participant while in the training program (X).

The difficulties raised by measurement error turn out to depend critically on which variable is mismeasured. If measurement error is random, the case usually treated in the literature, and it involves the dependent variable, there is no problem. The random residual in equation (1) now has a larger variance and the entire regression will explain less of the dependent variable, but as long as we are concerned with the value of the human investment coefficient, a_1, there is no reason why straightforward application of the regression technique will not give an unbiased estimate of this key coefficient.

But if measurement error affects either of the independent variables, things get trickier. The intuition behind this claim is that whatever value we record for the participant's X or Z, we are not recording the true value but some proxy that is randomly related to the true value. Accordingly, straightforward application of the regression technique will yield estimates of the coefficients that are averages of the true coefficient and zero, the coefficient we would get if we used a random variable instead of X or Z. Hence when we have measurement error in either of the independent variables, the relevant coefficients are biased toward zero, and some correction, such as grouping the data, must be made to average out the measurement error.

We might note the subtle difference between measurement error and the implementation problem discussed earlier. In both cases some outside factor is watering down the influence of the program variable, X. For the implementation problem, that something is that the program cannot be implemented properly; for measurement error, that something is that the program variable cannot be measured properly. In the implementation case it is not clear whether any correction should be made because perhaps the implementation problem is part of the whole program package. But in the measurement case it is clear that the evaluator should strive to eliminate the measurement error and get as accurate estimates as possible. The difference is that measurement error represents a potential problem with the evaluation, not with the program itself, and it is the evaluator's job to minimize problems with the evaluation and get accurate estimates of how well the program is really doing.

Selection Problems

Perhaps the greatest potential pitfall involves what is known as the selection problem. It was previously shown that when the observed outside variable affected the outcome measure, some technique such as regression analysis was necessary to correct for differences in Z and yield unbiased estimates of the program coefficient a_1. Were that not done, as shown in equation (4), the program impact would be confounded with the difference in Z, height in the example given, and we could not be sure whether the treatment or the difference in Z was generating the outcome difference. Precisely the same problem could exist with our random residual u_i, except that this time the problem is harder to solve because u_i is unobservable.

Referring to equation (1), suppose that there is some unobservable variable, call it ambition, that alters income. Other things being equal, ambitious participants in either the treatment or the control group will have higher incomes than lazy participants. If somehow we could magically assure that our treatment and control groups had the same proportions of ambitious and lazy participants, ambition would not lead to any bias in our estimate of the program's effect. But if not, there would be a bias.

What sort of a bias? That depends on how people were selected into the treatment and control group. If it is up to the subjects themselves, such as going to college or signing up for a training program, we might expect that the ambitious people will join the treatment group to a greater degree than the control group, and since we cannot observe and correct for differences in ambition as we can for observable Z variables, our estimate of how much the program raised income will be biased upward. The issue is called a selection problem because participants are self-selecting themselves into the program, and the correlation between the unobservable ambition factor and the outcome measure is slanting things in favor of the program. Precisely the same problem, this time known as "creaming", exists if program managers are allowed to select the participants they want for the program. There could be subtle ways in which they select the cream of the crop, and again the evaluation is slanted in favor of the program.

But there could be downward biases too. Sometimes program managers have such a strong social consciousness or believe so much in their program that they might actually select less ambitious participants, believing that the program can make them over. Or, sometimes participants in a program are selected from a waiting list of potential participants, some of whom no longer need the program when their number comes up. Suppose, for example, that there were a training program for unemployed workers, all of whom must sign up and wait for a period before the training begins. By the time the waiting period is over, the ambitious potential participants might have gotten jobs on their own and taken themselves off the list. In these cases selection bias could bias the estimate of a_1 downward.

Since the factor that determines outcomes is unobservable, it is very difficult to correct for selection problems with any sort of statistical technique. The only real solution is to have strict random assignment into the program. If an unbiased measure of program success is desired, selection cannot be left up to subjects or program managers, but only to the throw of the dice. It may sound heartless to control things this rigidly, but in the long run it will probably be better to have evaluations that yield more accurate and less biased information on which programs work well and which do not.

SOCIAL EXPERIMENTATION

This list of statistical difficulties could lead an aspiring evaluator to some pessimism. There are problems in implementing programs, problems in measuring inputs, and selection problems. Although some of these problems may not be terribly serious, and some can be corrected statistically, there are undoubtedly some that are serious and are resistant to any sort of statistical correction. Is there anything that can be done?

In fact, there is. In the late 1960s the federal government began to design large-scale social experiments to test social programs. The first set of experiments involved income maintenance, testing transfer programs that supported low-income families without a work requirement in several New Jersey sites, Seattle, and Denver. These plans varied according to basic support levels and the degree to which support was reduced as families earned income. Later came some similar experiments with health insurance schemes that varied the amount of deductible medical expenses and the sharing of expenses (coinsurance) between the family and the provider.[2]

Many of the problems previously discussed can be solved with social experiments:

> If the evaluator has trouble in measuring the impact of a certain program because there are not enough examples of it, or enough variation in the program variable, a social experiment can manufacture a broad range of program options.

> If the evaluator has trouble in distinguishing the impact of the program from the impact of other variables because their correlation is high, a social experiment can break the pattern by providing different program levels in a way designed to optimize the accuracy of the estimated program impact.

> If the evaluator has trouble with selection problems, an experiment can use random assignment of subjects to treatment and control groups, and to different types of subprograms.

> If the evaluator has trouble in gaining accurate measures of the Z, X, or Y variables, an experiment can be set up from the beginning with accurate measurement instruments.

At the same time, there are significant costs to social experiments. As research projects, they are quite costly—programs have to be manufactured, subjects must be paid or given treatments, and elaborate measurement and management groups have to be created. More than this, experiments take a great deal of time. The treatment period alone is five years for most social experiments, and it usually takes more than a decade from the initial proposal to the final data analysis. As in the income maintenance case we examine shortly, the policy proposal receiving the most interest can change dramatically between the start and the end of the social experiment. Perhaps for these reasons, the government has not initiated any large-scale social experiments for some time.

But there has nevertheless been some movement towards broadening evaluations in the direction of social experiments. The early social experiments were in programs that had not received legislative approval but were interesting as social research projects. More recently, the idea has been to couple programs that were being done anyway with random assignment of subjects into treatment and control groups, with reasonably complete measurement instruments, and with a broad range of program options, to gain many of the advantages of social experiments without the large costs.

THE SCALE OF THE EVALUATION

Whether one is planning a program evaluation or a social experiment, another matter that needs to be determined is the scale of the project. Does one survey 200 graduates of a human investment program, 400 graduates, or 1000 graduates? It turns out that the analysis is very similar to that of evaluating programs in general. As with any program, the optimizing strategy is to allocate funds to the evaluation until the marginal benefit of one last sample observation, in terms of greater precision of the program impact estimate, equals the marginal cost.[3]

Our estimate of the program impact, a_1, is really a sample statistic. If we have a small sample of subjects, the statistic may not be a good estimate of the true program impact for the entire population of subjects. But as we add to the sample, the law of averages implies that the sample estimate becomes a progressively more accurate estimator of true program impact, b. This is the benefit of getting a larger sample.

An illustration of this property is shown in Figure 9.1. Say that the true program impact is given by b. We are trying to estimate this true program impact by sampling subjects from the treatment and control group. If our total sample is of size N_1, a small sample, the relative frequency distribution of outcomes for our evaluation is as shown in the figure. The height of the distribution for each value of a_1, called the relative frequency of that estimate $[f(a_1)]$, rises to a peak at b and then declines again. But if we get a bigger sample N_2, the relative frequency distribution becomes more compact about the true estimate. As a convention, the area under each frequency distribution is set at one, so the frequency between any two a_1 values represents the probability of getting an estimate of the program's impact in that range.

Next, let us say that we estimate from program cost data how large the program's impact on outcomes would have to be to make it yield positive net benefits. Call this value b^*. In Figure 9.1 b^* is above the true estimate of program impact, as if the program would not pass a benefit-cost test if we had a large enough sample to make a precise estimate of its impact. This is done just for illustrative purposes: the entire analysis could be redone with $b > b^*$.

The benefit from increased sampling can then be defined as the greater probability of making a correct evaluation. Referring to Figure 9.1, if we have a sample size of N_1, the probability of a miscall—saying a program yields positive net benefits when it in fact does not—is the area $(A + B)$. As the

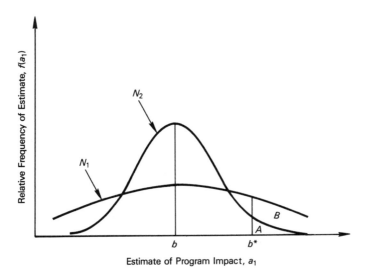

A small sample (N_1) yields the probability of saying a program has positive net benefits when it does not of area $A + B$.

A large sample (N_2) yields the probability of saying a program has positive net benefits when it does not of area A.

The gain in probability of an accurate estimate of the program's impact as we expand the sample from N_1 to N_2 is area B.

FIGURE 9.1 Sample Estimates of Program Impact for a Small and a Large Sample

sample size expands to N_2, the probability of a miscall falls to that denoted by area A. The area B then represents the marginal gain, in reduced probability of a miscall, from expanding the sample. It can be shown that if we label this probability of a correct evaluation as p, p will rise with N but at decreasing rates, a statistical law of diminishing returns.

The next task, as with any evaluation, is to express benefits from the evaluation in dollar terms. Benefits (B) are given by the expression

(6) $B = pqV$

where q is the probability that the evaluation will be important in political decisions on the project and V is the discounted present value of program costs. In addition to the fact that the probability of a miscall declines with N, this benefits function also tells evaluators not to spend scarce dollars if it is unlikely that the evaluation will be decisive in political decisions on the program, and not to spend scarce dollars if the stakes (present value of program costs) are small.

The evaluation cost function can be expressed in a straightforward manner as

(7) $C = c_0 + c_1 N$

where c_0 represents the fixed cost of the evaluation and c_1 the marginal cost, or the degree to which costs rise as the sample size rises. The optimal scale of the evaluation, as seen on Figure 9.2, is where the marginal benefit of one more sample observation, $\delta B / \delta N$, equals the marginal cost, c_1. This happens at sample size N^*, where both lines are parallel and the slopes are the same. The profit, or surplus, from doing the evaluation is measured by the difference between total benefits, B, and total costs, C. If the benefit function never rises to the cost function, the optimal sample for the evaluation is zero: do not do the evaluation for it is not worth its cost.

Although this is a reasonably clear conceptual framework for determining the scale of the evaluation, it could be difficult to operationalize. The reason is that just as information on the true program impact will not be known before starting, neither will the information on the distribution of this impact that is necessary to compute the benefits function. The best way to get around this difficulty is to go step by step. Start with a very small sample, a pilot test. Compute the estimate of a_1 and its standard error. Use this information to draw the frequency distribution and the probability of a miscall for this size sample. Compute the optimal sample size. Assuming this optimal sample size is greater than the small pilot sample, as it probably will be, draw a new sample, draw a new distribution, compute a new optimal sample size, and so forth. In this way the evaluator can work toward a final

FIGURE 9.2   Optimal Scale of the Evaluation

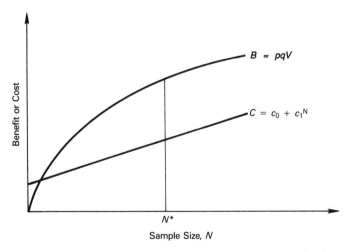

Sample Size, N

N^* is the optimal scale of the evaluation, where marginal benefits $\left(\dfrac{\Delta B}{\Delta N} \right)$ equal marginal costs (c_1) of an increase in observations.

solution of the estimated program impact, the probability of a miscall, and the optimal sample size for estimating both of these.

WELFARE REFORM

We now turn from these general issues to two specific human investment evaluations. One involves welfare reform for adults, the other enriched education for preschool children. But despite the diversity of the programs, the previously presented methodology can be used in both cases, and indeed, the results show broad similarities.

Regarding welfare reform, the first social experiments of the 1960s analyzed income maintenance programs where the government would just support the income of low-income families without any work requirement on the part of these recipients. Although it was generally found that welfare recipients worked almost as much in the presence of income support programs as in their absence (a small leak in the bucket), by the 1980s the policy interest had changed. By this time there was more of a feeling that low-income recipients should have to work for their support, and the welfare amendments of 1981 permitted states to experiment with different ways of combining work experience or requirements with welfare payments. The Manpower Demonstration Research Corporation (MDRC) conducted a random assignment evaluation of these welfare initiatives in eight states, with seven of the final reports being published by 1988. We show results for one of the most complete of these new-style social experiments in San Diego, California.[4]

Since 1982 San Diego has operated two innovative employment initiatives designed to increase employment and reduce welfare dependency. One, called the job search (JS) program, is a three-week job search workshop to teach welfare recipients how to search for jobs. The other, called the job search, work experience (JS,WE) program, takes over for those still unemployed and on welfare and gives recipients an unpaid public job for up to thirteen weeks. MDRC did a random assignment evaluation where 7,000 new welfare applicants were randomly assigned to either one of these treatment groups or to a control group, followed these applicants for two years, and did a benefit-cost analysis of the programs for the first five years following the time of application for welfare.

The results, in present value terms using a discount rate of 5 percent, are shown in Table 9.2. Total net benefits were $1,096 for the short JS program and $1,952 for the more elaborate JS,WE program, indicating that both programs passed the net benefit test quite handily. Applicants gained from $644 to $797 in the two programs, largely because of earnings gains which remained sizable for the two years of the evaluation period. As a result of these significant earnings gains, taxpayers gained as well—taxes paid by the applicants rose, transfers received by the applicants fell, and for the JS,WE

TABLE 9.2 San Diego Job Search (JS) and Work Experience (WE) Project
Net Present Value of Benefits per Applicant
1983 $, Discount Rate 5%, 5-Year Horizon

	APPLICANTS		TAXPAYERS		SOCIETY	
NET BENEFITS	JS	JS,WE	JS	JS,WE	JS	JS,WE
Output increase			3	205	-3	205
After-Tax income increase	1301	1861			1301	1861
Tax increase			235	371	235	371
Transfer decrease	-679	-1076	730	1158	51	82
Training saving	-4	-4	50	57	46	53
Operating costs			-534	-605	-534	-605
Allowance and expenses	26	16	-26	-31		-15
Total net benefits	644	797	452	1155	1096	1952

Source: Manpower Demonstration Research Corporation (MDRC), *California: The Demonstration of State Work/Welfare Initiatives*, (New York: MDRC, 1986), Table 3.

component, because of the imputed output gains from the public employment. Operating costs were all borne by taxpayers, but even considering this, taxpayers came out way ahead in the two programs.

Going through the other MDRC reports, we also see that these California results were more or less replicated in other states, with other samples of welfare recipients. The full list of results is shown in Table 9.3, with all evaluations done like that for California—random assignment, large sample, two-year observation period, five-year horizon, etc. Net benefits for society, the sum of the applicant gains and the taxpayer gains, are positive in ten of the eleven programs analyzed, by $1,000 or more per applicant in four of the

TABLE 9.3 Various State Work/Welfare Projects
Net Present Value of Benefits per Applicant
1983–85 $, Discount Rate 5%, 5-Year Horizon

STATE	TYPE OF PROGRAM	APPLICANTS	TAXPAYERS	SOCIETY
Arkansas	JS,WE	-363	711	348
California, AFDC	JS,WE	797	1155	1952
California, AFDC	JS	644	452	1096
California, AFDC-U	JS,WE	-1443	1414	-29
California, AFDC-U	JS	-1196	1239	43
Illinois	JS,WE	-35	283	248
Illinois	JS	-420	481	61
Maine	JS,WE	3182	-1129	2053
Maryland	JS,WE	547	65	612
Virginia	JS,WE	1134	667	1801
West Virginia	JS,WE	-84	734	650

Source: MDRC, various state reports, 1985–88.

eleven. Taxpayers come out ahead in ten of the eleven programs analyzed, by more than $1,000 per applicant in three of the eleven. Surprisingly, the applicants themselves do not come out as well—there are generally earnings gains, but given the tax and transfer adjustments, applicants actually lose in six of the eleven programs.

Given the political unpopularity of welfare and the widespread perception that welfare dependence is rising, these results are certainly encouraging. These MDRC evaluations cover numerous welfare recipients in many different states with a careful evaluation design. The fact that the results are so positive, particularly regarding the gains for taxpayers, is a hopeful sign, from the programmatic standpoint of reducing welfare dependency and the benefit-cost standpoint of being able to evaluate such program innovations. Perhaps taxpayer investment in welfare recipients is indeed a profitable investment.

PRESCHOOL EDUCATION

The MDRC evaluations were very strong cross-sectionally—they had a large sample in many different states. A different approach to doing human investment evaluations would be to get a much smaller sample, but to follow subjects for much longer. In so doing, one might better see the long-run returns, if any, from human investment programs. Nowhere would such a question be more relevant than for preschool education, where the investment takes place twenty years before the participants begin earning higher (or lower) incomes.

It obviously takes a great deal of patience to do such evaluations. Evaluators must record program data at the time of the evaluation, and then keep track of the participants in both treatment and control groups for another 20 to 25 years to make the evaluation. One project where the requisite patience has been shown is the Perry Preschool project in Ypsilanti, Michigan. The preschool treatment was administered to 58 randomly assigned disadvantaged black preschoolers from a low income area in Ypsilanti between 1963 and 1967, with 65 disadvantaged black preschoolers randomly assigned to the control group. Thirteen of the treatment students entered in the first year and participated in the treatment for one year; the rest participated for two years. All of these numbers are obviously minuscule compared to the scale of the MDRC evaluations, but the expense and logistic difficulties of both preschool education and long-term evaluations are such that no studies with larger samples are available. The treatment itself consisted of a morning classroom program during the academic year coupled with one home visit a week for the entire year.[5]

At the time of the latest data analysis in 1984, all participants were at least 19 years old. They had been followed and tested over the years, with remarkably small attrition of the sample (less than 2 percent). One finding was common to other such preschool programs—IQ scores of the treatment students rose right after the program but then fell back to the same level as for the control students.

But other differences persisted. The treatment students attended elementary school more regularly than the control students, they spent less time in special education, they were less likely to be classified as mentally retarded, they failed fewer grades, they received better grades in high school, they were more likely to graduate from high school, and they had more positive attitudes toward school at age 19. They also had better post-high school employment records, lower arrest records, received fewer transfer payments, and had a lower incidence of teen-age pregnancy. How all these good things could happen as a result of a relatively brief intervention program that only raised IQ scores for a short time is still something of a mystery to those in the field of education, but there are some plausible theories and these findings have been duplicated for other less elaborate evaluations of preschool programs.

The benefit-cost analysis summarizing all of these changes is shown in Table 9.4. All numbers are discounted present values, using a discount rate of 3 percent (other rates were also tried). Students are broken into the small sample in the one-year program and the larger group in the two-year program. Net benefits are further subdivided into those actually observed through age 19, and those extrapolated on the basis of these data past age 19. There was an attempt to value all changes but those in teen-age pregnancy.

The bottom right entries in the table suggest that discounted net benefits were between $23,769 and $28,933 per student in 1981 dollars, much larger than the totals for the welfare reform programs. Most of the gains are roughly the same between the one- and two-year programs: the difference in net benefits is because the discounted teaching costs are naturally almost twice as high. The big gains, as can be seen from the right columns, are in future earnings increases and welfare reduction, most of which are still projected; crime reductions, some of which have happened already and some of which are still projected; and the educational cost saving because students attended the expensive special education programs in lower numbers, which has happened already.

It is again remarkable that such a high share of the benefits of the Perry program go to nonparticipants—now about 80 percent of the net gains. These others still pay the initial education costs, but they gain the special education saving, the reduced crime expenses, the reduced transfer payments, and the higher taxes on participant earnings. The subjects themselves come out ahead as well, by more modest amounts. If the numbers can be believed, it makes even more sense for society to invest in the preschool education of disadvantaged black children than it does in reducing welfare dependency—though both are good investments.

TABLE 9.4   Perry Preschool Project
Net Present Value of Benefits per Pupil
1981 $, Discount Rate 3%

	PARTICIPANTS		OTHERS		SOCIETY	
NET BENEFITS	1 YEAR	2 YEAR	1 YEAR	2 YEAR	1 YEAR	2 YEAR
Measured to age 19	226	509	2,290	−2,389	2,515	−1,880
Preschool costs	—	—	−4,818	−9,289	−4,818	−9,289
Child care	290	572	—	—	290	572
Educational cost saving	—	—	5,113	4,964	5,113	4,964
Earnings increase	482	467	161	156	642	623
Welfare reduction	−546	−530	601	583	55	53
Crime reduction	—	—	1,233	1,197	1,233	1,197
Predicted from age 19	4856	4715	21,562	20,933	26,418	25,648
College costs	—	—	−704	−684	−704	−684
Earnings increase	19,233	18,674	4,580	4,446	23,813	23,120
Welfare reduction	−14,377	−13,959	15,815	15,355	1,438	1,396
Crime reduction	—	—	1,871	1,816	1,871	1,816
Total net benefits	5,082	5,224	23,852	18,544	28,933	23,769

Source: Berrueta-Clement, *et. al. Changed Lives: The Effects of the Perry Preschool Program on Youths Through Age 19* (Ypsilanti, MI: High Scope Educational Research Foundation, 1984). Tables 26 and 28. Components may not sum to total because of rounding error.

Of course one should remember that while the gains are larger here, they are not as reliable statistically. The sample sizes are very small and many of the gains are still projected, even twenty years later. At the same time, it is again heartening to know that at least some preschool education programs seem to be working well, and that benefit-cost analysis can be useful in identifying the successes.

SUMMARY

This chapter has discussed some of the ins and outs of human investment evaluations. Since these are investment projects, where resources are spent now in the anticipation of gains later on, it is necessary to be careful about timing, to make fairly long-term evaluations of gains and losses, and to do all comparisons in present value terms. The evaluations can be set up to show separately the gains and losses of participants and all others in society.

The main statistical difficulty in doing human investment evaluations is to measure properly the change in income following the treatment. One must control for other factors that might alter incomes, guard against selection bias, get large enough samples to reduce statistical uncertainty, and randomize assignment to the treatment and control group. These steps have been successfully negotiated, but there are lots of problems to watch out for.

The chapter looked at two specific human investment evaluations, both of which arrived at positive results. The MDRC evaluation of work-welfare initiatives in eight states had a very large and diverse sample, but followed subjects for a relatively short time. The High Scope evaluation of preschool enrichment programs had a tiny sample but followed subjects for a very long time. Both found positive net benefits overall. Participants came out slightly ahead, but the big news in both evaluations is how well nonparticipants did.

NOTES

[1]See James S. Coleman *et. al., Equality of Educational Opportunity* (Washington, D.C. Government Printing Office, 1966). Our criticism of the Coleman conclusions is taken from Glen G. Cain and Harold W. Watts, "Problems in Making Policy Inferences from the Coleman Report," *in* Peter H. Rossi and Walter Williams (eds.), *Evaluating Social Programs* (New York: Seminar Press, 1972).

The other report is by Christopher Jencks *et. al., Inequality: A Reassessment of the Effect of Family and Schooling in America* (New York: Basic Books, 1972).

[2]A great deal has been written on social experimentation. One of the most recent collections of pieces, along with further references, appears in Federal Reserve Bank of Boston, *The Negative Income Tax Experiment Then and Now*, 1987. An earlier summary was Jerry Hausman and David Wise (eds.), *Social Experimentation* (Chicago: University of Chicago Press, 1985).

[3]The analysis here follows that of George E. Johnson, "The Optimal Scale of Program Evaluation," Institute of Public Policy Studies Discussion Paper 86, University of Michigan, 1976.

[4]The following material is taken from MDRC, *California: The Demonstration of State Work/Welfare Initiatives* (New York: MDRC, 1986). Some of the MDRC reports on other states are also used.

[5]This information comes from J.R. Berrueta-Clement, L.J. Schweinhart, W.S. Barnett, A.S. Epstein, and D.P. Weikart, *Changed Lives: The Effects of the Perry Preschool Program on Youths Through Age 19* (Ypsilanti MI: High Scope Educational Research Foundation, 1984).

PROBLEMS

1. An educational program costs students $10,000 in tuition and living expenses, but it generates for them $20,000 in extra discounted after-tax earnings. The rest of society pays costs of $14,000 for scholarships but receives $2000 in discounted added tax revenues. Would the program pass the Kaldor-Hicks economic efficiency test? Is this the right test?

2. A training program costs $100 per participant in year zero and nothing thereafter. It generates benefits of *B* per year beginning in year one. These benefits decline by .2*B* each year, so that in the sixth year they are zero. All wages and prices rise by 5 percent each year, and the nominal discount rate is 7 percent. Find the level of *B* required to make the program a success.

3. A different training program costs taxpayers $400, all of which is spent in the first year. Five of its graduates were unemployed previously and now get jobs that pay $20 a year in the first year; the other five

graduates had jobs that paid $10 one year ago before they entered the program and now pay $20 in the first year. Labor economists observe that all wage gains from this type of program last for three years in real terms, and then drop to zero. Those who were unemployed received unemployment benefits of $5 a year before the program, and these benefits quit now that the workers have jobs. All prices and wages are stable, and the nominal discount rate is 2 percent. Find the gains or losses of the program to each of the three groups.

4. Recent health legislation mandates that some program money be put into evaluation. Assume that you are in charge of both the evaluation and the operation of a small program. Consultants tell you that to evaluate the program it will cost $3 million to hire the analysts and print the surveys, and that it costs exactly $20 for every subject surveyed. Your staff figures the benefits of the evaluation, in terms of improved knowledge about how the program works, to be given by the expression

$$B = \$4020N - \$2N^2$$

where N is the sample size. Find the sample size and the amount you will spend on the evaluation. Explain whether you would do the evaluation if it were not mandated.

TEN
INTERGOVERNMENTAL GRANTS

The typical evaluation study assumes that a government is simply spending money or using resources on some project. The social benefits of the project are then compared to its costs and the project either passes or does not pass a benefit-cost test. But classic prototype is coming to be an increasingly unrealistic description of the way most government spending programs actually work. As the role of government expands in the United States and many other countries, a more complicated federal structure is emerging. In the middle is a national government that conducts some programs on its own (defense, social security), but many more programs are conducted by way of grants to lower levels of government. Next are state or provincial governments that receive grants from the national government, conduct some projects on their own (highways, natural resources) but give still more grants to local governments. Most actual domestic services (education, police and fire, street maintenance, waste removal) are then provided by local governments, with grant assistance from both states and the national government.

This interlocking grant structure sets up a new evaluation complication. We now have to consider two new potential gainers and losers from any policy change—taxpayers outside the jurisdiction who may pay some of the cost of the program, and other citizens who may reap some of the benefits whenever spending changes.

In this chapter we deal with this new complication. We review the different types of grants and the theoretical rationale for each. We then show how the benefit-cost methodology can be extended to each type of grant. We go on to apply this methodology specifically to grants for highway construction and maintenance.

TYPES OF GRANTS

There are two broad types of grants—categorical and unrestricted. Categorical grants must be spent on a particular program or in a particular program area. Typically the federal government matches spending with the lower level of government, though sometimes the matching continues only up to some limit. Short of this limit, the federal government is lowering the price of the affected spending, the lower government will typically spend more, and one can do the usual type of efficiency evaluation of the change.

The other broad type of grant is an unrestricted grant. These come to lower governments as a matter of right or even treaty and can be spent or used for tax reduction as the lower government desires. Sometimes there are trivial conditions the local government must satisfy to obtain the grant, but the restrictions are much less onerous than for a categorical grant. Whereas for categorical grants the price is lowered, unrestricted grants make no change in relative prices and operate through the income effect alone. It is much harder to evaluate these grants, which entail a simple transfer of funds from one set of taxpayers to another, often without any economic efficiency change.

CATEGORICAL GRANTS

The rationale for categorical grants involves what are known as benefit spillovers. Referring to Figure 10.1, say that D represents the community demand function for some public good, the vertical summation of the marginal utility of all citizens in the community. But public goods will typically benefit citizens in other communities as well: cleaning up the water or the air lowers pollution in nearby communities, fire protection benefits citizens where fires could have spread, public health measures reduce risk of disease in other communities, and improving the roads or plowing the streets conveniences outsiders as well as the local citizenry. For this reason the higher demand function D_T represents the vertical summation of all who benefit from the public good—those who live inside and outside the community boundaries.

As in the case of public goods described in Chapters 2 and 3, it is clear that if outsiders benefit from, but do not pay for, public goods, too little public

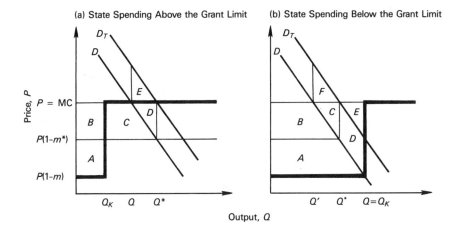

(a) State Spending Above the Grant Limit   (b) State Spending Below the Grant Limit

(a) When spending (Q) exceeds the kink point (Q_K), the matching rate (m) could be lowered to m^*, and the grant made open-ended. Spending would rise from Q to Q^* and the efficiency gain is area E.

(b) When spending equals or is below the kink point and the matching rate is lowered, spending would fall to Q^* and the efficiency gain is area E.

FIGURE 10.1 Comparison of Present Grants with Efficient Grants

goods output will be provided. If the marginal cost of the public good in question is $P = MC$ in the left panel, the community acting alone will choose Q units of public spending (at the intersection of community demand and the price line), whereas the social optimum level of public spending would be Q^* units (at the intersection of total demand and the price line).

One way to correct this suboptimality is for citizens in the nearby communities, or others who benefit from the public spending, to bribe the community in question to spend up to Q^*.[1] With only a small number of communities and programs with benefit spillovers, such a system of intercommunity bribes might work. But there are 82,000 local governments and special taxing districts in the United States, with benefit spillovers on a wide range of public spending programs. The sheer transactions cost of arranging the system of bribes would be immense. And there is a simpler way.

That is for the national government to identify some of the programs with important spillover effects—pollution treatment, transportation, community development, human investment, natural resource programs—and give matching grants for state or local government spending on these programs. Referring to the left panel of Figure 10.1, were the federal government to pay m^* of the cost of each unit of the public good, reducing its price from P to $P(1-m^*)$, public spending in the community would go from Q to the optimal level at Q^*. The pattern of gains and losses would not be precisely the same as with intercommunity bribes—federal taxpayers make the payment, and they are not the ones who benefit from the particular local spending—though such differences would average out for the nation as a whole. But for all communities the amount spent on public goods would be at the social optimum.

That argument gives a rationale for categorical grants, though the actual characteristics of these grants do not conform well to the characteristics suggested by this theoretical rationale. In fiscal 1987 federal government categorical matching grants to state or local governments totaled $96 billion, 2.2 percent of the GNP. More than half of this total, $54 billion, was in grants for income maintenance or health insurance for low-income people, a programmatic function often left over to the national government in other countries, and where the theoretical rationale for having the state or local government conduct the program is fairly tenuous.[2] The remaining $42 billion of grants was for programmatic functions where benefit spillovers are important, but where matching rates were completely out of proportion for the spillover rationale. The average federal matching rate (m) on these $42 billion of grants was .81—the federal government paid 81 percent of the cost. Studies of a few grants, the largest of which (for highways) is dealt with in more detail shortly, indicate that for most grants those inside the community got two-thirds or more of the benefits from the public spending, and those outside the community got one-third or less. Hence m^*, the social efficiency matching rate for the typical grant, should have been around .3, while in fact the actual matching rate was .81.

Were the federal government just to give out matching grants that lowered the price of public goods by 81 percent, as opposed to the 30 percent that might be considered optimal, there would be excess public spending and grants. To prevent that, there is another provision in these categorical grant programs—the funds are limited. Once local public spending rises to what will be called the kink point, Q_K in Figure 10.1, no more matching funds are available from the national government, and the price reverts to the full price, $P = MC$.

The price lines generated by these schemes are shown in both panels of Figure 10.1. The left panel shows the normal case where spending is above the kink point. The federal grant thus implies a deep price subsidy for a few units of the public program, but no subsidy at the margin. The effective price facing the state or local government is shown by the heavy line. Since the amount of grant funds is limited, these types of grants are called close-ended. Whereas the idea of the matching grant was to raise public spending to Q^*, since the close-ended grants contain no marginal price subsidy, public spending will not rise but remain at Q, the no-grant level of spending (assuming no income effects, which would generally be small for a particular grant program that makes a very small change in community spendable resources). We have the ironic result that excessively generous matching provisions have in effect defeated the purpose of the grant program, which now does not stimulate any state or local spending.

For the sake of completeness, the other possibility is shown in the right panel of Figure 10.1. Suppose for some reason the Congress legislated grant limits that were large relative to state spending on the public good. In the case drawn in the right panel, the grant is effectively open-ended and state or local spending goes to the kink point. Spending could conceivably even fall short of the kink point. The price line for such a grant is shown by the heavy line in the right panel.

An Efficient System of Categorical Grants

There is no mystery as to how to make the present system of categorical grants more efficient. All that needs to be done is to have the federal matching rate correspond to the share of marginal benefits from public spending received by those outside the community. The solution is exactly analogous to the system of Lindahl tax shares discussed in Chapter 3. As was the case there, there is a tendency to move to the efficient level of public output if the various taxpayers are paying at the margin what they receive at the margin. The only difference is that now we have extended the principle to those outside the community.

What would a Kaldor-Hicks evaluation of a move to an efficient level of grants look like? Beginning with the left panel of Figure 10.1, where the grant schedule kink point is low relative to existing levels of spending, making grants open-ended and shifting matching rates from m to m^* would straighten out the price line so it is at $P(1-m^*)$ for all levels of public spending. This in turn would raise spending from Q to Q^*, the efficient level. The change would affect the relevant groups as follows:

> Federal taxpayers lose area $(A + B)$ with the present system and would lose area $(B + C + D)$ with the new system. Their net gain is area $(A–C–D)$.
>
> State citizens gain area $(A + B)$ with the present system and would gain their consumer surplus, area $(B + C)$, with the new system. Their net gain is area $(C–A)$.
>
> Citizens in other communities gain the difference between the D_T schedule and the D schedule times the change in public spending, or area $(E + D)$.
>
> The sum of the net gains of the three groups, the Kaldor-Hicks or economic efficiency change, is area E.

That this sum is the correct answer can be seen from more direct reasoning. Output has changed by the difference between Q and Q^*, and the social valuation of this change is just the difference between marginal benefits and marginal costs summed over this interval, or area E.

We can do a similar calculation for the right panel in Figure 10.1, where spending is now low relative to the grant kink point, so the kink point is ineffective in constraining spending. Altering matching rates from m to m^* would make the new price line $P(1-m^*)$ again, and lower public spending from Q to Q^*. The change would affect the relevant groups as follows:

> Federal taxpayers lose area $(A+B+C+D+E)$ at present and area $(B+C)$ under the new system. Their net gain is area $(A+D+E)$.
>
> State citizens get the consumer surplus of area $(A+B)$ at present and the surplus of area B under the new system. Their net loss is area A.
>
> Citizens in other communities now lose the difference in demand schedules times the change in output, area D.
>
> The sum of the net gains of the three groups is area E.

Again, that this is the correct answer can be seen by direct reasoning—area E is the difference between marginal costs and marginal benefits summed over the change in output.

Thus the essential difference between the left and the right panel is that in the left panel spending is too low from a social standpoint, and the efficiency gain is the difference between marginal benefits and marginal costs over the increased output. By contrast, in the right panel spending is too large from a social standpoint, and the efficiency gain is the difference between marginal costs and marginal benefits over the decreased output.

Note that we have done both of these evaluations from the standpoint of all relevant groups, federal taxpayers, those inside the community, and those outside the community. The matter under investigation was a change in a federal policy, so such a perspective makes sense. But there could be changes initiated by the lower government, in which case it would make sense only to consider the welfare of the local citizens and to ignore that of federal taxpayers and outsiders.

Recent Changes in Categorical Grants

To tie all this in to real events in the United States, there was a great expansion in categorical grants of all types in the Great Society years of the 1960s. Since that time both Republican and Democratic Presidents have looked for ways to rein in federal spending on these grants. President Nixon invented a concept called special revenue sharing, which would have taken the entire categorical grant—area $(A+B)$ in the left panel of the figure—and converted it to a special revenue sharing grant that merely had to be spent in broad areas with no matching at all. Essentially this change would have converted these categorical grants to unrestricted grants where the community would receive area $(A+B)$ as an income transfer with no effect at all on the price of public spending at the margin. Whereas the efficient grant system previously described featured a marginal price of $P(1-m^*)$ to deal with benefit spillovers, special revenue sharing grants would feature a marginal price of

P. Many of the changes recommended by President Nixon have since been made: now the converted grants are called block grants.

A Kaldor-Hicks evaluation of the switch to block grants for the left panel would lead to pretty uninteresting results. The marginal price determining public spending was *P* before the change to block grants, and it remains *P* after the change. Hence there is no change in public spending, and no change in the welfare of those outside the community. There is no change in federal grants by assumption, and so also no change in the welfare of either federal taxpayers or state citizens. This all adds up to what might be called the Kaldor-Hicks null case: there is no change in the welfare of any group. There may be some saving in paperwork as a result of relaxed grant regulations, but beyond this it is hard to get either excited or upset by the change to block grants.

Things do get more interesting in the right panel of Figure 10.1, where the kink point is ineffective in constraining spending. The price line now would go from $P(1-m)$ to P, so state spending would be cut from Q to Q'. This change affects the relevant groups as follows:

> Federal taxpayers gain or lose nothing by assumption.
>
> State citizens get the consumer surplus of area $(A + B)$ before the change and the entire block grant payment, area $(A + B + C + D + E)$, after the change. They are better off by area $(C + D + E)$.
>
> Outsider lose the difference in demand schedules over the interval, area $(C + D + F)$.
>
> The Kaldor-Hicks summation of net gains is that block grants yield an efficiency gain of area $(E-F)$. Note that this gain may not be positive: that depends on a comparison of the size of the earlier overspending inefficiency that is now corrected (area E) with the size of the present underspending inefficiency that is now introduced (area F).

The trick in arriving at this latter result is to notice that the gain to state citizens from the present system is not the entire grant, only the consumer surplus from this grant. As the grant is converted from a price to an income subsidy, therefore, these state citizens are clearly made better off—they get the same money without the restrictions on how the money can be spent. Whether society is made better off then depends on how this gain stacks up against the loss to outsiders when public spending is reduced.

As a final historical matter, when the Reagan Administration was casting about for ways to reduce government domestic spending in the early 1980s, the Director of the Office of Management and Budget at the time, David Stockman, hit on an interesting variation on the block grant idea. He reasoned that since the move to block grants would make states better off, the states should be willing to give up a certain amount of their grant—25 percent in his proposal—and still not be hurt. The governors and mayors trooped to Washington and killed the formal proposal, though some block grants were later cut back fairly sharply when domestic spending was cut in the 1980s. But assuming the proposal had passed, how would one do an evaluation of the change?

We have already seen that if the kink point in the grant schedule were binding, in the left panel of Figure 10.1, the change would be fairly uninteresting. Prices at the margin are still unaffected by the Stockman block grant proposal and the welfare of outsiders is still unaffected. There is a simple distributional shift where federal taxpayers gain the area .25$(A + B)$ and state citizens lose the same amount. Hence there is no mystery why the governors and mayors trooped to Washington.

But if the kink point were not binding, in the right panel, the results are again more interesting. As without the Stockman proviso, the marginal price would rise from $P(1-m)$ to P, and public spending would fall from Q to Q'. The change then yields the following net gains:

Federal taxpayers gain their Stockman dividend, an area equal to .25$(A + B + C + D + E)$.

State citizens had the surplus of area $(A + B)$ before the change and the area equal to .75$(A + B + C + D + E)$ after the change.

Outsiders lose area $(C + D + F)$ as before.

The overall Kaldor-Hicks tally is for a net gain of area $(E–F)$, just as before. The difference is in how these social gains or losses are split up. Without the Stockman proviso, state citizens keep all the gains from the shift from price (categorical) to income (unrestricted) grants. With the Stockman proviso, the federal government extracts some of this new surplus. The amount extracted is precisely all of the new surplus when the area of the triangle $(C + E + D)$ is just one-quarter of the area of the rectangle $(A + B + C + D + E)$.

UNRESTRICTED GRANTS

Unrestricted grants can have a number of justifications. In some countries such as Australia they have come about by a treaty among the previously independent states that merged to form the new nation-state. In other countries they exist because the central government revenue system is alleged to be more efficient at collecting revenues than the state system.

In the United States these unrestricted grants did not exist before 1970. At that time the Nixon Administration began converting some formerly categorical grants to block form, as we previously saw, and it also introduced a new general revenue sharing program, the first major unrestricted grant from the national government to states and localities. This program lasted for a decade and a half, but in the mid 1980s was one of the casualties in the fight against budget deficits. Many states have also had, and still have, unrestricted grants to their local governments.

An important justification for the unrestricted grants of the national and state governments is income maintenance. Local communities in the United States finance most of their spending with a property tax, which falls more heavily on high-income groups with taxable property than on low-income groups. As can be seen in Figure 10.2, because of the upward slope of the tax function a high-income community with a great deal of taxable property and a high average income can finance a constant package of spending benefits with lower tax payments per household of given income. It is better to live in a community with lots of rich people to help finance your public goods than in a poor community.

If pure consumption goods such as yoyos were financed by public budgets, it would be inequitable to force residents of low-income communities to pay more for their yoyos than residents of high-income communities, but the inequity would not harm the long-run income prospects of the poor in any obvious sense. But when services that have a strong influence on the distribution of income in the long run, such as education, are financed by the public sector, the higher "tax price" that poor communities must pay for their education and other services is inequitable in both the short and long run. Communities make education available to provide opportunities for the poor to get ahead, but at the same time the financing provisions insure that poor communities have to pay more than rich communities for their schools.

There are several potential solutions to the problem. One, followed much more extensively in the nineteenth century in this country, is to consolidate governments. If poor central cities were able to annex their

FIGURE 10.2   Taxes and Expenditures for Various Income Groups

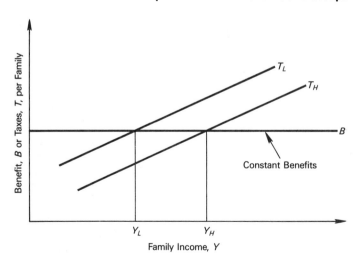

The high-income community can assess lower taxes for each income level to pay for a constant menu of benefits.

high-income suburbs, community income differences would be evened out and there would not be such a large variation in the tax price communities pay for public education. Another solution, used by many states for public education today, is "power equalization" grants, whereby poor communities get more favorable matching provisions than rich communities, again to even out community differences in tax price. A third solution is simply to give unrestricted grants to low-income communities. This could have been one rationale for the federal general revenue sharing program, though the funds were spread out so broadly among communities that the degree to which general revenue sharing actually bolstered relative public spending levels in low-income communities was very modest.

The evaluation of unrestricted grants follows that for the left panel of Figure 10.1, where there is no price effect. If the unrestricted grant contains no income effect as well, it is a simple matter of federal taxpayers giving up area $(A + B)$ and state taxpayers gaining the same amount. Even if there are benefit spillovers affecting outsiders, there would be no effect on outsiders because there is no change in public spending. If there is a change in public spending because of the income effect and if there are benefit spillovers, there would be an effect on outsiders from the unrestricted grant, but no economic efficiency change within the community as long as the marginal cost schedule is flat over the relevant range. The analysis in this case is essentially the same as that in Chapter 4, where demand shifts that vary output along a flat supply schedule yield no efficiency gains or losses.

FEDERAL HIGHWAY GRANTS

There are two main federal highway grant programs. The first, called the ABC program, was started back in 1926 to construct interurban highways. Under this program the federal matching rate is 67 percent. The second, called the Interstate Highway Program, was started in 1956 to build limited-access thruways along predetermined routes. There the federal government pays 90 percent of the cost. The combined grant for both programs, and now for some maintenance expenses on both sets of roads, was $13.3 billion in 1985, with an overall weighted average matching rate (m) of 83 percent.

On the benefit side, it is difficult to estimate exactly the benefits received by instate and outstate drivers on federally funded roads, but the Department of Transportation has done a driver survey of travellers on rural and urban interstate highways at random checkpoints in various states. Data from this survey are given in Table 10.1. Although there is some variation by state, overall six states the share of outstate drivers is 33 percent of the total. This share will be used to determine the marginal price reduction for an efficient interstate highway grant (m^*)—at the margin 33 percent of the benefits are outstate and 67 percent are instate.

TABLE 10.1   Interstate Highway Travel Study (Number of Drivers)

STATE	INSTATE	OUTSTATE	OUTSTATE TOTAL
Illinois	58,668	25,146	0.30
Indiana	122,599	49,653	0.29
Nevada	7,534	15,894	0.68
New Mexico	8,057	16,584	0.67
Pennsylvania	64,191	35,382	0.36
Virginia	105,424	37,944	0.26
Total	366,473	180,603	0.33

Source: Department of Transportation

As regards spending, state governments purchased $27 billion of goods and services to build and maintain highways in 1985. This represents the value for present spending, Q. Had they simply spent the entire federal grant of $13.3 billion at the prevailing matching rate of 83 percent, they would have spent $16 billion in all—$13.3 of the federal money and $2.7 billion of their own money. This calculation yields the kink point, Q_K. Note that of the $16 billion in spending, federal money is 83 percent of the total and state money is 17 percent.

Had the grant system been efficient, the open-ended matching rate would have been 33 percent and the marginal price would have been reduced by that amount. Assuming that the no-grant price is 1, the efficient price is .67, and the average price over the interval is .835. The formula for the arc elasticity given back in Chapter 4 then allows us to determine how high spending would be at the efficient price, Q^*. This formula is

(1) $E = (\Delta Q / Q) / \Delta P / P)$

where E refers to the arc elasticity, Q refers to the average of quantity before the change (27) and after the price reduction (27 + ΔQ), and P refers to the average price before and after the change (.835). It is not clear what value to use for this arc elasticity, but a wide range of studies have estimated absolute price elasticities of about .5.[3] Plugging in values, we get

(2) $.5 = \Delta Q / [(.5)(27) + (.5)(27 + \Delta Q)] / (.33 / .835);$
$\Delta Q = 6; Q^* = 27 + 6 = 33$

All of these values are shown in Figure 10.3, patterned after the left panel of Figure 10.1. Area $(A + B)$ is the present grant amount, $13.1 billion. Area $(B + C)$ is the present valuation of the grant to citizens of the state. Area $(D + E)$ is the gain to outsiders when the price falls and spending rises. The Kaldor-Hicks tally is shown at the bottom—federal taxpayers gain $2.4 billion, state citizens lose $3.4 billion, outsiders gain $2.0 billion from the

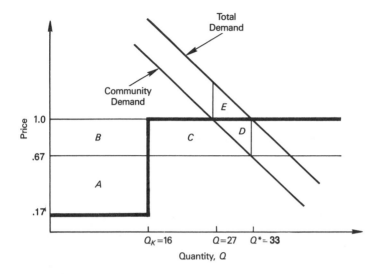

Area A = (.5)(16) = 8.0
Area B = (.33)(16) = 5.3
Area C = (.33)(30-16) = 4.6
Area D = Area E = (.5)(.33)(6) = 1.0

If grants are converted to efficient grants:
Federal taxpayers gain area (A-C-D)   = 2.4
State citizens gain area (C-A)   = -3.4
Outsiders gain area (D + E)   = 2.0
Net gain (area E)   1.0

FIGURE 10.3   Interstate Highway Grants, 1985 (Billions $)

higher spending, and the overall net gain from an efficiency standpoint, the sum of the three changes, is area *E*, $1.0 billion. The efficiency gain is only 7 percent of the grant, but what is perhaps more significant in this era when attempts are being made to cut federal spending is that the grant can be cut by 20 percent and at the same time made *more* efficient.

SUMMARY

This chapter has dealt with cases where policy is conducted at one remove through grants to lower levels of government, which in turn spend the money. When this happens, two new sets of constituents are added to the gain and loss calculation: federal taxpayers, who pay some of the cost of the project, and those living outside the community, who reap some of the benefits.

With these gainers and losers added to the calculation, the Kaldor-Hicks net benefit calculation for changes in grant provisions will turn on the marginal price paid for public goods. For most categorical grants in the

United States, the federal matching rate is very generous but the grant is not open-ended—states can benefit from this generous matching rate only up to a point, and then the price reverts to the no-grant price. As a consequence, even though matching rates are generous, there is actually too little spending from a social point of view on most grant-financed types of spending.

Past efforts to reform federal grants have featured conversion of categorical grants to block grant form. In converting categorical to unrestricted grants, there is no change in the marginal price of public spending, which was already the full price, and no change in money flows by assumption. Hence conversion of close-ended categorical grants to block grants leads to no efficiency changes whatever—federal taxpayers, instate, and outstate citizens are all just as well off as before the change. A better way to reform grants is by converting them to efficient grants, open-ended with the matching rate equal to the share of marginal benefits received by those outside the jurisdiction. In the one specific case looked at, for highway construction and maintenance, converting existing grants to efficient grants does make efficiency improvements and also cuts federal spending by twenty-eight percent of the initial grant.

NOTES

[1]This solution was pointed out by Ronald Coase, "The Problem of Social Cost," *Journal of Law and Economics*, October 1960.

[2]The rationale may be tenuous, but it is not absent. The issue is discussed in, and the other facts used here are taken from, Edward M. Gramlich, "Federalism and Federal Deficit Reduction," *National Tax Journal*, September 1987.

[3]Lists of empirical studies and the elasticities they have estimated are given by Edward M. Gramlich, "Models of Excessive Government Spending: Do the Facts Support the Theories?" in *Public Finance and Public Employment*, Robert H. Haveman (ed.) (Detroit: Wayne State University Press, 1982) and Robert P. Inman, "The Fiscal Performance of Local Governments: An Interpretive Review" in *Current Issues in Urban Economics*, Peter Mieszkowski and Malcolm Straszheim (eds.) (Baltimore: Johns Hopkins University Press, 1979).

PROBLEMS

1. Suppose the demand schedule for some state public spending program is given by
    $P = 100-Q$, where P is the price paid by state taxpayers and Q is the quantity of public spending. Outsiders gain an added 20 at each level of Q. The marginal cost of public spending to the state is 40.

    a. Find the level of public spending and the inefficiency from the standpoint of the whole society when there is no grant assistance at all.

    b. A grant is introduced with 90 percent federal matching for the first 50 units of output. Find the gains or losses of federal taxpayers, state taxpayers, and outsiders from this grant, along with the overall Kaldor-Hicks efficiency tally.

c. Design a grant that would maximize efficiency and compute the gains and losses of all three of the groups listed in b.

d. The present grant with 90 percent matching for the first 50 units of output is converted to block form. Find the gains or losses of all three groups with that change, and the Kaldor-Hicks efficiency tally.

2. Two equally large communities derive all their revenue from proportional income taxes on average family income, which is $10,000 in one of the communities but $20,000 in the other. Find the tax rate each community must levy to raise $500 per family of public spending. If a matching grant were given only to the poorer community, find the federal matching rate that would equalize tax prices between the two communities.

ELEVEN
TAX EXPENDITURES

Until now we have examined the benefits and costs of explicit spending programs. But there is another way in which governments can subsidize spending on various favored activities—through the tax system. If the income tax law allows taxpayers to deduct their expenses for charitable giving, mortgage interest, or whatever, taxpayers are subsidizing these activities just as if there were explicit spending programs in the same areas. That is the reason that the deductions in the federal income tax that favor particular activities are called tax expenditures.

The benefits and costs of tax expenditures can be analyzed in the same way as the benefits and costs of explicit government expenditures. Taxpayers give up something, those with a demand for the activity who benefit from the lower effective price because of the tax deduction gain, and other groups either gain or lose as spending on the activity changes.

In this chapter we examine the benefits and costs of tax expenditures. We first discuss the general advantages and disadvantages of this form of subsidy. We enumerate some of the large tax expenditures in the United States, a list common to many developed countries, and we show how to do a benefit-cost analysis of the third largest of these tax expenditures, the deductibility of state and local tax payments on the federal income tax.

GENERAL ADVANTAGES AND DISADVANTAGES
OF THE TAX EXPENDITURE APPROACH

The obvious difference between explicit expenditures and tax expenditures is that in the former case, the federal government is actually running the program, while in the latter case some other agency—another government, a private charity, or some other private sector agency—is. Some claim that the private sector is more efficient, and private agencies are easier to kill if they are not working well. On the other side, it can also be argued that any higher cost for federal agencies is due to the fact that they may feel more need to serve all potential clients, not just those favored by the supporters of the local government or private agency.

There is also a difference between the amount of spending on the activity and increases per dollar of cost to taxpayers. For explicit federal expenditures this gain in spending equals the taxpayer cost by definition. Not so for tax expenditures, which work by lowering taxable income. Assume first there is a proportional income tax at rate t where all taxpayers itemize deductions. With no allowable deductions a particular taxpayer would have paid tY dollars in income taxes, where Y is the taxpayer's income. If a certain activity is deductible, that same taxpayer would pay $t(Y-D-\Delta D)$ in income taxes, where D is the amount the taxpayer would have spent on the activity without the deduction and ΔD is the increase in spending as a result of the deduction. The increase in spending on the activity is thus ΔD, and the cost to the federal treasury is $t(D + \Delta D)$.

From the particular taxpayer's point of view, the cost of spending on the activity has gone from 1, the cost without deductibility, to $(1-t)$, the cost with deductibility. The increase in spending on the activity then depends on the elasticity of taxpayer response to the price change occasioned by the deduction. Using initial values as reference points, the percentage change in spending is $\Delta D/D$ and the percentage change in price is $-t$. Hence the elasticity (E) is

(1) $E = (\Delta D/D)/(-t) = -\Delta D/tD$

Since the gain in spending on the activity is ΔD and the taxpayer cost is $t(D + \Delta D)$, the ratio of gain in spending to taxpayer cost, which is one for an explicit expenditure, is

(2) $\text{Gain}/\text{Cost} = \Delta D/t(D + \Delta D) = -EtD/tD(1-Et) = -E/(1-Et)$

To try out a few values, if the elasticity is zero, there is no gain in spending on the activity. Here the deduction simply gives taxpayers a rebate for what they would have done anyway. It is a simple transfer from all taxpayers to those who itemize deductions. If the elasticity is close to -1 and the tax rate is low, the gain/cost ratio is close to one, about what it is for explicit expenditures. But if spending on the activity is very responsive to price with an elasticity more negative than -1, the gain/cost ration is greater than one. In this sense, the deduction approach yields more spending on the activity per dollar of taxpayer cost the more negative this elasticity.

As was shown in Chapter 5, things get even more complicated with a progressive income tax, where the average tax rate rises with income. In this case, the t in the preceding expressions equals the appropriate marginal tax rate facing each taxpayer, and because some taxpayers do not have enough deductions to make itemizing worthwhile, there is no reduction in price at all for nonitemizers. Then we have a situation where the tax deduction causes uneven reductions in prices and increases in ΔD across taxpayers:

> There is no price reduction and change in D at all for nonitemizers.
>
> Low-income groups with low marginal tax rates get a small price reduction and have a small change in D.
>
> High-income groups with high marginal tax rates get a large price reduction and could have a high change in D.

The implications of this situation are that the activities favored by tax expenditures are likely to be those that appeal to high-income, high marginal tax rate, taxpayers. This provides another contrast to spending on explicit expenditures, which would be voted on by the entire legislature whether or not the politicians represent voters that itemize.

Beyond these general statements, it is hard to say very much. The activities supported by tax expenditures, enumerated in the next section, are so diverse that any differences between explicit expenditures and tax expenditures depend on the particular conditions of the item being subsidized. Those same differences also make it impossible to do a generic benefit-cost analysis of a tax expenditure—the reason that in this chapter we only do a benefit-cost analysis of one particular tax expenditure.

EXISTING TAX EXPENDITURES

Although the concept of a tax expenditure is clear in principle, it has always been hard to compile a list of numbers, as one might do on the spending side of the budget. There are two reasons:

> Tax expenditures can only be defined with reference to the revenue that a normal tax system would bring in. Thus any provision in the tax code must be classified according to whether it is a tax expenditure (a deviation from the normal system) or merely part of the definition of that normal system.

Tax expenditures cannot be added up. If one is allowed to exclude a certain share of income from tax, one's propensity to itemize, one's marginal tax rate, and the value of any other deduction also change.

In view of these caveats, lists of tax expenditures always come with long explanations, and never come with overall totals. The list shown in Table 11.1 omits the long explanations and does give a total, but the caveats should be borne in mind—that total is a very crude approximation. In any case, the table does list the ten largest tax expenditures for the U.S. federal government, in terms of revenue loss, in fiscal 1989. The numbers, shown as a percentage share of GNP, are a good bit smaller than earlier because of the Tax Reform Act of 1986 (TRA). TRA eliminated many of the largest tax expenditures, and then reduced the remaining numbers in two other ways:

Since the standard deduction has increased, many fewer taxpayers are expected to itemize deductions. Before TRA about 32 percent of all tax returns claimed itemized deductions; by fiscal 1989 that share is expected to be about 25 percent.

Since marginal tax rates were lowered, the revenue loss from each particular itemized deduction is, too. Before TRA the marginal tax rate averaged 31 percent for all itemizers; by fiscal 1989 it should be down to about 19 percent.

But even with the changes, the U.S. federal treasury is still expected to lose more than 5 percent of GNP in fiscal 1989 because of tax expenditures. The largest by a big margin is the fact that pension earnings of employees either are not taxed or have the tax deferred. Other significant exclusions from taxable income are for employer health benefits, state and local interest,

TABLE 11.1   Significant U.S. Tax Expenditures, 1989 (Revenue Loss, as a Percentage Share of Gross National Product)

ITEM	SHARE
Exclusion of pension earnings	1.1
Deduction of mortgage interest	0.6
Deduction of state and local taxes	0.5
Exclusion of employer health benefits	0.5
Exclusion of state and local interest	0.3
Exclusion of social security benefits	0.3
Exclusion of capital gains at death	0.2
Deduction of charitable contributions	0.2
Exclusion of life insurance interest	0.1
Deduction of child care expenses	0.1
Total	5.6

Source: Office of Management and Budget, *Special Analysis: The Budget of the United States Government for Fiscal Year 1989.*

social security benefits, capital gains at death, and life insurance interest. Other significant deductions used in the determination of tax liability are for mortgage interest, state and local taxes, charitable contributions, and child care expenses.

THE DEDUCTIBILITY OF STATE AND LOCAL TAXES

The third largest of these tax expenditures, anticipated to cost the federal treasury $28 billion (0.5 percent of GNP) in 1989, involves the deductibility of state and local taxes. Federal taxpayers who itemize deductions can deduct their income and property tax payments to state and local governments from their federal taxable income, and so reduce their cost of state and local public goods below the cost of private goods. Because of the large revenue loss and the fact that tax deductibility would appear to subsidize spending by high-income itemizers, an initial Treasury Department tax reform plan proposed elimination of this tax expenditure. After much analytical and political debate, and many halfway proposals, deductibility was retained for income and property taxes but not for sales taxes in TRA.

Should this deduction have been retained? It is difficult to do a benefit-cost analysis of state and local tax deductibility because of three factors:

Since not all taxpayers itemize deductions, not all voters in a community will vote for increased public spending as a result of the deduction.

Since business taxes assessed by state and local governments are a cost of doing business and as such would be deductible, the deductibility of personal taxes can be said to keep these two revenue sources on the same footing.

Since the tax price of public goods for a high-income itemizer is higher in low-income communities, there is a possibility that the tax deduction will lower the price of public goods more in low-income communities, thus encouraging some mixing of income groups within communities.

We now show how each of these complications might be dealt with.

The Impact on State and Local
Public Spending

Suppose there are two types of voters in a community, low-income voters, who do not itemize deductions, and high-income voters who do. Initially state and local taxes are not deductible, but then they are made deductible. What would happen to state and local public spending?

Since state and local spending decisions are arrived at publicly, the question turns out to be complicated. It depends on how many voters have their desired public spending increased by how much by the tax deduction. The left panel of Figure 11.1 shows the case where there are no spillover

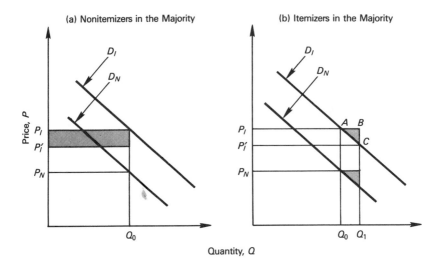

(a) Nonitemizers in the Majority

(b) Itemizers in the Majority

(a) When nonitemizers are in the majority, there is no change in quantity of public services demanded and no efficiency loss. The shaded area is a simple transfer from federal taxpayers to itemizers.
(b) When itemizers are in the majority, the quantity of public services demanded rises to Q_1. The efficiency losses from the change in deductability are represented by the shaded triangles.

FIGURE 11.1   Distortions due to Tax Deductibility

benefits of public spending outside the community and where before the deduction the community assesses perfect Lindahl tax shares, so that all voters favor the existing amount of spending. The demand functions for public goods for high-income itemizers and nonitemizers respectively are shown as D_I and D_N, with the high-income itemizers having a higher demand because of the presumed positive income effect, and also facing a higher tax price for public services. Apart from these differences, all voters are alike—all itemizers have the same demand function and face the same price schedule, and all nonitemizers have the same demand function and face the same price schedule.

In the left panel the homogeneous group of nonitemizers is assumed to have a voting majority. The introduction of tax deductibility does not change the spending demand of these nonitemizers at all, and because they are in a voting majority, deductibility does not change the community's desired spending. This is the case considered above where ΔD is zero—the tax deduction is a simple transfer of the shaded rectangle from all federal taxpayers to the high-income itemizers in a voting minority in this community. A benefit-cost analysis shows simply this transfer, with no overall efficiency gain or loss.

In the right panel we change things to give the homogeneous group of itemizers the voting majority. In this case the homogeneous itemizers will all desire an increase in spending from Q_0 to Q_1, and because of their voting majority, that will move community spending the same amount. Federal taxpayers now lose a slightly larger amount than before, $P_1BCP'_I$, because they now have to pay the deductibility cost on the expanded public output. The itemizers gain the consumer surplus trapezoid, $P_IACP'_I$. Hence for each itemizer there is a social loss of the top shaded triangle. Each nonitemizer loses the bottom shaded triangle, the difference between the nonitemizer's marginal cost and marginal benefit summed over the quantity change. The overall efficiency loss is then the sum of the top triangle for all itemizers and the bottom triangle for all nonitemizers.

This analysis may sound complex enough, but remember how simple we have made it. We have assumed that all itemizers are homogeneous, that all nonitemizers are homogeneous, and that all voters face perfect Lindahl tax shares. None of these assumptions are very realistic. And once they are relaxed, things become even more complicated. If tax shares are not Lindahl perfect, for example, nonitemizers might well demand more public services than itemizers even if nonitemizers are in the minority. In such a case deductibility could lead to gains for nonitemizers as well as itemizers. One can easily cook up many other such complications.

There is no way to work all this out short of going through data on individual voters. I made one such attempt to do this by using a survey of voters in Michigan in 1978, finding desired local spending and the impact on tax price of changes in deductibility, assuming a slope of the demand function, and working everything out.[1] The basic results are given in Table 11.2.

Beginning with the left column, this study grouped voters from Detroit, a low-income area, the Detroit suburbs, a high-income area, and the rest of the state, an area with an average income close to the overall average for the

TABLE 11.2   Impact of the Tax Deduction on Desired Local Government Spending Michigan, 1978

AREA	AVERAGE INCOME	SHARE OF VOTERS ITEMIZING (%)	CHANGE IN DESIRED SPENDING (%)	AVERAGE KALDOR-HICKS DISTORTION (%)*
Detroit	12,556	39.6	0	0
Detroit Suburbs	21,574	62.0	10.0	1.2
Rest of State	16,656	44.8	5.4	0.6
Total	17,544	49.0	5.0	0.6

*Average Kaldor-Hicks efficiency loss per voter computed as in Figure 11.1, as a percentage of expenditures.

Source: Edward M. Gramlich, "The Deductibility of State and Local Taxes," *National Tax Journal*, December, 1985.

state. We have already said that before TRA 32 percent of the tax returns claimed itemized deductions. That number was higher in the late 1970s when the standard deduction was lower, and it is also higher because a higher share of taxpayers who are of voting age itemize. When the sample was confined to voters alone, 49 percent of voters across the whole state itemized deductions. But because of income differences, only 39.6 percent of voters in Detroit itemized, while 62 percent of voters itemized in the high-income suburbs of Detroit.

Working out the individual spending demands with and without deductibility for each voter in the sample, and then computing the median for the sample with and without deductibility, we see that Detroit is a good example of the left panel of Figure 11.1. Median spending demand is not increased as a result of income tax deductibility, and one would expect no Kaldor-Hicks efficiency gain or loss there.

For the rest of the state, and in particular for the high-income suburbs of Detroit, things are different. Now deductibility raises median spending demand by up to 10 percent, and causes average per voter Kaldor-Hicks efficiency losses of up to 1.2 percent of expenditures. On pure efficiency grounds, income tax deductibility would fail the benefit-cost in these upper-income areas, though by fairly modest amounts.

The study did not include spillover benefits to those outside the particular area, but these could modify conclusions slightly. If the rise in spending in some communities does benefit outsiders, the overall efficiency loss would be less. On the other hand, were distributional considerations added to the evaluation, the verdict would be much more negative. Federal taxpayers are giving up revenue for the benefit of high-income voters in high-income communities, but not for low-income voters in low-income communities. Deductibility is the opposite of the compensatory revenue sharing plans mentioned in Chapter 10—it subsidizes communities and taxpayers with high incomes but not those with low incomes.

The Impact on Types of Taxes

A second type of shift deductibility could make is on the revenue side of the budget. If some taxes are made deductible and not others, the introduction of deductibility could alter the types of taxes used by state and local governments, and create yet new gainers and losers.

State and local taxes assessed on businesses have always been treated as a valid cost of doing business, and they have always been deductible. If personal and property taxes are not deductible, there would then be an incentive for states and localities to finance their expenditures by business taxes. This in turn would raise prices, generate consumer surplus losses, and so on down the chain. The removal of tax deductibility could then make consumers worse off in a benefit-cost sense.

But only if the removal of deductibility causes governments to alter their propensity to use different types of taxes. And it turns out to be very difficult to tell whether deductibility does cause government revenue shifts. Both personal and property taxes have been deductible since the personal income tax was first passed back in 1913, and it is impossible to get direct empirical observations on what would happen if personal and property taxes were not deductible. There has been a gradual tightening of the deductibility provisions over time—license fees were made nondeductible in 1964, gas taxes in 1978, and sales taxes in 1986—but nobody has been able to discern any predictable revenue shifts as a result of these changes. In fact, many states actually increased their sales tax after it was made nondeductible in 1986.

Some economists have tried to estimate empirical relationships based not on deductibility, but on some other causes of variation of the cost of particular taxes to local citizens. One such cause is the fact that some states can export some taxes to outsiders—a sales tax in Florida. Another such is that some local taxes are and are not deductible against their state taxes. As one would expect when the estimates are indirect, without much independent variation in the policy under investigation, the various estimates range widely—some economists report a strong sensitivity of taxes to deductibility provisions; others report very little. Pending some greater resolution of this empirical issue, there is little that can be done here in our benefit-cost analysis of deductibility.

The Impact on Community Income Mixing

Chapter 10 showed how taxpayers of a given income can face different tax prices for their public services in different communities. A particular taxpayer living in a community with extensive personal or business taxable wealth would face low property tax rates to support a standard public school system; one with the same income and wealth but living in a poor community would face much higher tax rates to support the very same school system.

This fact complicates the analysis of property or income tax deductibility. If taxes are deductible, the high tax price in the poor community might not bite so much, and there would be more incentive for wealthy taxpayers to remain in, or move to, poor communities. Deductibility might in this roundabout way cause more community income mixing, or less community stratification by income. And if it did that, a further set of gainers and losers would be added to the benefit-cost analysis.

As with the previous impacts, it turns out to be rather tricky to trace out this chain of events. High-income itemizing taxpayers face a higher tax price in poor communities, but they might not get more gains from deductibility than in rich communities because the quantity of public services purchased, and on which the deduction can be taken, is less.

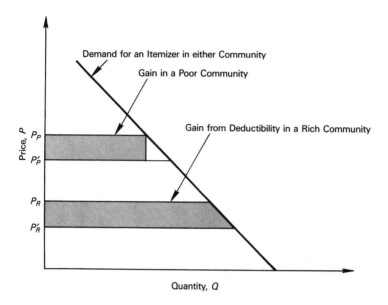

A rich taxpayer living in a poor community gains the top shaded area because of deductibility.

A rich taxpayer living in a rich community gains the bottom shaded area.

Which gain is larger depends on the elasticity of demand for public goods over the interval and the degree to which public output changes in either community.

FIGURE 11.2   Migration Incentives from Tax Deductibility

The point is demonstrated in Figure 11.2. The demand function shown is that for the high-income itemizer, assumed to be the same demand function whether this itemizer lives in a rich or a poor community. But if the itemizer lives in a poor community, he or she faces the high tax price P_P. At this high tax price, the itemizer, and the poor community, is assumed to consume the lower amount of public services. If property taxes are now made deductible, this itemizer will be in a minority, and we assume there is no change in the quantity of public services consumed. The gain to the itemizer from deductibility is the top rectangle.

In the rich community, the itemizer faces a lower tax price, consumes more public goods, and finds that the majority of voters want to consume more local public service output when there is property tax deductibility. The gain is the bottom consumer trapezoid. Is the gain in the poor community from deductibility greater than the gain in the rich community? There is no general answer—it depends on the disparity in tax price, what happens to the median voter in each community, and on the elasticity of demand for public services with respect to the tax price. Using the Michigan data referred to earlier, the average gain for high-income itemizers from deductibility is about 5 percent of tax payments greater in the poor community (Detroit), less than one percent of the annual income of this high-income itemizer. There could be some effect on income mixing, but it seems unlikely that differentials this small would influence living patterns very much.

Hence to do an overall benefit-cost analysis of state and local tax deductibility in poor communities like Detroit, it would seem to have no efficiency impact on spending and represent a simple transfer from federal taxpayers to high-income itemizers in a voting minority. In wealthy communities like the Detroit suburbs, it would still represent a transfer from federal taxpayers to high-income itemizers, but this time with efficiency costs of from one-half to one percent of expenditures. In neither community is there a clear impact on the composition of revenues and shifting tax burdens, though the jury is still out on this question. And it seems pretty unlikely to cause further gains and losses through migration. Deductibility comes out a slight loser on pure efficiency grounds, and a bigger loser when these efficiency changes are adjusted for distributional considerations.

SUMMARY

This chapter has analyzed tax expenditures—attempts by the government to induce spending in different areas through the tax system. These tax expenditures can, if the elasticity of the affected item is high enough, stimulate more spending per dollar of revenue loss than explicit expenditures. But if the elasticity is low, they can also stimulate less, and have the further disadvantage of only stimulating increased demand for those who benefit from greater income tax deductions. If someone is so poor that their taxable income is low or that they do not itemize deductions, tax expenditures will stimulate no more activity and simply represent a transfer from all federal taxpayers to high-income taxpayers who itemize deductions.

Some of the important tax expenditures in the United States involve the exclusion of employer fringe benefits—for pensions and health—and the deduction of expenses such as mortgage interest. Although it is impossible to do a generic benefit-cost analysis of this mixed bag of items, an analysis of the third-largest tax expenditure, the deductibility of state and local taxes from the federal income tax, arrives at fairly negative results. Deductibility of taxes is seen to generate no efficiency gains or losses, and to be mainly a transfer to high-income taxpayers, in areas such as Detroit where only a minority of taxpayers itemize. In richer areas, such as the high-income suburbs of Detroit, deductibility is still a transfer to high-income taxpayers, but this time it is with slight efficiency losses as well.

NOTES

[1]A more complete description of all these steps can be found in Edward M. Gramlich, "The Deductibility of State and Local Taxes," *National Tax Journal*, December 1985.

PROBLEMS

1. Suppose that the tax rate is 25 percent. Find the ratio of the gain in spending on the activity to the taxpayer cost for a taxpayer elasticity of giving of 0, -.5, -1, -1.5, -2. Find the elasticity for which this ratio of gain in spending to the taxpayer cost is exactly the same as for explicit expenditures.

2. Referring to problem 1 in Chapter 3, you have three consumers with the inverse demand functions for public services

    $$P_A = 26 - Q_A$$

    $$P_B = 28 - Q_B$$

    $$P_C = 33 - Q_C$$

    The cost per unit of public services is borne equally by the three consumers and is 60 without the deductibility of community taxes. A proportional national income tax with a 15 percent rate is now introduced, but community taxes are made deductible against this income tax. Community spending is always determined by the median spending demand of the three consumers.

    a. Find community spending, the dead-weight burden for each consumer, and the cost to national taxpayers if none of these taxpayers can itemize. Call this the base case.

    b. As compared with this base case, find community spending, the gain or loss to each consumer, and the cost to national taxpayers if only *C* can itemize. Do a Kaldor-Hicks evaluation of this change from the base case.

    c. As compared with the base case, find community spending, the gain or loss to each consumer, and the cost to national taxpayers if only *A* can itemize. Do a Kaldor-Hicks evaluation of this change from the base case.

    d. As compared with the base case, find community spending, the gain or loss to each consumer, and the cost to national taxpayers if only *B* can itemize. Do a Kaldor-Hicks evaluation of this change from the base case.

    e. Why do the results for individuals, national taxpayers, and the aggregate differ so much, depending on who can itemize?

CHAPTER TWELVE
SOCIAL REGULATION

Chapter 11 looked at how to extend the methodology of benefit-cost analysis to situations where the government does not carry out explicit spending programs but just makes available a tax subsidy to support some activity. In this chapter we extend the methodology further. Now we consider cases where the government regulates private behavior, simply requiring that some private agency do something. The benefits of such regulations are that certain harmful activities are no longer engaged in; the costs are the compliance costs borne by the private sector. One can do the usual sort of benefit-cost analysis to compare them.

There are many types of government regulation. In the nineteenth century the federal government first began to regulate the pricing behavior of railroads and trucks, later extending its regulatory scope to communications and air traffic. The general rationale for such regulations was the natural monopoly problem discussed in Chapter 2. The problem, as it developed over time, was that often the activities being regulated really were not natural monopolies at all—different modes of transportation must compete with each other, and with foreign providers. Moreover, the regulatory agencies often became captured by the industries they were supposed to regulate, allegedly keeping prices high and blocking new entry. In recent years many of these forms of regulation—for air traffic, railroads, trucks, and telephones—have been stripped away and these formerly regulated industries now operate with almost as much freedom as most other industries.

But another type of regulation has taken its place. Rather than just limiting price charged, as in the older style regulation of supposed natural monopolies, these newer style regulations try to prohibit certain undesirable byproducts of the production process—unsafe workplaces, air and water pollution, employment discrimination, unsafe consumer products. The past two decades have seen a rapid expansion of these social regulations. New regulatory agencies have also been introduced—the Occupational Safety and Health Agency (OSHA), the Environmental Protection Agency (EPA), the Equal Employment Opportunity Commission, the Consumer Product Safety Commission. Lately there has been some backing away from what was felt to be an excessive amount of social regulation, symbolized by President Reagan's only partially successful attempt to apply benefit-cost analysis to these regulatory activities.

In this chapter we see how one might apply benefit-cost analysis to social regulations. We first consider a model of occupational safety, where there is a regular market transaction between the injurer and the potential victim—the wage paid—but where there are no spillovers from regulatory actions to other firms. We then consider the reverse case of atmospheric pollution, where there is no regular market transaction between the injurer and the victim, but where there are extensive spillovers. The regulatory issues differ between the two cases, but the logic of the benefit-cost analysis turns out to be quite similar. We then go on to examine a specific regulation for occupational safety, the noise standard of OSHA, and a specific regulation for air pollution, the long-debated attempt to limit acid rain.

REGULATION WITH A MARKET TRANSACTION BUT NO SPILLOVERS

The model used here is where a firm engaged in production is injuring those it regularly transacts with—either through unsafe workplaces that harm its workers or unsafe products that harm its consumers. This regular transaction implies that there is already a way that the potential victims can protect themselves—workers can quit their jobs and work somewhere else; consumers can buy another product. As a result, it is not so clear that the market needs any regulation at all, and whether it does becomes the central benefit-cost question. At the same time, the lack of any regulatory spillovers means that the whole issue can be decided between the government and the firm, without bringing any other firms into the analysis.

Using the worker safety example, in Chapter 4 we saw that a careful examination of wage differentials was one way to value human lives—workers get compensation for engaging in risky activities, and the value of this compensation can be used to infer their own implicit valuation of their life (though perhaps only a lower bound estimate, as was discussed). The same argument suggests that workers will also demand higher wages to compensate for the risk of injury, and again empirical studies bear this out, although less strongly than when the injuries are fatalities.[1]

These wage differentials imply that worker accidents are costly to firms, and that firms will have a motive for preventing them even in the absence of any social regulation. Precisely the same statement can be made on the consumer side, if unsafe products can be shown to sell for a lower price than safe products. Whether firms engage in the optimal amount of accident prevention on either the worker or the consumer side is another matter. That depends on the degree to which wages are bid up or consumer prices are bid down.[2]

Suppose that there are two firms, one that is perfectly safe and pays a wage of W_2 and one that is not perfectly safe and pays a wage of W_1. Apart from the risk of injury, jobs in the two firms are exactly alike, requiring the same skill, having the same other working conditions, and so forth. Every time a worker gets injured, she loses h percent of her wages in the form of medical costs or days out sick, and for now we assume that she bears the entire burden of that cost. Hence the three possible outcomes for the worker are:

Work in firm 2 and not be injured, gain W_2.
Work in firm 1 and not be injured, gain W_1.
Work in firm 1 and be injured, gain $W_1(1-h)$.

If the accident rate in firm 1 is a, the expected wage in that firm, $E(W_1)$, can be computed by taking the weighted average of the probability of safety times that outcome and the probability of accident times that outcome

$$(1) E(W_1) = (1-a)(W_1) + aW_1(1-h) = (1-ah)W_1$$

If, for example, the accident rate is one-half, the expected wage is just the simple average of the no-injury wage and the injury wage.

If workers are neither risk lovers nor risk-averse but simply try to compare expected wages in all lines of work, and if they have good information about a and h, the market will equilibrate at the point where the expected wage for each firm is the same

$$(2) \ W_2 = E(W_1) = (1-ah)W_1$$

so that

$$(3) \ W_1 = W_2/(1-ah)$$

Since $(1-ah)$ is less than one, the risky wage W_1 is above the safe wage W_2 by just the amount necessary to compensate workers for their risk of accident in firm 1. When this model is expanded to include many firms with many different accident rates for the same type of work, actual wages paid by these firms should range on a continuum according to the firms' a and h values. And, to relate this equation to the discussion of Chapter 4, when we tried there to find the compensation a worker would require to undertake a risk of death, we knew a, W_1, and W_2 and worked backward to compute the implicit h workers placed on their own lives.

The cost of the unsafe workplace to firms is then simply the extra wages the firm has to pay to induce workers to work there. If the firm hires L_1 workers, this "consequences" cost (CC) is

(4) $CC = L_1(W_1-W_2) = L_1 W_2(1/(1-ah)-1) = ahL_1 W_2/(1-ah)$

This equation is drawn in Figure 12.1 as the CC curve. When a on the horizontal axis equals zero, the firm is perfectly safe, and the CC value read from (4) is zero. As a increases, the numerator rises proportionally with a, but the denominator declines, so CC rises more than proportionally with

FIGURE 12.1   Total Costs of Accident Prevention

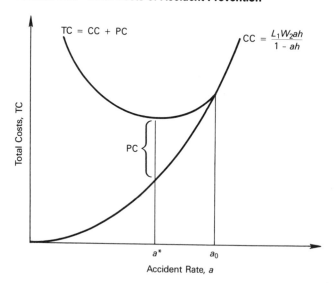

Total cost (TC) = Consequences cost (CC) + Prevention cost (PC)
TC minimized at a^*

At a^* $\dfrac{\delta TC}{\delta a} = \dfrac{\delta PC}{\delta a} + \dfrac{\delta CC}{\delta a} = 0$

$-\dfrac{\delta PC}{\delta a} = \dfrac{\delta CC}{\delta a} = \dfrac{L_1 W_2 h}{(1-ah)^2}$

increases in a. For those with some calculus, the latter condition is simply that both first and second derivatives of CC with respect to a are positive.

Before going on, we can inquire about factors that would shift this CC curve. If either the size of the work force required by firm 1 or the general level of wages in firm 2 rose, the consequences of injury for firm 1 would rise for each accident rate, and the CC curve would pivot up. The reason is that firm 1 is being forced to pay compensating differentials either to more workers (L_1) or on a higher wage base (W_2). More important for our theory, if workers became more risk-averse and began insisting on a higher premium for bearing the risk of injury, their own psychological h would rise and the CC curve would again pivot up.

Paying for accidents is only one of the options open to the firm: the other is to prevent them from happening in the first place. If firm 1 also spends on accident prevention, we can define its total accident-related costs, TC, as the sum of its consequences costs, CC, and its prevention costs, PC

(5) $TC = PC + CC$

These prevention costs are then added on to the consequences costs in Figure 12.1 to derive the total costs. Total costs are shown as TC in the figure, with PC equaling the difference between TC and CC by definition. Say a_0 is the accident rate the firm would have if it spent nothing at all on prevention, where $PC = 0$. Moving left from that point, TC is higher than CC by just the amount spent on prevention. Notice that this PC curve is drawn as if there were diminishing marginal returns to accident prevention—the first few are cheap to prevent; after that it gets more costly. Most engineering studies of firms' production processes confirm this general property.

From the figure it is obvious what a profit-maximizing firm will do. If all other aspects of its production behavior (output, prices, labor input, etc.) are unaffected by worker accidents, it can maximize profits by minimizing accident-related costs. It finds this minimum where the TC curve is minimized, at a^*. At any accident rate to the right of a^*, the firm would save more on consequences by reducing accidents than it would spend on prevention. At any accident rate to the left of a^*, the firm would save more on prevention than it spends on consequences.[3]

Hence safety freaks can find some good news and some bad news in this model. The good news is that even with no government regulation at all, the firm is guided by the invisible hand of the free market to prevent some accidents. The bad news is that there will not be a totally safe work environment—the optimizing firm is encouraged to compare the costs of preventing accidents and letting them occur to find the optimal accident rate, which will not normally be zero.

The matters dealt with here are easier to see if we switch from the total costs of accident prevention in Figure 12.1 to marginal benefits and costs,

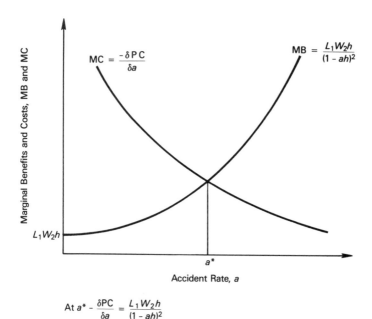

At a^* $-\dfrac{\delta PC}{\delta a} = \dfrac{L_1 W_2 h}{(1-ah)^2}$

　　　　　MC = MB

The a^* shown here is exactly the same as shown in Figure 12.1.

FIGURE 12.2　Marginal Benefits and Costs of Accident Prevention

shown in Figure 12.2. The marginal benefit to a firm in preventing accidents is the saving on consequences costs, or the change in CC with respect to a unit change in the accident rate. From calculus we have

$$(6)\ MB = \delta CC/\delta a = \delta[ahL_1W_2/(1-ah)]/\delta a = hL_1W_2/(1-ah)^2$$

This curve is drawn on Figure 12.2 as the MB curve. When a is zero, its value is the intercept, hL_1W_2. Again as a rises, the denominator falls and MB rises disproportionately.

On the cost side, the marginal cost of prevention is the increase in PC as the accident rate falls by one unit, or $-\delta PC/\delta a$. Again from calculus, we know that when TC is minimized in Figure 12.1, $\delta TC/\delta a = 0$. Substituting into (5) we have

$$(7)\ 0 = \delta TC/\delta a = \delta PC/\delta a + \delta CC/\delta a$$

This means that

$$(8)\ MB = \delta CC/\delta a = -\delta PC/\delta a = MC$$

With these changes, we can convert the total cost diagram of Figure 12.1 to a marginal benefit, marginal cost diagram of accident prevention, shown in Figure 12.2. The a^* that minimizes TC in Figure 12.1 is precisely the same value that equates MB and MC in Figure 12.2. As before, when a is above a^*, the MB from accident prevention—the cost of the higher wage differentials—is greater than the relatively cheap cost of prevention and the firm is led to more and more prevention, until the rising marginal cost of this accident prevention equals the falling marginal benefit represented by the smaller wage costs of allowing accidents to happen.

We have seen that the accident rate a^* is the one that maximizes firm profits. Is it also the right accident rate from society's standpoint? That depends on whether workers had the right information on a and h to make good decisions, and enough bargaining power to bid the wage for the risky firm above that for the safe firm. When workers were short of either information or bargaining power in Chapter 4, we found that market wage differentials could undervalue human lives. Here if workers are short of either information or bargaining power, market wage differentials could lead to too little accident prevention.

To see how this works, refer to Figure 12.3. Suppose now that workers do not have good information on either a or h, so they charge too low a wage

FIGURE 12.3   Market and Social Benefits and Costs of Accident Prevention

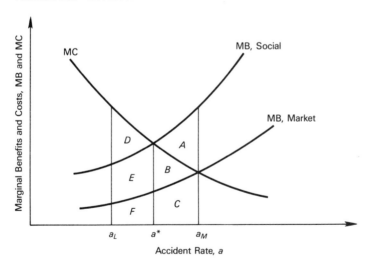

As the accident rate is lowered from market rate of a_M to social optimum rate a^*, the gain is area $(A + B + C)$, while the cost is area $(B + C)$. The net gain is area A.

But as the accident rate is lowered from the social optimum rate of a^* to the low accident rate of a_L, the gain is area $(E + F)$ while the cost is area $(D + E + F)$. The net loss is area D.

differential to firm 1—the true cost of accidents to workers is greater than that implied by the $W_1 - W_2$ observed in the market. In this case there will be two MB curves, one based on market wage differentials and one based on the true social cost of accidents. The right accident rate from the point of view of society is still a^*, but since workers undercharge firms for accident risk, firms will go to the accident rate a_M.

This model gives the basic case for regulation when there exists a regular transaction between the firm and the potentially injured party. If the potentially injured party, whether a worker or a consumer, is well-informed about the risks and has bargaining power, the market will work in the usual way to give the right amount of accident prevention. Adam Smith's invisible hand is alive and well. If workers or consumers do not have enough information to act in their long-run best interests, or enough bargaining power, firms will be led to too little accident prevention.

The same reasoning illustrates how one might do a benefit-cost analysis of a regulation. Suppose first that the market is not working well, the existing accident rate is a_M, and the social optimal accident rate is a^*. The government could then force the firm to get its act together and lower its accident rate to a^*. The benefits of moving from a_M to a^* are given by the area under the social marginal benefits curve, area $(A + B + C)$. The costs are the added prevention costs that the government has forced on the firm, the area under the MC curve, area $(B + C)$. The net gain from this regulation is area A.

But of course the government can overregulate. Suppose now that the market is working well already, the firm already had the social optimum accident rate a^*, but the government then forces the firm to lower its accident rate still further to the low rate a_L. The gain of the new tightening of the regulation is the area under the MB curve over the interval from a^* to a_L, area $(E + F)$. The cost is the area under the MC curve over the same interval, area $(D + E + F)$. This time the net loss is area D.

Social Insurance

Government regulation is not the only way, or perhaps not even the best way, to correct the market inefficiency of underprevention of accidents. Suppose there were social insurance for workers who were injured, as most developed countries now have in the form of worker compensation systems. A perfectly functioning worker compensation system will be defined as one that compensates workers the full accident cost, h, when they get injured, financing the expected present value of this compensation out of a trust fund that charges firms on an "experience-rated" basis for their accidents. Firm 2, our safe firm, has no accidents and has to pay nothing to our worker compensation fund under a perfect experience-rated system. Firm 1, our risky firm, has to reimburse the fund the full present value cost of the compensation it pays under a perfect experience-rated system.

Most actual worker compensation systems fall short of this perfect ideal on both counts:

> They do not pay the full cost of accidents to workers—they generally pay more than is appropriate to some workers and less than is appropriate to others.
>
> The premia they charge firms are not fully experience-rated—they generally charge less than is appropriate to some firms and more than is appropriate to others.[4]

Just to see how worker compensation might work, however, let us assume away these defects and suppose that our worker compensation fund compensates and charges appropriately.

Such a worker compensation system eliminates the need for workers to earn more from firm 1—workers have nothing to fear in working there because they will be compensated fully for any accidents incurred. But it does not eliminate the consequences costs of accidents to firm 1—in fact, by charging an experience-rated premium, it forces firm 1 to pay the full cost of its accidents to the fund. This characteristic alone brings the market and the social MB schedules into equality with each other, and makes the invisible hand of the market again provide the proper amount of accident prevention. The market will work as long as firms are charged the full present value cost of accidents, and a perfectly functioning worker compensation system can be viewed as one way to make the market function well. Putting it another way, a perfectly functioning worker compensation system either has no effect on the accident rate, if workers already charge appropriate wage differentials, or it eliminates the market inefficiency, if workers do not charge appropriate wage differentials. For this reason, it can also eliminate the need for social regulation of worker safety.

So the basic case for regulation now hinges on whether workers have sufficient information and bargaining power to charge firms the full cost of their injuries, or if they do not, whether worker compensation funds compensate workers appropriately and charge firms the full experience-rated costs of their accidents. We will examine a specific real world case study shortly, but for now we might hypothesize that these conditions might well be fulfilled for minor, repetitious accidents and stable firms. But for major accidents or safety defects where the risks take a long time to develop—asbestos-related cancer being the best example—it is hard to see how workers could charge the right premium or worker compensation funds could either. Moreover, if firms enter and leave the industry, firms no longer in operation cannot very well be given the proper incentives to produce safely, or be charged the proper amount by the worker compensation fund.

Inputs or Outputs?

The model so far has characterized the government regulation by the accident rate, whether a^*, a_M, or some other rate. In fact, things are not this simple, and there is a real question of how the government should regulate occupational safety.

There are two broad approaches:

Regulate outputs. Keep records of firm safety performance over time and tax it, such as through rises in its experience-rated premium, if it permits too many accidents.

Regulate inputs. Inspect and monitor firms' actual production process, prohibiting the use of harmful substances or dangerous processes.

The basic argument for the output approach is to leave the firm as the master of its own destiny. For good social reasons it is told that it will be charged a certain amount for its accidents, and it then goes on to do the optimizing calculation on this basis. It can seek out the cheapest way to prevent accidents, and find the minimum total cost of prevention given now the right market signals from a social standpoint. Over time, it can even set its engineers to work to find cheaper ways to prevent accidents, which in turn can shift down the MC curve, and lead to more safety, and cheaper safety, in the long run.

But there are some good arguments on the other side as well. Sometimes the cost of using hazardous substances—asbestos—are very high, so high that if the firm were charged, it would go out of business. Sometimes firms will disappear by the time the worker compensation fund calls the day of reckoning. And, it may be more costly for the enforcement agency to monitor accidents over time and work out all the present values than simply to inspect firms to see if they are using hazardous materials or dangerous procedures. In such cases it is easier and better to regulate inputs. Hence there is no one right answer to this question—it depends on relative costs and benefits. Indeed, one could actually do a benefit-cost analysis that compares the costs and benefits of the two different regulatory approaches.

Prices or Quantities?

A similar question involves the price or quantity approach to regulation. Should the government just charge firms an experience-rated premium for its accidents (a price approach), or should it enforce a certain maximum accident rate on firms (a quantity approach)?

If there is no uncertainty about the benefit or the cost schedule in Figure 12.3, it does not matter. The right accident rate is a^*, and the firm will go to this value if the government shifts up the MB schedule appropriately by a tax, or if the government simply forces the firm to bring its accident rate down to a^*. Either way, the firm is moving along the same MC schedule to the same optimum point.

But if there is uncertainty about either of these schedules, the answer is just as indefinite as for inputs and outputs. It depends on a comparison of the potential losses due to uncertainty.

Two opposing cases are shown in Figure 12.4. In both panels the accident rate a_M is the one that results with no worker compensation tax. The left panel shows the case of uncertainty on the cost side. Regulators figure the firm's prevention cost schedule will be given by the MC line, but they are not sure. The marginal physical costs of having the firm prevent accidents could be higher than expected, along the MC_H schedule, or lower, along the MC_L schedule. Whatever the case, if the tax is perfectly experience-rated, it will automatically provide the right amount of accident prevention at the intersection of the social MB curve and whatever MC curve happens to be in force. By contrast, the imposition of a quantity control on the accident rate, even if it is the accident rate that is socially optimal given the expected MC curve (a_R), will lead to the inefficiencies shown by the shaded triangles. If the prevention cost happens to be high, forcing the firm to a_R will lead to some uneconomic accident prevention where the marginal cost exceeds the marginal benefit (the top shaded triangle). If the prevention cost happens to be

FIGURE 12.4   Taxes or Regulations?

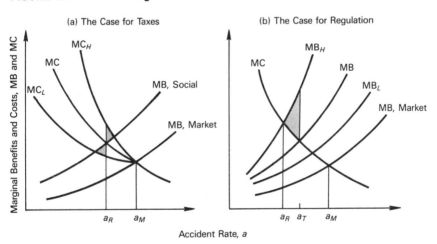

(a) When there is uncertainty about the cost of preventing accidents, a tax system that simply imposes the social costs of accidents on firms is usually the most efficient approach. Regulating firms to a_R will generate the top shaded dead-weight inefficiency if marginal prevention costs are higher than anticipated; the bottom shaded inefficiency if lower than anticipated.

(b) When there is uncertainty about the benefits, or consequences, of preventing accidents, a tax system imposing the MB schedule could lead to inefficiencies if the consequences of accidents are worse than expected (along the MB_H curve). In such a case it may be better to impose the low accident rate, a_R, until more is known.

low, forcing the firm to a_R will not induce it to prevent those accidents where the marginal benefit exceeds the marginal cost. Hence uncertainty about the costs of preventing accidents generally argues for the tax approach—just charge firms the cost of accidents and let them optimize.

But that is not the end of the story. Suppose now that there is perfect certainty about the costs of preventing accidents, but that there is uncertainty about the marginal benefits. A new substance or technique is introduced where proper experience-rated premium cannot yet be computed or charged. Compared to the free market outcome of a_M, the marginal benefits of prevention might be modest—given by the MB_L schedule—or dramatic—given by the MB_H schedule. In this case, even if the present value premium were computed correctly at MB on average, accidents could be too low or too high depending on the ultimate consequences, unknown at the time the worker compensation tax was actually imposed. In such a case there is an argument for simply preventing use of the new technique or substance until more is known about it. The conservative regulatory approach of enforcing the low accident rate of a_R, either directly or by preventing use of the new process until further study, will save the shaded triangle in some portion of the cases. That may not seem like much, but we could be talking about saved lives, where the true MB schedule turns out to be quite steeply upward-sloping and the shaded triangle very large.

In either case, the essence of the problem involves uncertainty. And generally uncertainty about both costs and benefits will be dispelled over time—firms will experiment with exactly how cheap it is to prevent accidents or not use particular substances and more will be known about the benefits of avoiding these substances. Appropriate taxes and/or quantity controls can then be instituted, and some of these issues may wane in importance.

Uniform or Particular Standards?

A final interesting question involving social regulation is that of whether standards should be particular to firms and industries or uniform across all firms and industries. This time a more definitive answer can be given. Even when the marginal benefits of accident prevention are the same across firms, there is no rationale for imposing uniform accident rates as long as the marginal cost of prevention differs by firm or industry.

The reasons are shown in Figure 12.5. In an industry or firm where accident prevention is costly, such as coal mining, the efficient accident rate is a_H; where it is cheap, such as college teaching, the efficient accident rate is a_L. A tax or worker compensation scheme will lead the two firms or industries to these accident rates, and we will observe different levels of accidents in the two.

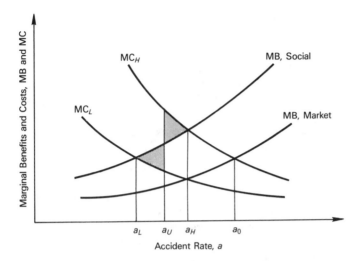

One approach is to tax firms for the consequences of accidents and have the firm where it is expensive to prevent accidents go to a_H and the firm where it is cheap go to a_L.

The alternative approach is to regulate both firms to the uniform rate a_U. That causes too much regulation in the high-cost firm and the top shaded triangle; too little regulation in the low-cost firm and the bottom shaded triangle.

FIGURE 12.5   Uniform or Particular Standards?

What if, instead, we forced all firms to the uniform accident rate a_U? This policy might appear to be fairer, but it is not, and it certainly is not economically efficient.

The market has already established fairness by letting workers be compensated for accidents, either before the fact by wage differentials or after the fact by social insurance. In either case, workers should be indifferent between working for the safe and the risky firms even if their accident rates differ.

Moreover, uniform standards will prove to be very inefficient, as is shown in the figure. There will be too much accident prevention where it is costly, too little where it is cheap. If the high cost firm were told to reduce its accidents from the optimal rate at a_H to the uniform rate a_U, the top shaded triangle gives the excess of marginal costs over benefits. Similarly, the cheap prevention firm will be underpreventing accidents, as shown by the bottom shaded triangle where marginal benefits exceed costs. Given the compensating wage differentials that already exist in the market, because of information or social insurance, establishing uniform accident rates in addition is regulatory overkill—high-cost firms will be going to enormous expense to prevent injuries, and low-cost firms will not be preventing accidents that could be prevented very cheaply.

REGULATION WITHOUT A MARKET TRANSACTION
BUT WITH SPILLOVERS

We now shift the focus to cases where there is no regular transaction between the injurer and the potential victim, but where there are spillovers so that the degree to which one firm is regulated affects the degree to which another firm should be regulated.

Whereas occupational safety is the classic example of the previous regulatory situation, air pollution is the classic example of this one. With all the major forms of air pollution—acid rain, the greenhouse effect, depletion of the ozone layer—the injured parties are far removed from the polluting firms or consumers and are not linked by any regular transaction. With acid rain, the main offenders are power companies in the Ohio River Valley and the main costs are borne by those who use lakes in New England or Canada. Similar problems exist in northern Europe and elsewhere around the globe. With the greenhouse effect, the main offenders are those who burn fossil fuel and cut down forests; the main victims cannot even be identified yet and might or might not even be alive. With ozone depletion, the main offenders are users of chloroflourocarbons and halogens; the main victims are again yet to be identified and perhaps yet to be born.

Not only are the victims unlinked to the offenders, but the danger of the offense depends on what everybody else is doing. Generating acid rain, burning fossil fuels, and using chloroflourocarbons would all be much less costly to the environment if no one else were doing it; all activities would be much more costly if everyone else were doing much more. We no longer have the simple case examined previously where we just try to get one firm down to the accident rate a^* and then go on to the next firm. Now the question of how much we regulate any one firm determines how much pollution there is in the air and how much we should regulate any other firm.

These two differences simplify and complicate the regulatory problem at the same time. On the one hand, the simple question of whether there should be any social regulation seems much easier to answer. With occupational safety the answer depends in a fairly complicated way on whether compensating wage differentials for risky firms are high enough to protect workers and whether existing social insurance arrangements are adequately experience-rated. With atmospheric pollution, by contrast, there is no apparent way to limit the offending actions at all without governmental social regulation. If the problem can be shown to be potentially dangerous, and the three preceding ones certainly can be, there is a good case for at least some type of environmental regulation.

On the other hand, the existence of spillovers suggests that limits should be designed for a whole system or region, not just one firm. Somehow the regulating agency must determine how much pollution the atmosphere can bear, region by region, and then work out efficient allocations of the requisite reductions in emissions.

The way this can be done is demonstrated in Figure 12.6. Suppose the regulatory agency has decided that, given existing pollution levels and dangers, a total reduction of emission of E is required to protect the atmosphere. The calculation behind this determination follows roughly that described in Figure 12.3, where the difference between the no-government level of pollution (analogous to a_M) and the optimal level (analogous to a^*) is determined by a comparison of marginal benefits and costs of pollution reduction. Suppose further that the source of the pollution does not matter.

Given the total desired reduction, E, how should it be allocated across potential polluters? In Figure 12.6 we assume there are just two potential sources of pollution (they could be firms or regions), though the analysis could easily be extended to many sources. The first source has the prevention

FIGURE 12.6 Efficient Allocation between Two Polluters

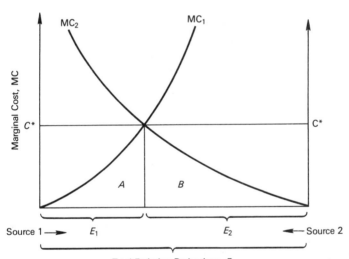

Suppose the total amount of emission reductions required by the control authority was E. The optimal allocation is where the MC curves cross.
- (a) The optimal emission charge for both sources is C^*.
- (b) At C^*, source 1 will control E_1, and source 2 E_2, with $E_1 + E_2 = E$.
- (c) Total cleanup cost borne by source 1 is area A, that borne by source 2 is area B.
- (d) Total costs need not be the same. The efficient allocation is where marginal costs are the same.

schedule given by MC_1, starting from the left origin and rising with the amount of emissions prevented at source 1. The second source has the prevention schedule given by MC_2, starting from the right origin and moving left, with marginal prevention costs again rising as we move leftward and source 2 prevents more emissions.

The optimal allocation of this predetermined emission reduction is given by the intersection of these MC curves, at C^*. Were the marginal cost of prevention not the same for each source, we could always reduce total emission reduction costs by having the source where marginal costs are low reduce emissions more, and the source where marginal costs are high reduce emissions less. At the optimal allocation, where source 1 is reducing emissions by E_1 and source 2 by E_2, the total reduction is E by definition. Source 1 spends a total of area A on emission reduction; source 2 spends a total of area B. It is important to note that this efficient allocation condition is that the marginal cost at both sources is the same, not the total cost. Hence at the optimal allocation point, $MC_1 = MC_2 = C^*$ and the total prevention cost of area $(A + B)$ is minimized. But there is no reason why each source's total prevention cost is equal (area A does not necessarily equal area B).

How can a regulatory authority achieve this optimal allocation? The simple answer is for it simply to assess the charge of C^* and let sources respond. The problem with this simple answer is that it may be difficult for the regulatory to determine C^*. Usually the only information possessed by the regulatory agency is how much emission the atmosphere can tolerate; the agency is unlikely to know the marginal prevention cost implied by this tolerated emission level.

But there is another way. The regulatory authority could just give out permits to pollute. It would monitor air quality in the neighborhood of these polluting sources, to determine whether the two sources were polluting too much. Suppose we have the situation depicted in Figure 12.7, where the MC schedule from each source is exactly that shown in Figure 12.6. The regulatory initially decided on some arbitrary basis to require source 1 to reduce emissions by E_1 and source 2 by $E-E_1$, so that total emissions reductions were the desired amount E. If the permits were nontransferable, source 1 would reduce emissions by E_1 and spend area I, the cumulative sum of marginal costs between zero and E_1, on pollution reduction. Source 2 would reduce emissions by $E-E_1$ and spend total costs of area $(B + F + G + H)$.

This allocation fails our marginal cost test because the marginal costs of prevention are not equal for the two pollution sources. We could reduce total emission reduction costs by having the high marginal cost source 2 reduce less and the low marginal cost source 1 reduce more. The regulatory agency could, of course, accomplish this end by transferring some permits from source 1 to source 2. But to do this requires having the regulatory agency

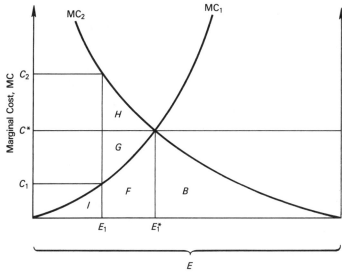

Suppose nontransferable permits were given that forced source 1 to reduce emissions by E_1 units and source 2 by $(E-E_1)$ units. The marginal cost for source 1 is C_1, that for source 2 is C_2.

If these permits were made transferable, source 1 (where it is cheap to control) would like to sell emission permits to source 2 until E_1^*. The equilibrium price of permits is C^*.

Source 1 sells $(E_1^* - E_1)$ permits to source 2 at C^* per permit, but is forced to spend area F more on cleanup. Its net gain is area G.

Source 2 buys $(E_1^* - E_1)$ permits from source 1 at C^* per permit, but is forced to spend area $(F + G + H)$ less on cleanup. Its net gain is area H.

The net social gain from making permits transferable is area $(G + H)$.

FIGURE 12.7   Nontransferable and Transferable Emission Permits

know the marginal cost at each source, which it generally is not equipped to do. All it has to do instead is to allow pollution permits to be transferable, or saleable. Source 1, the low-cost source, might sell some permits to source 2, the high-cost source. It would begin selling until its own marginal prevention cost equaled the price it could get for a permit. Source 2 would buy until the buying price fell to its own marginal prevention cost. In equilibrium the price of a permit to pollute would equal the marginal cost of each source, or C^*. At this equilibrium marginal costs are again equated and total reduction costs are minimized.

We can find the exact gains from making permits transferable by doing a benefit-cost analysis. The gains are as follows:

Source 1 sells $E_1^*-E_1$ permits to source 2 at a price per permit of C^*. Its gain from selling the permits is area $(G + F)$, but because it sold the permits, it does have to reduce pollution by $E_1^*-E_1$ units. This costs area F, making for a net gain of area G.

Source 2 spends area $(G + F)$ on the permits, but because it bought, it has to reduce emissions by less. Its saving on pollution reduction costs is area $(F + G + H)$, making for a net gain of area H.

The Kaldor-Hicks net gain from making permits transferable is area $(G + H)$, exactly the dead-weight inefficiency in the previous case where permits were not transferable.

Both sources gain, showing why the transaction in pollution permits is in the best interest of both parties.

The idea here is straightforward. The regulatory agency knows the amount of pollution reduction required, but it does not know marginal costs at the two sources and the optimal allocation. It can start with any old allocation of pollution permits that gives the desired overall reduction. As long as these permits are transferable, and firms are competitive, sources or firms can be relied on to buy and sell until the marginal cost is equal at the various sources, which in turn implies that aggregate reduction costs are minimized.

The initial allocation of permits does not matter from an overall efficiency standpoint—we end up at E_1^* and C^* whatever the initial allocation. But this initial allocation of permits is still important in another sense, because it influences the ultimate distribution of gains and losses in the fight against air pollution. To see this, compare the distribution of costs if the regulatory had magically given out the right amount of permits from a cost-minimization point of view with the case we just considered. If the initial allocation of permits had been cost-minimizing, no permits would have been traded and source 1 would have spent area A (equal to area $(I + F)$) and source 2 area B on cleanup. If, on the other hand, the initial allocation to source 1 were E_1, source 1 still spends area A on cleanup in the end, and source 2 still spends area B. But in the meantime source 1 has sold permits to source 2 and received area $(G + F)$ for the sold permits. In efficiency terms the final equilibrium point is independent of the initial allocation of permits, but the gains and losses received by the different parties are not independent of the initial allocation of permits.

Pollution permits were not transferable in the early days of environmental regulation in this country, but recently the EPA has begun experimenting with some new transfer schemes. The offset program is a device by which new polluting sources can enter a market, provided they purchase offsetting emissions reductions from existing sources of pollution. The bubble policy allows each existing source to make trades to minimize total costs. The emission banking procedure is a procedure whereby a source can get credit for emission reductions beyond those required, with the credits able to be used subsequently or sold.[5]

REGULATION WITH A REGULAR TRANSACTION:
OSHA'S NOISE STANDARD

We now examine one particular case of a social regulation where there is a regular market transaction but no spillovers, to be followed by one where there is not a regular market transaction but where there are spillovers. The first involves the Occupational Safety and Health Act (OSHA) noise standard.[6]

One of the first standards handed down by OSHA was its interim noise standard. This standard limited the average noise level to which workers could be exposed to 90 decibels (roughly the level of a noisy subway train), with a maximum exposure at any time of 140 decibels, a two-hour maximum average of 100 decibels, and a four-hour maximum of 95 decibels. OSHA's research agency also recommended a more stringent standard that cut each of these averages by 5 decibels, a tightening that may not seem like much but in fact sounds only three-fourths as loud on average, and has only half the energy level.

OSHA then commissioned a prominent noise consulting firm, Bolt, Beranek, and Newman (BNN), to estimate compliance costs for the 85 and 90 decibel standards. These costs came out to be $31 billion and $18 billion, respectively, in 1974 dollars for all manufacturing firms.

There are at least four ways to estimate the benefits of noise reduction:

The market approach. The argument is simply that if workers are well-informed and find noise disorienting, they will bid up wages appropriately. For the entire manufacturing sector, workers should have adequate bargaining power, and they certainly should be well-informed about the costs, if they are not already deaf. The implication of this approach, of course, is that any further regulation will have negative net benefits.

The capital values approach, from housing values. Robert Smith looked at a number of studies comparing housing values in the vicinity of noisy airports, along the lines suggested in Chapter 4, and he found that the annual marginal benefit of going to the 90 decibel standard from no standard was about $6 billion in 1974 dollars, and the annual marginal benefit of going to the 85 decibel standard from the 90 decibel standard was another $6 billion. There are a number of limitations to such studies, as discussed in Chapter 4, and in any event the numbers should be viewed as upper bound estimates.

The direct estimation approach, from the value of hearing loss. There is general agreement that workers exposed to noise levels above 90 decibels over a long period of time will suffer some hearing loss, but the loss is slight and the exposure must be prolonged, for twenty years or more. Both OSHA and BBN estimated that the incidence of long-term hearing loss for retirees who spent their whole career in a noisy workplaces declined by five percentage points from no standard to 90 decibels, and another nine percentage points from 90 to 85 decibels. Combining these estimates with worker compensation awards, OSHA and BBN arrived at direct hearing loss values of $2 billion from no standard to 90 decibels and $4 billion from 90 decibels to 85 decibels. These

TABLE 12.1   Benefits and Costs of the OSHA Noise Standards (Billions of 1974 $)

ITEM	MOVING FROM NO STANDARD TO A 90 DECIBEL STANDARD	MOVING FROM A 90 DECIBEL STANDARD TO AN 85 DECIBEL STANDARD
Cost	13	18
Benefits, Capital Values	6	6
Benefits, Hearing Loss	2	4
Net Cost, Capital Values	7	12
Net Cost, Hearing Loss	11	14
Net Cost, Sum of Benefits	5	8

Source: Robert S. Smith, *The Occupational Safety and Health Act: Its Costs and Achievements* (Washington, D.C.: American Enterprise Institute for Public Policy Research, 1976), Chapter 3.

numbers would again be upper bound estimates because most workers do not spend their whole career exposed to excessive noise.

The behavioral approach, from workers' propensity to wear earplugs. It turns out that the noise level experienced by workers with specially fitted earplugs is well below that implied by either of the standards. Earplugs are quite cheap to produce, though there may be some costs in terms of comfort to employees in wearing them. But almost every attempt to outfit workers with free earplugs, even in very noisy workplaces, has had to be abandoned for lack of worker interest. Whatever the cost of noise to workers, it seems to be below that of wearing earplugs.

The first and fourth methods of estimating the benefits of controlling noise do not give quantitative numbers, though they do recommend against adopting either of the noise standards. The second and third methods do give numbers, and they also recommend against adopting either of the standards, as shown by the information in Table 12.1. Even if we estimate benefits by summing two upper bound estimates, implying some double-counting of benefits, we find that benefits are less than costs and that the noise standards should not be adopted.

As a final note, OSHA had imposed the 90 decibel standard in 1972, though it was never vigorously enforced. After these studies, and almost a decade of delay and argumentation, the agency decided not to enforce the 85 decibel standard, though it kept the 90 decibel standard in force. As of now, firms still operate under a very loosely enforced 90 decibel standard.

REGULATION WITH SPILLOVERS: ACID RAIN

One of the most actively debated pollution issues is acid rain. As is probably well-known, acid rain is created by the emission of sulfates and nitrates, which form acidic compounds in the atmosphere and later fall to the earth and damage structures, kill trees and fish, and possibly impair human health. A large percentage of the relevant emissions come from utility companies in the Ohio River Valley, and a large share of the costs are borne in the Adirondack Mountains of New York State, mountains and lakes in New England, and in Canada. The main limitation on emissions at present is from the Clean Air Act of 1978, but this limitation forces only new utility boilers installed since 1978 to be fitted with scrubbers that reduce sulfate and nitrate emissions. Emissions from older plants are by and large unrestricted, though the Congress has debated imposing tougher standards for many years now.

Various regulatory approaches have been suggested to limit acid rain. The traditional approach would simply require polluters to reduce emissions of sulfur dioxide, the main pollutant, and pay whatever cost. Were firms free to reduce emissions in the cheapest possible way, they would simply substitute low sulfur coal from the south, midwest, and west for the high sulfur coal presently mined in parts of Appalachia and Illinois. But this would entail a big reduction in demand for high sulfur coal and concomitant economic dislocation in these mining communities, already generally poor areas. So other measures have been proposed that limit fuel-switching to protect high sulfur coal. This limitation would force older utilities to retrofit their burners with scrubbers, which significantly increases the cost of reducing emissions. Other measures suggested to limit emissions are electricity taxes, subsidies for high sulfur coal scrubbers, emissions taxes, and taxes on the sulfur content of fuel. The economic costs of all of these measures were recently computed by the Congressional Budget Office.[7]

Here we make use of the CBO numbers to illustrate the preceding points made. First of all we compare the costs of a specific amount of pollution reduction with and without the limitation that protects the high sulfur coal industry. We then examine the statewide allocation of emissions reductions and the pattern of marginal costs, to see whether the mandated reductions are cost-minimizing.

Man-made emissions of sulfur dioxide totaled about 27 million tons in 1985, of which 16 million came from electric utilities. Emissions from utilities are anticipated to grow to about 18.5 million tons by 1995, and proposals to limit acid rain have called for reductions of between 7.2 and 9.2 million tons from this amount. Since emissions reductions are usually measured against emissions in 1980, the peak year, these two reductions plans are commonly referred to as the 8 and 10 million ton reduction plan.

There are two ways in which the reduction plans under debate are not cost-minimizing:

The scrubber requirement, which forces older utilities into very costly prevention programs. For 1995, CBO computed that the 8 million reduction plan cost $1.9 billion ($265 per ton of reduced emissions, in 1985 dollars) with no limitation on fuel-switching, and $2.1 billion ($293 per ton) with the limitation on fuel-switching. Both of these numbers, and the extra costs due to scrubbers, are much higher for the 10 million ton reduction plan.

The arbitrary assignment of emissions reductions. Reductions are assigned to states through an excess emissions formula (EEF) based on emissions in excess of a specified amount, but not on marginal costs. Since permits are not transferable, there is no assurance that the pattern of reductions will be efficient.

Although the published data are fragmentary, it is possible to use these data to find a reduction plan that costs less than that given by the EEF assignments. The general principle is the simple one just described—compute the marginal cost by state and have the low cost states reduce more and the high cost states reduce less, exactly what would happen if the EEF emissions were made transferable.

The basic numbers to do this are shown in Table 12.2. Ten states, seven of which are located in the Ohio River Valley, account for 80 percent of the excess emissions. The emissions these ten would bear under the 8 million ton EEF reduction plan are shown in the first column. The costs borne by utilities in the particular states to make these reductions are shown in the second column. The quotient, the state cost of emission reduction per ton between zero and the 8 million plan, is shown in the third column and labelled MC−,

TABLE 12.2   Acid Rain Emission Reductions, 1995 Utility Plants Only, No Constraints

STATE	EEF 8 MILLION TON REDUCTION (MILLIONS TONS)	COST (MILLIONS $)	MC−($)	MC+($)	REALLOCATE (MILLIONS TONS)	COST Δ (MILLIONS $)
Ohio	1.054	158	150	150	+.334	50
Missouri	.775	113	146	367	+.188	69
Indiana	.634	107	169	130	+.246	32
Pennsylvania	.600	199	332	1,322		
Illinois	.576	124	215	760		
West Virginia	.531	153	288	367	+.093	34
Kentucky	.284	68	239	7130		
(Ohio Valley)	(4.454)	(922)	(207)	(838)	(.861)	(185)
Wisconsin	.474	98	207	877		
The Carolinas	.457	127	278	345	+.029	10
Tennessee	.340	40	118	118	+.140	17
Other	1.522	732	481	599	−1.030	−495
Total	7.247	1,919	265	677	0	−283

EEF Cost/Ton = 1,919/7.247 = 265

Reallocated Cost/Ton = (1,919−283)/7.247 = 226

Cost/Ton with Constraints = 293

Source: Congressional Budget Office, *Curbing Acid Rain: Cost, Budget, and Coal-Market Effects* (Washington, D.C.: Government Printing Office, 1986).

the marginal cost in the interval zero to 8 million tons. The CBO report also gives the data for each state between the 8 million reduction plan and the 10 million reduction plan. These data are transformed to give MC+ in the fourth column, the marginal cost between 8 and 10 million tons. In effect, MC– is the relevant marginal cost if a state reduces emissions less than in the EEF plan, and MC+ is the marginal cost if the state reduces emissions more.

Both columns of MC numbers show sizable differences, so we might suspect that the EEF reduction plan is not cost-minimizing. We can derive a cheaper plan in the following simple way—expand emissions reductions in states where MC+ is low, contract emissions reductions in states where MC– is high. Whenever we find some MC+ numbers below the MC– numbers, we can save on costs.

And we can. The groups of states where it is most costly to reduce emissions under the EEF plan is "Other", where the MC– is $481 per ton. That is four times the value of the lowest MC+ (Tennessee), and well above the MC+ in five other states. In the plan labelled "Reallocate" we simply expand emissions reductions as much as possible (given the published CBO data) in these six low-cost states, replacing emissions in the high-cost states. The numbers are worked out in the table. The aggregate cost saving from this switch is $283 million, yielding a new overall cost per ton of emissions reduction of $226. Even our simple technique saved more than the limitation on fuel-switching cost.

It would be possible to do even better with more complete data. We only have two cost values in one year, between zero and the 8 million reduction, and 8 and 10, for each state, all in 1995. With continuous data on the marginal cost curve in each state over time, we could go to the point of exact equation of discounted marginal costs across states and save even more. This is, of course, precisely what a transferable scheme would do, and in fact there is no obvious reason why EPA could not allow emissions trading across states to achieve cost reductions.[8]

These calculations show how important it is to worry about the efficient cost-reduction package. Limitations such as that on high sulfur coal obviously get in the way of cost minimization. Arbitrary allocations of emissions reduction do as well, though their potential for excess cost is much more subtle.

SUMMARY

This chapter has examined two types of social regulation—that for worker safety where there is already a protective mechanism—and that for air pollution—where there is not a protective mechanism, but where there are complex spillover effects. In the former instance the case for social regulation is unclear: it depends on how much workers bid up wages for accident-prone firms and on the properties of any social insurance schemes that compensate workers for accidents. In the latter, the case for social regulation is generally quite compelling.

But just arguing for regulation does not end the matter. Regulation can be on outputs (the accident record of a firm) or inputs (the substances and processes used), by way of taxes or controls on the accident rate. For any particular situation it is hard to tell which approach is best *a priori;* that depends on the details of the case. But it is generally unwise to try to force firms to uniform accident rates when their benefit and cost schedules differ.

When spillovers are present, the degree to which one polluting source should be regulated depends on the degree to which others are. The cost-minimizing approach here is for the regulatory agency to determine how many emissions in aggregate the atmosphere can stand, and then allocate these emissions, or emission reductions, across sources so that the marginal cost of prevention is the same for all sources. Schemes such as making pollution permits transferable will accomplish this end.

The chapter also looked at two particular social regulations. There seem to be slightly greater costs than benefits in having OSHA limit noise in the workplace, as it has in a loose way since 1972. There are presumably greater benefits than costs in having EPA mandate reductions in emissions that cause acid rain, though it would be possible to make the calculus even more favorable by reallocating emissions reductions across states.

NOTES

[1] Robert S. Smith, "Compensating Wages Differentials and Public Policy: A Review," *Industrial and Labor Relations Review,* 1979, finds six studies that report cempensating wage differentials when industry injury rates are high and ten that report compensating wage differentials when industry fatality rates are high.

[2] The model used to examine the case comes from Walter Oi, "On the Economics of Industrial Safety," *Law and Contemporary Problems,* Summer-Autumn 1974.

[3] This standard was first enunciated by a lawyer, Guido Calabresi, in *The Cost of Accidents: A Legal and Economic Analysis* (New Haven, Yale University Press, 1970).

[4] Robert S. Smith, *The Occupational Safety and Health Act: Its Goals and Achievements* (Washington: American Enterprise Institute for Public Policy Research, 1976).

[5] A more complete discussion can be found in Tom Tietenberg, *Environmental and Natural Resource Economics,* 2nd edition (Glenview, IL: Scott, Foresman and Company, 1988), Chapters 14 and 15.

[6] The following information comes from a summary by Smith, *The Occupational Safety and Health Act,* Chapter 3.

[7] Congressional Budget Office, *Curbing Acid Rain: Cost, Budget, and Coal Market Effects* (Washington: Government Printing Office, 1986).

[8] Such a policy has been proposed by Tom Tietenberg, "An Innovative Market-Based Approach to Acid Rain Control: Acid Rain Reduction Credits," *Challenge,* March-April 1989.

PROBLEMS

1. Fancy Wheels Skateboard Company employs 50 testers who occasionally fall and break their arms. These testers could earn $9,800 in perfectly safe occupations, but when they break their arms, they lose an average of 20 percent of annual wages. The company could repave its sidewalks with extra soft asphalt, and lower the probability (a) of an arm break, according to the following schedule

a	Cost, $
0	80,000
.1	40,000
.2	20,000
.3	10,000
.4	4,000
.5	0

   a. If workers are risk-neutral, how much will FWSC spend on repaving? What would be the added cost to FWSC if OSHA required repaving until testing was absolutely safe?
   b. A new generation of daredevils comes along, and they love skateboarding so much that they are willing to test for $9,800—despite the fact that some fall and break their arms. What will FWSC do now? What is the extra cost of the OSHA regulations?
   c. The city council is debating an ordinance to outlaw skateboarding on city streets. The cost of this legislation would be the loss of personal freedom; the benefit would be the fact that the city would no longer have to treat the broken arms of vagabond skateboarders. Can you use the information given here to estimate, or bracket, benefits? Why or why not?
2. Power plants in Ohio and Indiana generate acid rain that kills trees and fish in New York State. EPA decides that to save the lakes and forests in New York, it will be necessary to reduce power plant emissions from Ohio and Indiana by 12 tons. The prevention cost schedules for each state are

$$MC_O = E_O$$

$$MC_I = 2E_I$$

   where MC are in billions of dollars per ton, the emission reductions (E) are in tons, and the subscripts are obvious.
   a. Initially EPA forces both Ohio and Indiana to reduce emissions by 6 tons. Find the amount spent on emission reduction in both states, the total amount spent, and the marginal cost in each state.

b. You go to work at EPA and argue that this is not the optimal allocation. Design a minimum cost scheme, find the amount spent on emission reduction in both states, the total amount spent, and the marginal cost in each state. How much have you saved?

c. Although your scheme minimized the total cost of pollution reduction, it made one of the states worse off. How could you have gotten to the optimal allocation and made both states better off? By how much are they better off?

d. A hostile President takes over and eliminates EPA. Ohio and Indiana go back to polluting as usual. Is there anything Governor Mario Cuomo of New York State can do?

THIRTEEN
GETTING STARTED

Rather than recapitulating the whole book, this chapter will be used to give a pragmatic guide for the aspiring benefit-cost analyst. One can read through the theory about this, that, or the other thing, and still not have a very good idea of how actually to do a benefit-cost analysis. In this chapter we give a sample list of the steps one might take. It should go without saying that this list is simply illustrative: one can do perfectly good work following a totally different path. But these steps nevertheless represent what would seem to be a reasonable logical sequence most of the time.

CHOOSING THE RIGHT POLICY

Benefit-cost analysis is a good tool to use when considering the impact of a policy measure that changes the allocation of resources. It is not as good at analyzing the impact of purely distributional measures, such as a marginal expansion in transfer programs, general revenue sharing, or progressive tax rates, though there will be some allocational impacts even for these measures. It is not the right tool to use for analyzing questions of property rights, such as a measure to return lands to native Americans. It is not well-adapted to entitlement questions, such as whether older Americans deserve catastrophic health care. Nor is it well-adapted to questions of basic rights, such as whether federal employees should be administered drug tests.

Saying that there is a lot that benefit-cost analysis cannot do is not meant as a council of despair. As this book has tried to illustrate, there are a great many important policy questions on which benefit-cost analysis can provide helpful advice—physical investments such as dams, roads, defense goods, and public housing; human investments such as education, health, welfare reform, and day care; mixed distribution-allocation programs such as minimum wages and public employment; agricultural subsidies; categorical grants; tax subsidies; tariffs, quotas, and excise taxes; regulations where there is a market transaction; regulations involving externalities. There ought to be enough on this plate for almost anybody.

Regarding the process question, fledgling analysts might fall into two groups. One group is students taking a course such as this who are required by their hard-nosed professor to do a course project and need a topic. The main advice to this group would be to start with an issue interesting to you, whether drawn from the experience of a national, state, or local government, involving a university, a service agency, or a lobbyist group. Then think of some policy measures that deal with this question—good ideas, crackpot ideas—everything is eligible. Before you know it, you have a list of projects on which one might do a benefit-cost analysis. More on whittling down this list momentarily.

The other group of fledgling analysts are out there in the world practicing. Governments, universities, service agencies, and lobbyists really do benefit-cost analysis, or at least they are in the business of criticizing benefit-cost analyses done by others. This group has lots of problems, but generally choosing a topic is the last worry—the topic is there, and the analyst just has to do the work.

WHO GAINS AND WHO LOSES AND WHY?

Assuming now that we have got a policy measure to be analyzed, or at least a short list of them, what next? The main suggestion would be to start with the basics: what will this policy do, who gains or loses, and why? Let's not worry about real numbers yet—we will get to quantification issues shortly. For now, act like any self-respecting economist and *assume* that you can get whatever numbers you need.

You can defer numerical questions, but at this stage you should be clear about the potential impacts of your policies. Physical investments such as dams and roads have been analyzed countless times, and for them it is fairly straightforward to compile your list—that given in Chapter 8 for the Tellico Dam will generally do the job. National defense projects are harder, but the typical defense project should be enhancing security, it may benefit defense suppliers, and it would generally make taxpayers worse off, sometimes quite a bit worse off. For trade policy questions the distortions dealt with in Chapters 4 and 5 are key. For human investments the list given in Chapter 9 for welfare reform and the preschool education project will generally be adequate. For the regulations with market transactions the list given in Chapter 12, with adaptation depending on the problem at hand, should generally suffice. But for disparate policies like tax subsidies, categorical grants, or regulations involving externalities, the policy in question can do so many different things that one will have to be quite inventive at this stage.

VALUING THE GAINS

This is one of the key steps, perhaps the key step, in most benefit-cost analyses. More often than not, how well this step is negotiated tells how good the study is. For most projects the gains will somehow be read from market outcomes. For dams, roads, and recreational areas there will be one or many relevant demand curves, and all of the issues confronted in Chapters 4 and 8 arise. What is the shape of the demand curve, what shifts it, what is the interaction with the supply curve, does the relevant market clear, can one apply the travel cost method or something like it?

For some projects, most notably agricultural projects in developing countries, one must worry about secondary markets. If farmers grow more rice, they grow fewer groundnuts. In these cases one should be working out all the secondary changes and tracing them through. As mentioned in Chapter 5, that can be rather difficult to do, and fortunately there is a new technology—that of general equilibrium simulation—that is coming to the rescue. It takes a bit of economics to be able to do this, but even fledgling economists should be able to specify demand and supply functions with interactive effects—the supply of one crop lowers the supply of others. And once this is done, the new technology allows one to plug into a microcomputer simulation disk and compute social net benefits and other outcome variables of interest.

For projects that save lives or time, or alter capital values, we must turn to allied markets. As was indicated in Chapter 4, one must give some thought to which allied markets. Saving lives saves lives, not the labor services of the same individual. That is why the RC standard is a good starting point, but the DFE standard is not. Projects that save time can save different kinds of time for different people, and it can be quite tricky to get a good allied market valuation. The capital value approach can be quite useful in a wide range of applications, but one must guard against double-counting gains, which is quite easy with something like capital values that summarize the impact of many changes. The same cautionary words go for evaluations of sumptuary activities like drinking and smoking, and taxation of same. Does the demand for cigarettes or liquor include the user's psychological adjustment for the long-run personal costs of these activities or not? The results will depend critically on the decision, and the analyst must be ready to deal with the issue.

We have talked about direct markets and allied markets, but not so much about what to do when there are no markets. One would be hard-pressed to come up with any market to use to value the MX missile, the value of reduced roadside litter for trash pickup or bottle return bills, the value of reduced emission of sulfur dioxides or chlorofluorocarbons, and on down the list. What to do then?

It sounds paradoxical, but the best approach is to do nothing at all. Benefit-cost analysis is often criticized for undervaluing things that cannot be valued, but if done properly, that criticism is wide of the mark. If things cannot be valued by any known technique, just be honest about it and keep that limitation up front. First, suppose we have two programs that make similar nonquantifiable improvements in society's welfare—for example, the MX missile and the Midgetman missile. Then one could certainly work out all of the costs and the timing of these costs, all the present values, and just present these projects as alternative ways to accomplish the same end. Or, one could do the same analysis for a city that is comparing the use of trash compactors with buying more land for a landfill dump. Or, one could find the least cost way to reduce sulfur dioxide emissions. As mentioned, these types of studies are known as cost effectiveness analyses, a jargon word for simply finding the least cost solution to some problem. Such studies can be very useful policy analysis projects—net benefits of the policy cannot be measured, but the analyst is showing how they can be maximized.

Alternatively, suppose there is just one way to accomplish some end. A mandatory bottle return bill will reduce roadside litter, and there are not many other measures one can think of that will. Then the benefit-cost approach would be to value everything else that can be valued—the production cost increases, the time cost of returning bottles or sorting trash, the saving on trash pickup or landfill costs—and just do a consumer information evaluation. Considering everything, it costs the average citizen $x to institute a mandatory bottle return program. Do you citizens want to pay or not? Precisely that decision is made routinely by every consumer almost all of the time. What is wrong with doing the same thing for public sector decisions? These decisions could then be made in a much more informed manner, and that is the basic point of the whole enterprise.

For human investment programs there really are not markets to analyze. These programs' benefits are usually measured by a statistical analysis of experience with related programs, or inference from data somehow. There is no point in repeating the list of potential pitfalls given in Chapter 9, but all the issues raised there involve the basic question of how relevant these data are for the program the analyst is interested in. Analysts looking at other projects have to worry about how allied are allied markets; analysts looking at human investment projects have to worry about how allied are the data from allied programs.

VALUING THE COSTS

This step is normally easier than valuing the gains. For most projects, even including human investment projects, these costs are simply budget costs, or are well-estimated by budget costs.

The few exceptions to this rule are noted in Chapter 4. When the government as a buyer is important enough to influence market prices, budget costs may overstate true social costs to a slight extent. When market imperfections push the market supply above the true marginal social cost, budget costs may overstate true costs to a greater extent.

The main area where this problem arises is on the "jobs" issue. Politicians are wont to try to obtain programs, and others to defend them, because they create jobs. At this point the benefit-cost analyst can ask some hard questions—are these temporary or permanent jobs, will the job gains here result in overall employment gains, or will other employment just go down, in which case using labor here is a real social cost? Moreover, do new workers here even benefit at all—are they going to make more than they made somewhere else? And, are the workers even here now? Even if the analyst is analyzing the program from the perspective of one state, ignoring losses to other states, if workers on a project are new immigrants to the state, the job gains make no one in the present jurisdiction any better off. The whole jobs issue is a potential alibi for large-scale fudging of numbers, and the benefit-cost analyst should be ready with a sharp whistle and a sharp pen.

For nonbudgetary programs such as regulations, the costs are no longer budget costs but now compliance costs to be borne by firms. These raise a new set of problems. The principle of equating marginal costs to marginal benefits, or equalizing marginal costs across different sources of pollution, is clear, but unlike with budget costs, the measurement issues become much trickier. Obviously one should try as hard as possible to get good data, but an alternative approach suggested in Chapter 12 is to design policies, such as transferable pollution permits, that minimize costs whatever they are. The connection to the cost effectiveness studies is obvious—often one can make valuable policy initiatives, or at least good policy decisions, without being in possession of all the relevant data.

DEALING WITH TIME AND UNCERTAINTY

Once the basic structure of the evaluation is in place, one should guard against simple mistakes in putting the results together. For uncertainty, one would generally just compute the expected value of outcomes—the probability of this outcome times this result plus the probability of that outcome times that result. We have given examples of such calculations at different points in the book. In rare cases, mentioned in Chapter 4, the uncertainty will be large enough for certain groups that there might be some additional adjustment for risk. If certain groups can gain or lose enormously from a project, with no obvious way to insure themselves, one might include less than the expected value of gains as their true, risk-discounted gain from a project. If workers are uninformed or insufficiently risk-averse, they may charge firms less than the actuarial risk for potential accidents, and one might work this into the analysis.

For projects that have differential patterns of benefits and costs over time, it is also important to get the time discounting right. Everything should be put in terms of present values, and one should avoid silly mistakes like discounting nominal benefits with real discount rates, or the reverse. Decide at the outset whether it is most convenient to use nominal or real values and stick to one set or the other. Regarding risk, it is sometimes argued that discount rates should be altered to adjust for risk, but that suggestion is misleading. Just deal with risk as shown in Chapter 4, and compute risk-adjusted present values in the usual way.

On the discount rate itself, modern thinking pegs that at the social rate of time preference, somewhere around 3.5 percent in the United States (see the discussion in Chapter 6). When a project displaces consumption—is to be financed by taxation—benefits should simply be discounted by this social rate, compared with current consumption costs, and that is the end of it. When a project displaces investment—is to be financed by borrowing—benefits should be discounted by the borrowing rate faced by the government. When economies are open to capital movements and tax factors are minor, as is true in the United States, the borrowing discount rate and the social discount rate will be quite similar, but in other times and places, they could differ substantially.

SENSITIVITY TESTING

On completion of all of these steps, one has in essence done a benefit-cost analysis. But that is not the end of the job, because it is necessary to think about a few presentation issues.

One involves sensitivity testing. In all likelihood, measurement uncertainties will pervade any benefit-cost study. There are ranges of plausible values for the slope of a demand function, for the slope of a supply function, for use if markets do not clear, for cross-elasticities of demand or supply, for values of lives or time computed from allied markets, for assumptions on whether capital values or the demand for liquor and cigarettes really includes adjustment for personal harm, for discount rates and uncertainty adjustments. One can be as insightful and inventive as possible, and still have substantial uncertainty about the actual numbers.

What to do? A first step is to list the sources of uncertainty and go through them one-by-one. Put everything else at expected values and vary the discount rate. Or, put everything else at expected values and vary the slope of the demand curve. The calculations sound laborious, but in fact are quite simple and straightforward if one has the data on a microcomputer spreadsheet program. And if one goes through the numbers in this manner, one first gets an idea of which types of uncertainty are important in influencing the overall results. Those conceptual uncertainties that are unimportant can simply be dismissed, with the writeup noting that fact.

For those conceptual uncertainties that are important, a full range of numbers should be shown—using, for example, the lowest and highest plausible values for the discount rate. The writeup should explain how the choice affects the overall results, why, and then give some guidance about whether a low, high, or middling value should be used. And the writeup should be honest in describing the results—if the uncertainties really are dominating, one should say so. If one feels that while uncertainties are there, the weight of the evidence points in one direction, say that too.

GAINS AND LOSSES OF DIFFERENT GROUPS

Once the results are computed, with sensitivity ranges if necessary, the analyst then has to display results. The overall Kaldor-Hicks net benefit tally has been mentioned and computed throughout the book, and this one number will probably always be the most important number for most programs. But it certainly should not be the only number shown.

Politicians have to make decisions that create gainers and losers. They run for office voluntarily and presumably are comfortable making such decisions, but they are quite visible and they do not have a high degree of job security. They like to know what monsters lurk in the forest if they were to come out for policy measure x, before they come out for x. That means that it is important for them to know who is gaining and losing how much in this program, with what degree of statistical confidence. It should be a routine requirement of benefit-cost analysis that all distributions of gains and losses for various groups should be shown. These could be put in one table and added up at the end, as we did in Chapter 9 for human investment programs. With the human investment programs we considered, for example, the fact nonparticipants came out ahead in both programs may well predict the ultimate political success of these programs much more than the Kaldor-Hicks overall net benefits tally.

MAKING THE DECISION

At this point if it were left up to the analyst, the last step is reasonably clear. As long as gains and losses of different groups are not to be weighted, just find the program that maximizes net benefits. Do not even get tempted to show benefit-cost ratios—they can just get you into trouble.

If the gains and losses are to be weighted, or if certain gains and losses—such as those of outsiders—are to be excluded altogether (given a zero weight), things get trickier. On excluding gains altogether, the analyst is working for taxpayers. If they are national taxpayers and the program is national, there would be very few outside gains and losses that should be excluded altogether. If the program is local, external benefits should in general be given a low weight, and perhaps counted at zero.

On distributional weights, the advice is similar to that for the jobs question mentioned previously. Distributional weighting is fine, provided that there is some reason for believing that society is not on its optimal income distribution, and providing that one does not overdo it. Chapter 7 showed how to keep any distributional weights used within a reasonable bound, and reasonably close to one, with reference to the inefficiencies implicit in transfer programs. The relevant comparison is between a program and a marginal expansion of transfer programs as an alternative way to raise low incomes, and we should choose the cheapest approach. That is insured by not using distributional weights that exceed $1/(1-c)$, as shown in Chapter 7.

Of course, benefit-cost analysis is really an exercise in how to advise politicians, so for the most part the analyst will not be called on actually to make a decision, or a choice of programs. Politicians get elected because they want to do this, and do it they will most of the time. The only advice that can be given here is the advice that every sports fan keeps in mind—you cannot win them all. Sometimes the decision will come out the way the analyst wants it, or the way indicated by the benefit-cost study. Other times it will not. Do not get discouraged; just go onto the next project. If your work is good, over time it will make a difference.

ANSWERS TO PROBLEMS

CHAPTER 3

1. a. Sum the inverse demand functions to get the social demand function of $D = 87 - 3Q = 60$; $Q = 9$.
   b. At $Q = 9$, $P_A = 17$, $P_B = 19$, $P_C = 24$.
   c. Insert $P = 20$ into the first demand function to get $Q_A = 6$, $DWB_A = 4.5$. Do the same for the others to get $Q_B = 8$, $DWB_B = 0.5$; $Q_C = 13$, $DWB_C = 8$.
   d. Consumption would go to the median voter level at $Q = 8$. At this point $DWB_A = 2$, $DWB_B = 0$, $DWB_C = 12.5$.
   e. C would be willing to bribe up to 4.5 (the difference in DWB_C) to move from $Q = 8$ to $Q = 9$. A's bribe would have to be at least 2.5, B's at least 0.5.
      The Clarke taxes can be computed as follows. A and B together chose $Q = 7$ (their Samuelsonian maximum). When C joins the group, $Q = 9$. DWB_A goes from 0.5 at $Q = 7$ to 4.5 at $Q = 9$. DWB_B does not change from $Q = 7$ to $Q = 9$. C's Clarke tax is then 4.
      A and C together choose $Q = 9.5$, which we round off to $Q = 9$. When B joins, $Q = 9$. B's Clarke tax is zero.
      B and C together choose $Q = 10.5$, which we round off to $Q = 10$. When A joins, $Q = 9$. DWB_B goes from 2 to 0.5. DWB_C goes from 4.5 to 8. A's Clarke tax is 2.

f. The Kaldor-Hicks gain is the amount C is prepared to bribe, 4.5, less the amount A and B require, 3, to equal 1.5. At Q = 8, the social willingness to pay is 63, and the social gain in moving to Q = 9 is (.5)(3)(1) = 1.5.

2. Between Q = 6 and Q = 8, A is for 6 and B and C are for 8.
Between Q = 8 and Q = 13, A and B are for 8 and C is for 13.
Between Q = 6 and Q = 13, A and B are for 6 and C is for 13.
When this winner (Q = 6) is matched against Q = 8, Q = 8 prevails.
When C's preferences are not single-peaked, between Q = 6 and Q = 8, A and C are for 6 and B is for 8.
Between Q = 8 and Q = 13, A and B are for 8 and C is for 13.
Between Q = 6 and Q = 13, A and B are for 6 and C is for 13.
When this winner (Q = 6) is matched against Q = 8, Q = 6 prevails.
The lesson is that there is no clear victor when preferences are not single-peaked.

3. The net benefits and benefit-cost ratios are listed as follows:

DAM	B	C	B–C	B/C
1	40	20	20	2.0
2	30	10	20	3.0
3	30	20	10	1.5
4	10	20	−10	0.5
5	15	10	5	1.5
6	15	20	−5	.75

For the optimal sized budget, take all where net benefits (B − C) are positive, dams 1, 2, 3, and 5. The budget cost here is 60. If the budget were held to 20, net benefits would be maximized by taking dams 2 and 5. Note that we do not take dam 1 even though its benefit-cost ratio is greater than that of dam 5. If the dams are substitutes, build dam 3 and gain 10. Again the benefit-cost ratio does not help.

CHAPTER 4

1. The inverse linear demand function is $P = 15 - Q$. When the price is raised from $P = 10$ to $P = 12$, the loss is the trapezoid given by $(.5)(2)(5 + 3) = 8$. When the price is lowered from $P = 5$ to $P = 3$, the gain is the trapezoid $(.5)(2)(10 + 12) = 22$. For a given change in P the change in consumer welfare is greater the lower is P, because Q is larger.
The arc elasticity (E) between the points is given by $E = (5/7.5)/(-5/7.5) = -1$. This inverse demand function between $P = 5$ and $P = 10$ can also be expressed as $P = 50/Q$.

2. When $P = 10$, $Q = 10$. When $P = 9$, $Q = 11$. The gain for consumers is the trapezoid $(.5)(1)(10 + 11) = 10.5$. If the supply function is flat, there

is no producer surplus gain for producers, so the social gain is just this 10.5.

When $P = 1 + Q$, $Q = 9.5$ and $P = 10.5$. When $P = Q$, $Q = 10$ and $P = 10$. The gain for consumers is $(.5)(.5)(9.5 + 10) = 4.875$. The gain for producers is $(.5)(10)(10) - (.5)(9.5)(9.5) = 4.875$. The social gain is the sum, 9.75. It is slightly smaller than the gain in the flat supply function case because the rising cost lowers the gain on the new output.

3.   a.   Solve the old demand function for $Q = 150 - 25P$. The new one is then $Q' = 200 - 25P$. The new inverse is $P' = 8.0 - .04Q$.
     b.   Set $6.0 - .04Q = .02Q$, $Q = 100$, $P = 2$.
     c.   Set $8.0 - .04Q = .02Q$, $Q = 133.3$, $P = 2.67$.
     d.   Budget cost is $(2.67)(50) = 133.5$.
     e.   Consumer surplus loss is $(.5)(.67)(100 + 83.3) = 61.4$.
     f.   Producer surplus gain on old units is $(.67)(100) = 67.0$.
     g.   Producer surplus gain on new units is $(33.3)[2.67 - (.5)(1 + 1.33)] = 50.1$.
     h.   Net social cost is the sum: $133.5 + 61.4 - 67.0 - 50.1 = 77.8$.

4.   a.   Demand is given by $2 = 92 - L$, $L = 90$. Supply by $2 = .02L'$, $L' = 100$. Unemployment is the difference, 10.
     b.   The budget cost is $(2)(5) = 10$. The average valuation of work effort by those willing to work at $W = 2$ is 1, so the social cost is $(1)(5) = 5$.
     c.   The social cost would be unchanged by these transfers, though the incidence of gains and losses would be altered.

5.   a.   Set $1000 - H = H$, $H = 500$, market clearing rent is 500.
     b.   With rent control the supply is 400, demand is 600.
     c.   Landlords lose $(.5)(100)(400 + 500) = 45,000$.
     d.   Renters gained $(.5)(500)(500) = 125,000$ before the law. With the law the average valuation of those getting an apartment is 700, so the gain with the law is $(400)(700 - 400) = 120,000$. The net loss to renters is 5,000. Note that renters lose because there is no way to insure that high demanders get apartments.
     e.   Kaldor-Hicks net losses are $45,000 + 5,000 = 50,000$.
     f.   The losses felt by landlords are the same as before, 45,000.
     g.   Graduate students gained 125,000 before the law. With the law there are only half as many rentable units, so the gain with the new version of the law is $(200)(700 - 400) = 60,000$. The net loss of graduate students rises to 65,000.
     h.   The poor gain $(200)(50) = 10,000$.
     i.   Kaldor-Hicks net losses are $45,000 + 65,000 - 10,000 = 100,000$.

6.   The workers require $200 to accept a death risk of .001. The value of a life by this method is $(\$200)(1000) = \$200,000$. All of the problems recounted in the text would make this estimate a lower bound estimate.

7.   a.   Expected income is $(.5)(144) + (.5)(56) = 100$, the same as that of the certain package.
     b.   Expected utility is $(.5)(12) + (.5)(7.5) = 9.7$, less than that (10) of the certain package. There is a utility loss with the project.

CHAPTER 5

1. a. Before the innovation set $10 - R = 2 + R$, $R = 4$, $P_R = 6$. Insert this value into the corn demand and set $16 - C = C$, $C = 8$, $P = 8$.
    b. After the innovation set $10 - R = R$, $R = 5$, $P_R = 5$. Insert this value into the corn demand and set $15 - C = C$, $C = 7.5$, $P = 7.5$.
    c. Rice consumers gain $(.5)(1)(4 + 5) = 4.5$. Rice producers gained $(.5)(4)(4) = 8$ before and $(.5)(5)(5) = 12.5$ now, for a net of 4.5. The social gain of the innovation in the rice market is 9.
    d. Using the method described in the text, corn consumers gain the trapezoid $(.5)(.5)(7 + 7.5) = 3.625$. Corn producers lose $(.5)(.5)(7.5 + 8) = 3.875$. The net loss in the corn market is 0.25.
    e. The Kaldor-Hicks net benefits are $9 - .25 = 8.75$.
2. a. Everything in the rice market is as before. Before the innovation the solution to the corn market is $16 - C = 2 + C$, $C = 7$, $P = 9$. After the innovation the solution to the corn market is $15 - C = 2 + C$, $C = 6.5$, $P = 8.5$. In the corn market the innovation gains consumers $(.5)(.5)(6 + 6.5) = 3.125$; it costs producers $(.5)(.5)(6.5 + 7) = 3.375$. The net social loss in the corn market is the loss in tax revenue, $(2)(.5) = 1$, the loss in producer surplus $= 3.375$, less the gain in consumer surplus 3.125, or 1.25.
    b. In this case the answers given above have not fully accounted for the net benefits because as the price of corn falls, the demand function for rice is shifted back. In general one looks for secondary market effects when there are price changes in these other markets, or when there are quantity changes in the presence of distortions.

CHAPTER 6

1. The present value of B is highest ($11.61) but both have positive present values, so both should be done (A = $7.50). When $r = .11$, A has a present value of $2.70 (do it), and B of $1.78 (do it). When $r = .15$, both present values become negative and both projects become uneconomic. Note that as r increases, both projects look worse, but B, with more deferred gratification, gets worse faster.
2. Using the formulas in the text, the present value of the stream is $1,000 when $r = .1$, $2,000 when $r = .05$, and $1,428.57 when $r = .03$ and $d = .04$. If the stream is in real dollars and the real discount rate is .04, the present value is $2,500—general price inflation can be ignored because it cancels out. But if there is expected to be specific price inflation that raises benefits more than nominal interest rates, it does not cancel out and the present value is $3,333.33.
3. The present value for three years is 28.8. For ten years it is 89.8. If the stream lasts forever, the present value is 500. If benefits decay to 9 in

year two, the decay rate is .1 and the present value of the stream is 10/(.02 + .1) = 83.3. If the decay is to 9 in year two, we can think of this as a stream of benefits of 9 forever, the present value of which is 9/.02 = 450, plus the discounted value of 1 in year one, making for a net present value of 450.98. The value of a stream of 5 forever is 250. The value of the first three years of that stream is an extra 14.4 (just half of what was computed above for 10). The net present value of the whole stream is 264.4.

4. You would pay 4 for the lottery ticket if you are risk-neutral, but you would prefer A with a present value of 5. When A is converted to a lottery, its expected present value is zero—you are indifferent. Since the present value of the package with the certain 10.50 is 5, already worked out, you would pay an insurance premium of up to that amount for the package.

5. First off, this net benefit pattern is not unreasonable. Suppose gross benefits are 48, 24, and 12 in the three years, and costs are 38 and 46 in the first two years. Solving the quadratic equation gives i values of 0 and .2, both of which are plausible internal rates of return. The present value of the project when r = .07 is –.08. Based on the present value rule, you should decide against the project. There is no way to decide anything based on the internal rate of return.

6. The equilibrium condition is sy = nk, giving k = 16 and y = 4. Over time levels of labor, capital, and output all grow at the rate of .05 per year. The private discount rate is the marginal product of capital, which can be computed as .125 (you need calculus to do this). The social rate of time preference is n = .05. Since the economy is under-saving, for tax-financed projects the ABFK rule uses a discount rate of .05 when benefits last forever. For bond-financed projects the discount rate is .125 when both benefits and private capital last forever.

When the economy is open, the marginal product of private capital and the discount rate for bond-financed projects falls to .06. What happens to the social rate of time preference and the discount rate for tax-financed projects becomes something of a mystery—one could defend either .05 or .06. One could even split the difference.

CHAPTER 7

1. According to the Kaldor-Hicks standard we just sum the gains and find net benefits equal to 1.6 for A and 1.2 for B—A is preferable. If the first set of tax rates is used to get weights, w_p = .2/.15 = 1.33 and the weighted benefits of A are (.5)(1.33) + 1.1 = 1.77 for A and 1.53 for B. If the second set is used, the weighted benefits of A are (.5)(3) + 1.1 = 2.6 and of B are (1)(3) + .2 = 3.2. To find the weight that makes society indifferent, set .5w_p + 1.1 = w_p + .2, w_p = 1.8.

2. Refer to the answers for problem 5 in Chapter 4. If all renters are low income, there is no weight that makes the rent control law a winner because low income renters lose.

With the constraint on who can rent, high income landlords lose $45,000, high income students lose $65,000, and total high income losses are $110,000. Low income gains are $10,000, giving a weight of 11 necessary to make the program's weighted net benefits equal to zero. This law would then be as efficient in transferring income as a transfer program with a leaky bucket coefficient (c) computed as $1/(1 - c) = 11$, $c = .91$.

3. a. Without the minimum wage, $W = 2$ when demand is equal to the fixed supply of 8. With the minimum of 5, $L = 5$. The gain to workers is $(3)(5) - (2)(8 - 5) = 9$. The loss to consumers is $(.5)(3)(5 + 8) = 19.5$. The Kaldor-Hicks loss is 10.5. The w_p necessary to make weighted net benefits equal zero is $9w_p - 19.5 = 0$, $w_p = 2.17$ if all low wage workers were from low income families; and $4.5w_p - 19.5 + 4.5 = 0$, $w_p = 3.33$ if half of the low wage workers were from low income families.

   b. With the new supply function, $10 - L = .25 L$, $L = 8$ and $W = 2$ in the market without minimum wages, and $W = 5$, $L = 5$ with minimum wages, just the same as before. The loss to consumers is also just the same as before, 19.5. But the gain to low wage workers now differs, because of the new supply assumption. Before the minimum, workers gained producer surplus of $(.5)(2)(8) = 8$. With the minimum, the average valuation of effort of those who get the jobs is 2.5 and the gain is $(5)(5 - 2.5) = 12.5$. The net change in worker surplus is 4.5. If all low wage workers were from low income families, $4.5w_p - 19.5 = 0$, $w_p = 4.33$. If half, $2.25w_p - 19.5 + 2.25 = 0$, $w_p = 7.67$. What has happened is that the minimum wage has become a less efficient device to transfer income because the supply elasticity means that jobs will not be allocated efficiently among the low wage workers.

4. For the low income market, the pre-tax equilibrium is found by setting $10 - L = L$, $L = 5$, $W = 5$. The post-tax equilibrium is found by setting $10 - L = 1.5L$, $L = 4$, $W = 6$. The tax raises $(2)(4) = 8$, the loss in consumer surplus is $(.5)(1)(4 + 5) = 4.5$, the loss in workers' producer surplus is also $(.5)(1)(4 + 5) = 4.5$, and the excess burden in this market is $9 - 8 = 1$.

   For the high income market, the pre-tax equilibrium is where $30 - L = L$, $L = 15$, $W = 15$. The post-tax equilibrium is where $30 - L = 1.5L$, $L = 12$, $W = 18$. The tax raises $(6)(12) = 72$ and consumers and producers both lose $(.5)(3)(12 + 15) = 40.5$. The excess burden is $91 - 72 = 19$. The Kaldor-Hicks burden from the redistribution program is $1 + 19 = 20$. The net gain for poor families is thus $-4.5 + (.5)(8 + 72) = 35.5$. The net gain for nonpoor families is $-4.5 - 91 + (.5)(8 + 72) = -55.5$. Note that the sum of these changes equals the Kaldor-Hicks excess burden. The leaky bucket coefficient is found from the expression $35.5 =$

$(1 - c)(55.5)$, $c = .36$. The w_p* value for this leaky bucket coefficient is 1.56.

CHAPTER 8

1. When the consumer surplus does not decay at all, the present value of net benefits is $200/.05 - 1000 = 3000$. When it decays at the rate of 5 percent, the present value of net benefits is $200/.1 - 1000 = 1000$. When it decays at the rate of 10 percent, the present value of net benefits is $200/.15 - 1000 = 333$.

   If the discount rate is 5 percent, the benefit decay rate is 5 percent, and environmental costs also decay 5 percent a year, the present value of net benefits is $200/.1 - 1000 - 20/.1 = 800$. If environmental costs do not decay, the present value of net benefits is $200/.1 - 1000 - 20/.05 = 600$. If environmental costs rise at 5 percent a year, the present value of these environmental costs is infinity, and the dam becomes a big loser. These various rates of change are important in determining how things come out.

2. The number of users when the full cost of using the area is $7 is given by $100 - Q = 7$, $Q = 93$. The consumer surplus loss is $(.5)(100 - 7)(93) = \$4,325$ per day.

3. a. First off, we can ignore the general price inflation because we know the real discount rate is .03. The present value of the oil is $50[1 + 1.01 + (1.01)^2 + (1.01)^3 + (1.01)^4] = 255$, and the present value of the wolverines is $5/(.03 - .01) = 250$ (note that here the environmental resources can not be restored). There are positive net benefits from drilling, meaning that drilling passes the first test of the chapter, but these benefits rise over time, failing the postponement test. You should postpone development.

   b. Since all prices are now rising at .04 indefinitely, the real discount rate is $.07 - .04 = .03$, just the same as before, and z, the rate of benefit appreciation, is zero. The present value of the benefits now falls to $50[1 + .97 + (.97)^2 + (.97)^3 + (.97)^4] = 235$ and the present value of the wolverines is just as before. Now you do not drill because drilling does not pass the net benefits test.

   c. In fact, there is no steady price appreciation that makes it worthwhile to drill now. If z is .03 or lower, drilling fails the net benefit test. If z is .03 or higher, drilling fails the postponement test. The only way to make drilling economic now is to raise the present price of oil, hence raising net benefits, and to assume low appreciation, making it economic to drill now instead of later.

CHAPTER 9

1. Net discounted benefits of students are $10,000, and net discounted costs of others are $12,000. The program clearly fails the Kaldor-Hicks

test. But that may not be the right test. If this is a program that helps low income students, we may want to put a weight on their gains. The w_p necessary to make weighted net benefits equal to zero is only 1.2, so perhaps the program passes the transfer efficiency test.

2. We can find the B necessary to make the program a success by solving $B[1/1.02 + .8/(1.02)^2 + .6/(1.02)^3 + .4/(1.02)^4 + .2/(1.02)^5] = 100$, B = 34.9.

3. Those who had jobs previously gain $10(1 + .98 + .96) = 29.4$. There are five such workers, so their total gain is $(5)(29.4) = 147$. Those who did not have jobs previously gain $15(1 + .98 + .96) = 44.1$. There are five of these workers, so their total gain is $(5)(44.1) = 220$. Taxpayers lose 400 but gain back $(5)(5)(1 + .98 + .96) = 73.5$ on the reduced unemployment payments, for a net loss of 326.5. The Kaldor-Hicks gain is $147 + 220 - 326.5 = 40.5$.

4. Total benefits are given by $4020N - 2N^2$ and marginal benefits by $4020 - 4N$ (from calculus). Total costs are given by $3,000,000 + 20N$ and marginal costs by 20. To find the optimal sample size, equate marginal benefits and marginal costs, $4020 - 4N = 20$, $N = 1000$. This number is easy to compute with calculus; if you do not know calculus, you can also simply insert various N's into the total benefits and costs equations and see where the net benefits are maximized. This value of $N = 1000$ is the optimal sample size whether or not the evaluation is done, and the sample size you would draw if the evaluation were mandated. To ask the deeper question of whether or not you would do the evaluation if it were not mandated, insert $N = 1000$ into the total benefits and total costs equation. Total benefits are 2.02 million and total costs are 3.02 million (the amount you would spend if mandated), so it does not make sense to do the evaluation.

CHAPTER 10

1. a. When there is no grant assistance at all, set $100 - Q = 40$, $Q = 60$. But to find the social efficiency point, set $120 - Q = 40$, $Q = 80$. The excess burden of the externality is $(.5)(20)(20) = 200$.
    b. The close ended grant amount is $(.9)(40)(50) = 1800$. This amount is lost by federal taxpayers and gained by state taxpayers. There is no change for anybody else.
    c. Suppose we had a grant that got the state to spend 80, the efficient amount. State marginal willingness to pay at $Q = 80$ is 20, so the grant would have to be open ended with a matching rate of .5. If this grant were to replace the existing grant, federal taxpayers would save 1800 but spend $(.5)(40)(80) = 1600$, for a net saving of 200. State taxpayers would lose the 1800 but gain the consumer surplus $(.5)(.5)(40)(60 + 80) = 1400$, for a net loss of 400. Outsiders would gain $(20)(20) = 400$. The Kaldor-Hicks gain is 200, just the initial excess burden.

d. If the present grant were converted to block form, there would be no change for any group. The marginal price is unaffected, output is unaffected, outsiders are unaffected, and taxpayers at both levels are unaffected.

2. The proportional tax rates can be computed from t(10,000) = 500, t = .05 in the poor community and t(20,000) = 500, t = .025 in the higher income community. Putting it another way, a constant tax rate will not buy as many public services in the poor community. A matching grant with a federal matching share of .5 will be needed to even out the tax prices.

CHAPTER 11

1. Using the formula given in the text, we get:

E	G/C
0	0
−0.5	0.44
−1.0	0.80
−1.5	1.09
−2.0	1.33

We can also find the elasticity for which the G/C ratio is the same as for expenditures, 1, by setting the equation equal to one and solving −E/(1 − .25E) = 1, E = −1.33.

2. a. Desired spending demands are just as given for problem 1d in Chapter 3: $Q_A = 6$, $Q_B = 8$, $Q_C = 13$, median Q = 8. At Q = 8, $DWB_A = 2$, $DWB_B = 0$, $DWB_C = 12.5$. Obviously tax costs are zero.

b. If only C can itemize, C's price goes from 20 to 17 and C's desired spending goes from $Q_C = 13$ to $Q_C = 16$. But the median voter does not change, so there is no change in community spending. The only change is that C does not pay as much in national taxes. C can claim deductions of (20)(8) = 160, C's taxable income goes down this amount, C gains (.15)(160) = 24, and national taxpayers lose 24.

c. If only A can itemize, A's price goes from 20 to 17 and A's desired spending goes from $Q_A = 6$ to $Q_A = 9$. Now things get tricky because Q = 9 becomes the spending demand of the median voter (A). The DWB_B goes from zero to 0.5 and the DWB_C goes from 12.5 to 8. On the existing Q = 8 units of output, national taxpayers lose (.15)(20)(8) = 24 and A gains the same amount—this is just a transfer. As output goes from Q = 8 to Q = 9, national taxpayers lose 3 and A gains the triangle defined by the valuation at $Q_A = 8$, $P_A = 18$, the valuation at $Q_A = 9$, $P_A = 17$, and the cost at 17. This triangle has an area of 0.5. Hence A gains 24.5, national taxpayers lose 27, B loses 0.5, and C gains 4.5. The net Kaldor-Hicks gain from all this is 1.5. In problem 1d in Chapter 3, this is also the Kaldor-Hicks gain from going from the median voter point at $Q = 8$ to the Samuelsonian point at $Q = 9$.

d. If only B can itemize, B's desired spending goes to $Q_B = 11$, which becomes the median voter spending level. At $Q = 11$, DWB_A goes from 2 to 12.5 and DWB_C goes from 12.5 to 2—this part is a wash. National taxpayers lose $(3)(11) = 33$ and B gains $(.5)(3)(8 + 11) = 28.5$ from the consumer surplus. The net Kaldor-Hicks loss is 4.5. That too turns out to be just the Kaldor-Hicks loss in going from $Q = 8$ to $Q = 11$ without tax deductibility.

e. The results depend on who is the median voter and how much the different voters lose at different spending levels. All of this changes depending on who can itemize.

CHAPTER 12

1. a. The expression for consequences cost is $CC = (50)(.2a)(9,800)/(1 - .2a)$. The text shows how to minimize costs with calculus, but here we just evaluate CC and PC at different levels of a:

a	PC	CC	TC
0	80,000	0	80,000
.1	40,000	10,000	50,000
.2	20,000	20,417	40,417
.3	10,000	31,277	41,277
.4	4,000	42,609	46,609
.5	0	54,444	54,444

The optimal point is where $a = .2$, where FWSC spends $20,000 on repaving. Were OSHA to require absolute safety, costs would rise by $39,583.

b. With the daredevils, market CC would be zero and TC would be minimized where there was no repaving. FWSC would not repave and the cost of the OSHA regulations would be $80,000.

c. You cannot use this information, or you can only use it if the FWSC testers have the same distaste for breaking their arms as do the vagabonds.

2. a. Ohio has an $MC = 6$ and spends $(.5)(6)(6) = 18$. Indiana has an $MC = 12$ and spends $(.5)(6)(12) = 36$. Total emission reduction costs are 54.

b. At the optimum the MC in each state is equal and total emission reductions is 12. Letting E_I equal $12 - E_O$, we have $E_O = 2(12 - E_O)$, $E_O = 8$, $E_I = 4$, and $MC = 8$ in each state. Ohio spends $(.5)(8)(8) = 32$, Indiana spends $(.5)(4)(8) = 16$, total costs are 48, and you saved 6. Nice going.

c.   Suppose you gave each state emission permits of 6 less than they were emitting before the regulation. Ohio sells permission to pollute 2 more tons to Indiana for 8 a ton. Ohio gains 16 from the sale of permits, spends 14 more on pollution prevention, and comes out ahead by 2. Indiana spends 16 on the emission permits but cuts down its cost of pollution reduction by 20, coming out ahead by 4. Note that the net Kaldor-Hicks gain of 6 is just what you saved by reallocating emission reductions, except that this new scheme made neither state worse off and did not require you to know the MC schedules in the two states.

d.   The only thing would be to bribe Ohio and Indiana to reduce pollution. If Governor Mario knew the MC schedules, he could get away with a cost of 48, or he might even work out his own transferable emission scheme.

INDEX

244